CAMPAIGN CRAFT

Recent Titles in the
Praeger Series in Political Communication
Robert E. Denton, Jr., *General Editor*

CAMPAIGN CRAFT

The Strategies, Tactics, and Art of Political Campaign Management

Revised and Expanded Edition

DANIEL M. SHEA
and
MICHAEL JOHN BURTON

Praeger Series in Political Communication

Westport, Connecticut
London

Library of Congress Cataloging-in-Publication Data

Shea, Daniel M.
    Campaign craft : the strategies, tactics, and art of political campaign management / Daniel M. Shea and Michael John Burton.—Rev. and expanded ed.
      p. cm.—(Praeger series in political communication, ISSN 1062–5623)
    Includes bibliographical references and index.
    ISBN 0–275–97093–0 (alk. paper)—ISBN 0–275–97094–9 (pbk. : alk. paper)
    1. Campaign management—United States. I. Burton, Michael John. II. Title. III. Series.
JK2281.S49 2001
324.7'0973—dc21   00–052423

British Library Cataloguing in Publication Data is available.

Library of Congress Catalog Card Number: 00–052423
ISBN: 0–275–97093–0
     0–275–97094–9 (pbk.)
ISSN: 1062–5623

First published in 2001

Praeger Publishers, 88 Post Road West, Westport, CT 06881
An imprint of Greenwood Publishing Group, Inc.
www.praeger.com

Printed in the United States of America

The paper used in this book complies with the
Permanent Paper Standard issued by the National
Information Standards Organization (Z39.48–1984).

10 9 8 7 6 5 4 3

Copyright Acknowledgments

The authors and publisher gratefully acknowledge permission for use of the following material:

Adapted from Jesse Marquette, "How to Become a Wise Consumer of Campaign Polling," in Daniel M. Shea, *Campaign Craft: The Strategies, Tactics, and Art of Political Campaign Management* (Westport, CT: Praeger, 1996). Copyright © by Daniel M. Shea. Reproduced by permission of Greenwood Publishing Group, Inc., Westport, CT.

Contents

CONTENTS

Series Foreword

Those of us from the discipline of communication studies have long believed that communication is prior to all other fields of inquiry. In several other forums I have argued that the essence of politics is "talk" or human interaction.[1] Such interaction may be formal or informal, verbal or nonverbal, public or private, but it is always persuasive, forcing us consciously or subconsciously to interpret, to evaluate, and to act. Communication is the vehicle for human action.

From this perspective, it is not surprising that Aristotle recognized the natural kinship of politics and communication in his writings *Politics* and *Rhetoric*. In the former, he established that humans are "political beings [who] alone of the animals [are] furnished with the faculty of language."[2] In the latter, he began his systematic analysis of discourse by proclaiming that "rhetorical study, in its strict sense, is concerned with the modes of persuasion."[3] Thus, it was recognized over twenty-three hundred years ago that politics and communication go hand in hand because they are essential parts of human nature.

In 1981, Dan Nimmo and Keith Sanders proclaimed that political communication was an emerging field.[4] Although its origin, as noted, dates back centuries, a "self-consciously cross-disciplinary" focus began in the late 1950s. Thousands of books and articles later, colleges and universities offer a variety of graduate and undergraduate coursework in the area in such diverse departments as communication, mass communication, journalism, political science, and sociology.[5] In Nimmo and Sanders's early assessment, the "key areas of inquiry" included rhetorical analysis, propaganda analysis, attitude change studies, voting studies, government and the news media, functional and systems analyses, technological changes, media technologies, campaign techniques, and research techniques.[6] In a survey of the state of the field in 1983, the same authors and Lynda Kaid found additional, more specific areas of concerns such as the presidency, political polls, public opinion, debates, and advertising.[7]

Since the first study, they have also noted a shift away from the rather strict behavioral approach.

A decade later, Dan Nimmo and David Swanson argued that "political communication has developed some identity as a more or less distinct domain of scholarly work."[8] The scope and concerns of the area have further expanded to include critical theories and cultural studies. Although there is no precise definition, method, or disciplinary home of the area of inquiry, its primary domain comprises the role, processes, and effects of communication within the context of politics broadly defined.

In 1985, the editors of *Political Communication Yearbook: 1984* noted that "more things are happening in the study, teaching, and practice of political communication than can be captured within the space limitations of the relatively few publications available."[9] In addition, they argued that the backgrounds of "those involved in the field [are] so varied and pluralist in outlook and approach, . . . it [is] a mistake to adhere slavishly to any set format in shaping the content."[10] More recently, Swanson and Nimmo have called for "ways of overcoming the unhappy consequences of fragmentation within a framework that respects, encourages, and benefits from diverse scholarly commitments, agendas, and approaches."[11]

In agreement with these assessments of the area and with gentle encouragement, in 1988 Praeger established the series entitled "Praeger Series in Political Communication." The series is open to all qualitative and quantitative methodologies as well as contemporary and historical studies. The key to characterizing the studies in the series is the focus on communication variables or activities within a political context or dimension. As of this writing, over seventy volumes have been published and numerous impressive works are forthcoming. Scholars from the disciplines of communication, history, journalism, political science, and sociology have participated in the series.

I am, without shame or modesty, a fan of the series. The joy of serving as its editor is in participating in the dialogue of the field of political communication and in reading the contributors' works. I invite you to join me.

Robert E. Denton, Jr.

NOTES

1. See Robert E. Denton, Jr., *The Symbolic Dimensions of the American Presidency* (Prospect Heights, IL: Waveland Press, 1982); Robert E. Denton, Jr., and Gary Woodward, *Political Communication in America* (New York: Praeger, 1985; 2d ed., 1990); Robert E. Denton Jr., and Dan Hahn, *Presidential Communication* (New York: Praeger, 1986); and Robert E. Denton, Jr., *The Primetime Presidency of Ronald Reagan* (New York: Praeger, 1988).

2. Aristotle, *The Politics of Aristotle*, trans. Ernest Barker (New York: Oxford University Press, 1970), p. 5.

3. Aristotle, *Rhetoric*, trans. W. Rhys Roberts (New York: The Modern Library, 1954), p. 22.

4. Dan Nimmo and Keith Sanders, "Introduction: The Emergence of Political Communication as a Field," in *Handbook of Political Communication*, eds. Dan Nimmo and Keith Sanders (Beverly Hills, CA: Sage, 1981), pp. 11–36.

5. Ibid., p. 15.

6. Ibid., pp. 17–27.

7. Keith Sanders, Lynda Kaid, and Dan Nimmo, eds. *Political Communication Yearbook: 1984* (Carbondale, IL: Southern Illinois University, 1985), pp. 283–308.

8. Dan Nimmo and David Swanson, "The Field of Political Communication: Beyond the Voter Persuasion Paradigm," in *New Directions in Political Communication*, eds. David Swanson and Dan Nimmo (Beverly Hills, CA: Sage, 1990), p. 8.

9. Sanders, Kaid, and Nimmo, *Political Communication Yearbook: 1984*, p. xiv.

10. Ibid.

11. Nimmo and Swanson, "The Field of Political Communication," p. 11.

Preface

A few years ago, I set out to write a book that would help bridge the gap between what scholars understood about modern elections and what campaign operatives knew about the process. It was to be a book that would help students, both in and out of the classroom, better appreciate new-style elections. I looked to merge theoretical information, such as the history and rationale behind different campaign activities, with practical information on how electioneering is done. The first edition of this volume was the end product, and apparently the model worked; the book has been well received.

One of the themes of the first volume, however, is that modern campaign technologies evolve quickly and that a true student of the process must be willing to shed old practices for new. When I wrote the book (fall 1995), I felt fairly confident that I was abreast of technological developments, centered mostly around modes of communication and data analysis. I noted, for instance, the virtues of CD-ROMs when it came to accessing demographic data. Well, the pace of the Information Age has outdated many of the pages. Almost all of the demographic data that one would ever expect to use can be downloaded from the Internet in a few moments. Who could have imagined that a former professional wrestler—a third-party candidate no less—could be elected governor using the Net to rally followers? Our first "cybergovernor"? Such are the fascinating times we live in.

So this new edition is designed as a "technological update," so to speak.

But it is also a good bit more than an update. Instructors, reviewers, and colleagues have noted a good many minor glitches and confusing sections in the first edition, so these, too, have been corrected. Mostly, in considering the types of changes that I thought important in a second edition, a fuller strategic element jumped to mind. The book needed a finer sense of nuance—something garnered from years in the trenches—on the front line. Given that my "front line" for the last seven years has been in the classroom, it seemed plain that I needed some help in this regard. A campaign is, to be sure, more than the sum of its parts.

Michael John Burton heeded my call for assistance. Mike and I were good friends and classmates during our graduate school days at the University at Albany, but we headed down different paths thereafter. I went to the "ivy towers," and Mike went to the "real world." It came as no surprise that Mike would excel. Within a few years of moving to Washington he joined the Clinton–Gore team at the White House. Mike kept up the staggering pace of a White House staffer for five years. As assistant political director to Vice President Al Gore, he had the opportunity to see inside a wide variety of campaigns—from mayoral races to Clinton–Gore '96. It is a unique understanding that will serve him well in his new career.

Mike returned to academia as an assistant professor of political science at Ohio University in 1998. He is slated to take the scholarly/publishing world by storm, and it has been a privilege to work with him on this project. His handiwork and keen insight fill this volume—particularly the powerful concluding chapter. It is, I suggest, a much better volume due to his efforts.

So, the reader will find many new sections, updated graphics and data, scores of recent stories and anecdotes, technological innovations, and, I hope, a finer sense of how each piece of the campaign process might be pulled together. It has been a joy to rework, and I hope readers find the "new and improved" version helpful.

Daniel M. Shea
Allegheny College

Acknowledgments

We would like to thank the many scholars and practitioners who provided feedback on the first edition of this book, as well as on revised sections. At Praeger, Jim Sabin was most helpful, as were Linda Ellis-Stiewing, Liz Leiba, and Marcia Goldstein, who helped move the draft through its final stages. Also, portions of the book owe a great debt to Jesse Marquette and Mark R. Weaver, who contributed chapters to the original edition of this book.

Dan would like to thank the Department of Political Science at Allegheny for providing a supportive and constructive environment. He owes a special tribute, of course, to his beloved partner, Christine Gatto-Shea.

Mike would like to thank the Department of Political Science at Ohio University for its patience and understanding, as well as Molly Park, Steven "The Book" Petrovic, David Boisture, and James Moore for their attention to some of the details. Additionally, he would like to thank his family, especially his mother, Dr. Grace Burton, whose comments on Chapter 6 will save readers from at least a bit of math anxiety. Finally, Mike would like to express a deep appreciation to all the political professionals who taught him the craft. (The wisdom is yours; any mistakes can be blamed on him—as always.)

Together, Dan and Mike would like to dedicate this book to the Department of Political Science at the State University of New York at Albany. Our advisers and mentors—indeed, the whole faculty—contributed to this book in ways that are visible only to Dan and Mike. It is a debt that we cannot fully repay but one that we will always remember.

Chapter One

Introduction: Consultant-Centered Campaigns

The presidential election of 1896 was among the most intensely fought races in American history. It pitted Democrat William Jennings Bryan, a fiery ex-congressman from Nebraska, against Republican William McKinley, who had served in Congress prior to being elected governor of Ohio. Bryan was a gifted orator in the classical tradition. At the time, economic misfortune was dividing the nation by region and class, and many saw the gold standard as a threat to debtors and a boon to financiers. Bryan delivered an impassioned speech at the Democratic convention. In defiance of his adversaries, Bryan declared, "You shall not press upon the brow of labor this crown of thorns, you shall not crucify mankind upon a cross of gold" (Bryan 1913, 249). Taking his "Silver Democrat" message to twenty-six states, talking to an estimated 5 million people, distancing himself from the failures of the incumbent Democratic administration, Bryan cast himself as the champion of the "common man" (Dinkin 1989, 114).

Sensing trouble, McKinley harnessed the talents and ingenuity of his longtime friend and political godfather Marcus A. Hanna—arguably the first modern campaign consultant. Hanna fashioned the McKinley race along "business principles," putting together an elaborate organization designed to handle every phase of the race (Troy 1991, 105). He created different bureaus for different constituencies—Germans, African Americans, wheelmen, merchants, and even women, who did not yet enjoy universal suffrage. Hundreds of speakers were deployed, and countless pamphlets were distributed, many of them printed in foreign languages for use in ethnic neighborhoods. To finance this high-priced strategy, Hanna systematically approached captains of industry, raising more money than had ever been raised for a presidential race—estimated at $3.5 million to $4.0 million (S. Jones 1964, 283; Glad 1964, 169). Mark Hanna's spending record would stand for nearly a quarter century.

Bryan's travels notwithstanding, the customs of the 1800s held that presidential candidates actively campaigned only if they were in trouble. McKinley rightly feared that campaigning would make him look weak and, more importantly, that it would give Bryan a chance to upstage him. Hanna therefore orchestrated a series of finely tuned "pilgrimages." The candidate did not go to the people. The people went to the candidate.

Hanna enlisted the aid of leading GOP railroad moguls who offered excursion passes to those wishing a journey to McKinley's front porch in Canton, Ohio (Jamieson 1984, 18). Once these delegations reached the candidate, every step was choreographed, and the press was given prime seating. Introductory speeches delivered by supporters were carefully scrutinized by Hanna's team to ensure consistency of message. McKinley's front-porch campaign captured the attention of the nation: "The desire to come to Canton has reached the point of mania," reported Francis Loomis (Troy 1991, 105). From midsummer until the election, McKinley gave over 300 speeches and had perhaps 1 million callers at his door. Such a phenomenon had the ordeal become that many people snatched twigs, grass, stones, and even pieces of the famous porch as souvenirs.

Election Day saw one of the largest voter turnouts in history. McKinley won with just 51 percent of the vote, thanks, in large measure, to the skill of his top aide, Mark Hanna.

Hanna's accomplishment was a low-tech affair. Telephone communication was still novel. A couple decades after the McKinley victory, wireless radio was accelerating communication and setting the stage for astonishing technological change in the second half of the century. Television was introduced following World War II and, within ten years, fully two-thirds of the nation's households had at least one television set. Satellite communications soon became a standard part of local television newscasts. The Cable News Network (CNN) took its place in the White House, often reporting international news to the president's staff before the intelligence agencies could. At the turn of the twenty-first century nearly every home had a television, two-thirds were wired for cable, and at least 30 percent of American adults had access to the Internet—a technology that few could have imagined as recently as 1990. College students walk around campus with digital phones, radio stations broadcast on the Net, and start-up businesses issue hand-held personal digital assistants to incoming employees. One can only imagine what Hanna would have dreamed up for the World Wide Web.

The technological revolution is changing education, transportation, personal communications, the job market, and the way that people think about the future. Less obvious, but no less profound, are the corresponding adjustments made to the American system of governance. Government at all levels is going online. Voters are tracked by ever-growing databases. Large campaigns cannot survive without hiring someone who knows how to uplink video to a satellite. In March 2000 the Arizona Democratic Party held a cyberprimary, allowing citizens to cast their votes for Al Gore and Bill Bradley over the Web. Although the constitutional structure of the United States remains much as it was in the late 1700s, the Framers might not recognize the way that Americans now elect public officials.

In the recent past, not unlike the days of the nation's founding, campaigns were conducted by armies of volunteers, usually local party activists and the candidate's network of friends and family. Time-honored methods were used, mostly face-to-face canvassing and the distribution of printed material (e.g., pamphlets, posters, and newspaper advertisements). In the 1950s "retail" politics was the way of the world. Massachusetts pol Tip O'Neill, who would later make his mark as Speaker of the House, could view politics as a sociable affair: hands are shaken, deals are made, and no one gives his or her vote until asked (O'Neill 1987). As a retired legislator, O'Neill lamented, "If I were running today, I probably would have to use all the modern techniques of political campaigning: hiring a political consultant, polling extensively and making ads targeted to TV audiences" (1994, xi–xii).

O'Neill was living in the twilight of retail campaigns. The shift toward professional campaigning that began with Mark Hanna's work in 1896 was hastened by Dwight D. Eisenhower's 1952 campaign for president. Eisenhower hired an advertising team, which produced some of the first television campaign commercials. Using the product-tested technique of name repetition, a jingle went, "Ike for President, Ike for President; You like Ike, I like Ike, Everybody likes Ike." By the mid-1960s, the skills and tactics used by product marketing specialists had moved down to the realm of congressional elections. Carefully conducted, random-sample surveys, for example, proved to be a better and more cost-effective means of identifying the wishes of voters than just walking around and consulting other party leaders. In this transformation, Joe McGinniss, who detailed Richard Nixon's advertising strategy, saw a loss of innocence: "With the coming of television, and the knowledge of how it could be used to seduce voters, the old political values disappeared" (1969, 28).

Today, pure grassroots campaigning seems archaic for all but the humblest races. Political operatives dismiss it as "old-style." Even city council races are starting to use expensive, high-tech methods, and the newfound tricks of the 1980s were considered passé a decade later. Instead of large-scale polls, narrowly targeted focus groups came into vogue. By the mid-1990s it was normal to see videotapes distributed en masse. Satellite feeds were replacing smoke-filled rooms and blast-faxes rendered hand-distributed press releases obsolete. Of course, the advent of the World Wide Web brought about fundamental changes in daily campaign communications. No other area of American politics has so drastically changed over the last few decades than the manner in which candidates pursue votes.

The revolution in campaign technology has had, and will continue to have, a substantial effect on elections. It intensifies the importance of money in the election process. Candidates with access to financial resources can bypass traditional party screening mechanisms, which once began with loyalty and hard work. Traditional political parties, the center of campaign activity for over 150 years, have lost ground to campaign consultants and political action committees (PACs), though they have maintained relevance by adopting the ways of these competitors. Political parties, which once served as the organizational foundation of American politics, have become "service-oriented" organizations that allocate financial resources and expertise to candidates (White and Shea 2000, 84–107). The money that a candidate receives from the party and other sources is spent on a variety of specialized services, from sophisticated polling to high-budget media production. All politics may be local, as Tip O'Neill often said, but the campaign industry has become distinctly national in its scope and power.

Inevitably, the types of campaign information provided to voters have also changed. Viewers now see thirty-second television spots and six-second sound bites. In 1994, three years after Arnold Schwarzenegger's *Terminator 2* thrilled audiences with a new cinematic effect—image morphing—Republican candidates ran ads that showed the faces of Democratic candidates slowly dissolving into that of President Bill Clinton. The technique was roundly criticized as an oversimplification of serious issues, but it was effective.

Some argue that, with the new media, "style becomes substance" (McGinniss 1969, 30). The volume of negative campaign advertising runs at a fever pitch. The media often seem more interested in who is ahead in the polls and in how each campaign is being run than in the policy stands of the candidates. There is even some evidence to suggest that the type of person willing to undergo the rigors of modern campaigning has changed, leading to a much different crop of public officials and a new approach to governance (Ehrenhalt 1991).

THE STUDY OF CONTEMPORARY ELECTIONS

Do campaigns matter? Several of the earliest election studies, conducted in the 1950s and 1960s (e.g., Berelson, Lazarsfeld, and McPhee 1954), found little evidence that they did. Voters, it was believed, vote according to party affiliation rather than campaign message. Only when a dramatic, crosscutting issue divided the electorate would voters be swayed by candidate appeals. Partisan stability was believed to be especially strong at the local level. Scholars found little value in studying individual campaigns because electioneering seemed to have little bearing on election outcomes.

Today, many researchers agree that campaigns deserve close attention. Fewer voters are guided by party preference alone. Especially for the growing number of alienated voters, campaigns matter (Nimmo 1970). The amount of money spent by candidates at all levels has skyrocketed, and the candidate with the most money usually wins. Although the machinery of urban party organizations has broken down, parties are providing candidates with greater and greater assistance. Several studies during the last decade have underscored the growing import of party organizations at all levels of electoral politics (see, e.g., Frendries and Gitelson 1999). Finally, by the early 1970s, students of congressional elections detected a sharp increase in the reelection rate for incumbents. Concerned about the competitiveness of the election process, scholars attempted to specify the nature of the incumbency advantage. Each of these elements underscored the need for shifting the analysis from the voter to the campaign process itself.

While an aggregate-level view of elections is important, it is only part of the picture. Scores of studies have been published in recent years on voter alienation, distrust, turnout, candidate-centered elections, PAC money, candidate motivation, media gatekeeping, negative campaigning, and the contours of incumbency. But with the exception of a modest body of literature on campaign strategy, scant attention has been paid to campaign management and technology. Critical questions go unanswered. Political scientists know that favorable news coverage gives candidates a big boost, but how, precisely, does one go about getting it? Money is the mother's milk of elections, but how does a campaign raise it? In short, how do campaigns work?

It has been said that an electoral politics that once was "party-centered" has become "candidate-centered" or even "campaign-centered" (Menefee-Libey 2000). As political scientists reconceptualize the process, they must think about the new constellation of campaign actors that has come to light in American politics— contemporary managers, consultants, and party operatives. We know the forest, but not yet the trees.

CAMPAIGN MANAGEMENT LITERATURE

Campaign management and technology have not been altogether neglected. Several books emerged in the 1970s, most notably those of Robert Agranoff (1972), Joseph Napolitan (1972), and James Brown and Philip M. Seib (1976). In the 1980s Larry Sabato (1981) drew attention to the emerging campaign profession. Marjorie R. Hershey (1984), Ann Beaudry and Bob Schaeffer (1986), and Barbara L. Salmore and Stephen A. Salmore (1989) shed much needed light on the inner workings of electioneering. Edwin Diamond and Stephen Bates (1992) and Karen S. Johnson-Cartee and Gary A. Copeland (1991) provided in-depth examinations of campaign advertising; Kathleen Hall Jamieson (1992) explored the rise of "dirty politics"; Steven Ansolabehere and Shanto Iyengar (1997) analyzed negative advertising; and Gary W. Selnow (1994) took account of computer technology in elections. Several new works have examined the growing importance of consultants in the process, including those of Johnson-Cartee and Copeland (1997) and Kerwin C. Swint (1998). James A. Thurber and Candace Nelson also edited two volumes (1995 and 2000), both of which provide a mix of theoretical and applied material. Robert V. Friedenberg (1997) has outlined an important segment of the campaign industry, communications consultancy.

In addition to scholarly work, one may study the literature of practitioners. One of the most frequently used texts in this area has been Sabato's edited book (1989), a collection of reprinted articles from *Campaigns & Elections,* a trade magazine for campaign consultants. *Campaigns & Elections* currently offers, in second edition, *The Road to Victory,* another compendium of past articles (Faucheux 1998). Beyond edited collections, there are a variety of campaign manuals, usually written by elected officials and campaign professionals, that give readers a sense of ground-level campaign tactics. These books, like the *Campaigns & Elections* articles, are strong on detail. Judge Lawrence Grey's *How to Win a Local Election,* for example, tells campaign operatives, "A clear coat of varnish can extend the life of a sign, and one good tip is to take the stack of signs as they come from the printer and use a roller with varnish to seal all the edges" (1999, 194–95). Dick Simpson, an academician and former campaign consultant, penned a venerable handbook dubbed *Winning Elections* (1996). Robert Thomas and Doug Gowen have written a short work on running for local office (1999). Campaign manuals such as these explore strategic issues, but they do so in the absence of a larger intellectual construct. It is not their mission to locate new-style politics in the broader context of the Digital Age.

This book is designed to merge theory and practice and to help fill a gap in the campaign management literature. It is meant for students of new-style electioneering, combining theoretical knowledge with practical information about the nature and function of "real-world" election activities. Each chapter reviews a segment of the new campaign craft, its logic and importance, as well as relevant tactics, technologies, and illustrations. More than anything else, the goal of the book is to help take the mystery out of this complex aspect of American policy.

NEW-STYLE CAMPAIGNING

The term "new-style" campaigning is used frequently in the pages that follow. Originally advanced by Robert Agranoff (1972), it continues, with some modification, to symbolize the state of modern electioneering. The distinctions between "old-style" and "new-style" campaigning can be drawn along four dimensions: (1) new players, (2) new incentives, (3) new tactics, and (4) new resources.

New Players

The exact role of candidates in elections has changed a great deal in the past few decades. Each party offers a candidate, the person with the most votes wins, and the candidates remain the stars—but the supporting cast of contemporary campaigns is vastly different from what it was in the "golden age of parties."

From the 1830s into the 1960s, candidates did not run for office by themselves—they stood for election with their campaigns largely driven by party organizations, and their fortunes linked to the success or failure of the party. Candidates were expected to contribute to their election effort, of course—often a donation to party coffers was a precondition of nomination—but a great deal of voter contact was left to party activists. If there were people who could be called "professionals," they were professionals only in the sense that they were the most seasoned party workers. Training was provided by the party as operatives moved up the organizational ladder. Formal education was no match for trial by fire.

George Washington Plunkitt, a powerful Democratic leader in New York City's old Tammany Hall organization, was clear on this point:

> We ain't all bookworms and college professors. If we were, Tammany might win an election once in four thousand years. Most of the leaders are plain American citizens, of the people and near the people, and they have all the education they need to whip the dudes who part their name in the middle and to run City Government. We got bookworms, too, in the organization. But we don't make them district leaders. We keep them for ornaments on parade days. (Riordon 1995, 45)

Experience, not scientific outlook, was the organizing force of Tammany politics.

Tammany and other such organizations drew their power largely from the distribution of government jobs and other benefits to new immigrants in return for demonstrated party loyalty. But at the turn of the twentieth century, the Progressive movement began to hammer away at city machines. Progressive reformers pushed for civil service rules (which reduced opportunities for patronage), the secret ballot (which rendered vote promises unenforceable), and direct primary elections (which removed the selection of nominees from party leaders and gave it to the voting electorate). In some states good government groups even pressed for nonpartisan municipal elections. Decreased immigration, increased mobility, broad-based education, and changing family patterns all worked to reduce the power of political parties.

Old connections were fading. Of John F. Kennedy, O'Neill wrote, "I'd have to say that he was only nominally a Democrat. . . . To work for Jack [in his congressional races], the Kennedys recruited a group of energetic and talented volunteers, most of whom had never worked in a political campaign" (1987, 76). It was a pattern that would repeat itself time and again for one candidate after another. By the 1970s, presidential nomination reforms had stripped party leaders of the role that they once had in selecting their party's candidate, and campaign finance reform led to the proliferation of labor, business, and ideological PACs, further diminishing the relative weight of party assistance to candidates. In effect, the smoke-filled rooms were taken out of the process. Some observers were left to conclude that "the party's over" (Broder 1971).

Without parties, it was assumed that candidate "image" would replace party-based appeals. Beginning first at the presidential level, students of American elections noticed a growing number of candidates running without benefit of significant party help. "Candidate-centered" politics was said to have emerged. Television was perfectly suited to campaign appeals based on individual candidates. With television ads being purchased by individual contributions, candidates at all levels soon found that they could go it alone. It became common for people to say, "I vote for the candidate, not the party," even when they consistently voted for one party or another. Voters, like candidates, surrendered much of their party allegiance.

New-style election consultants quickly emerged, responding to the new demands of candidates—and in some ways fueling that demand (Sabato 1981).

Familiar with the tools of public relations and product marketing, campaign professionals met the needs of a changing campaign environment. Consultants were able to measure voter preferences and then aim specific campaign messages toward specific groups. Strategy was mapped on slide rules, then on calculators, and, later, on desk-top computers. As the campaign industry began to take off in the early 1970s, one scholar counted some thirty branches of the campaign profession (Agranoff 1972, 17). The number soared over the next three decades.

New Incentives

Incentives for helping candidates prior to the 1970s were manifold. Party organizations controlled the reins of government—regulating patronage disbursement and managing government contracts. Some people would assist a candidate because they believed in the person or the party, while others were family friends showing personal loyalty. It was also common to find campaign workers expecting that after the election they would get a job on the elected official's staff.

More recently, although volunteers continue to help, and some people are surely hoping for a government job, independent professionals are the core of the campaign team. It is gainful employment. Top consultants can earn hundreds of dollars per hour, often charging a sizable percentage on media expenditures. At the very top of the profession, where consultants compete for a slice of the presidential campaign pie, the numbers are astronomical. Dick Morris, who advised the 1996 Clinton campaign, told the *Washington Post,* "I made about $500,000 in 1995 . . . and I made about a million in 1996" (Harris 1998). Consultants strongly differentiate themselves according to party (Thurber, Kolodny, and Dulio 2000). There are Democratic media consultants and Republican media consultants, if for no other reason than because candidates do not trust freelancers willing to serve both sides of the aisle. (Morris is an exception to that rule.) But consulting is a profit-based enterprise, as is readily seen in *Campaigns & Elections* magazine, which features scores of ads run by campaign professionals of all descriptions. Whether one needs a pollster, a direct mailer, a database manager, a media-buyer, a grassroots organizer, a phone-banker, a television producer, or even a Webmaster, a political consultant will be there to help (for a fee).

New Tactics

If the medium is the message, then the technology is the tactic. Television and radio allow candidates to enter more living rooms in thirty seconds than party foot soldiers might have reached in a month. Computers are used in direct mail, survey research, list development, fund-raising, targeting, and just about every other campaign function. About the only thing that computers do not do is directly ask for votes—but this may be changing as well. New technologies allow a candidate to simultaneously meet with several groups of voters via satellite hookups, and "actualities" can be fed to radio news stations digitally. The Internet allows voters to see policy papers, family photographs, and even television ads. In Campaign 2000, presidential candidate John McCain reportedly raised $5.5 million on the Web (Hockaday and Donatelli 2000, 73).

The difference is not just the medium of message dissemination, but the strategy that new-style electioneering sustains. Early uses of mass media took a shotgun approach. The candidate's media strategy—to the extent that it had a well-planned line of attack—would seek to broadcast the message widely. The goal was to reach as many people as possible. This meant getting the message out through newspapers, rallies, and district-wide, door-to-door canvassing. Each of these tactics was effective in contacting people, though not always the most persuadable voters. Little was done to link the right message with the right person. In the new millennium, scrupulous efforts are made to discover voter preferences through survey research. A carefully honed message is directed to each persuadable voter group. Contemporary electioneering uses a rifle, not a shotgun. It is the art and science of modern campaign "targeting."

New Resources

New-style campaigns survive on money. Nearly all of the tactics of this emerging profession hinge on financial resources. Some candidates win despite lagging funds, but examples are rare. There is a startlingly close correlation between campaign money and electoral success. Few new-style consultants would trade cash for volunteers. The reason is simple: if a campaign is short on volunteers for a phone bank, it can buy the services of a telemarketing firm; if, however, the campaign is short on money, surplus volunteers will not pay the long-distance bills.

The weight of financial necessity on recent elections has created a plethora of new questions. Where should the money come from? What do contributors expect? How are the funds raised? And, how much is enough? The rising cost of elections and the growth of special-interest money have astounded observers of the democratic process. Agranoff, for example, seemed surprised in 1972 when he noted that state legislative campaigns might cost between $10,000 and $20,000 (1972, 27). By the late 1990s, ten times this amount was customary in some states. In the 1998 Democratic three-way gubernatorial primary in California, business executive Al Checchi spent $40 million only to finish last, and in 2000, Jon Corzine spent $60 million to become the junior senator from New Jersey. Moreover, national and state parties, and even outside interest groups, are spending increasingly large amounts of "soft money" on television advertising (Magleby 2000). Despite frequent calls for reform, there is little agreement as to what should be done.

CONSULTANT-CENTERED CAMPAIGNS

Agranoff's view of new-style campaigning goes a long way toward describing the state of affairs at the beginning of the new millennium, but it is not a perfect fit. Two adjustments must be made to the traditional view: we should understand that, in some ways, the party organizations have made a comeback, and, at the same time, the modern campaign, often called a candidate-centered operation, might actually be "consultant-centered."

The Resurgence of Party Organizations

It was taken for granted by the mid-1970s that political parties no longer mattered in electoral politics. Voter partisanship was down, presidential candidates ran on their own hook—sometimes blasting the official party apparatus—and legislators were inclined to stray from the wishes of the party leaders. Nevertheless, the national party organizations and thousands of state and local party units throughout the nation hung on. They did not completely disappear, as many expected they would.

The Party Transformation Study (PTS), undertaken by Neil Cotter and his colleagues in 1984, systematically surveyed thousands of party leaders across the nation. Their principal finding was that, contrary to popular wisdom, most party organizations remained vibrant and, in fact, were often stronger than at the turn of the twentieth century. Although the relative weight of party activity had declined in light of PACs, parties were by far the largest single source of assistance to candidates. Office seekers relied upon parties to carry petitions, organize volunteers, give money, make telephone calls, and canvass door to door. The PTS was followed up by a number of other studies, all of which found basically the same thing—"the party goes on" (Kayden and Mahe 1985).

At first the contradiction seemed puzzling. How could it be that fewer voters tied themselves to a partisan label and that legislators saw fit to abandon the party at will when, at the same time, party organizations were expanding? Joseph Schlesinger (1991) has provided a possible answer: it is precisely because partisanship does not matter among the voters, he argued, that elections have become more competitive and less predictable. In this new environment, party organizations have been forced to adapt, and adaptation has taken the form of greater campaign service. Moreover, because candidates face uncertain elections, they look to merge with others in the same predicament as a form of collective protection.

Today, aggressive local party organizations can be found across the nation. Many have moved into the Digital Age and boast computer targeting systems, direct-mail operations, survey apparatus, and telemarketing centers. The same 1970s-era campaign finance reform measures that gave limited direct party payments to candidates also opened up what is now called the "soft-money loophole." Direct donations to federal candidates are tightly regulated, but money given to the parties is not. As a result, political parties at all levels can make big-money media buys promoting their party and its members.

The national and state party organizations have developed new structures specifically designed for legislative elections. These "campaign committees," such as the National Republican Campaign Committee (for Republican members of Congress) or the Democratic Legislative Campaign Committee (for Democratic state legislatures), serve as leading-edge consultancy operations. Now found in almost every state, legislative campaign committees (LCCs) provide a host of campaign services (Shea 1995a). In some states, such as New York, Ohio, California, Michigan, and Wisconsin, they have become dominant players in state legislative elections—far surpassing the efforts of PACs and special-interest groups. In New York, for example, the Democratic Assembly Campaign Committee (just one of four) spends nearly $5 million each election (Shea 1995a).

The services and resources provided to candidates by national and state committees are vast. They give money, but, more importantly, they provide expertise and assistance. Promising congressional candidates can expect to be invited to Washington, DC, or the state capital to attend training sessions. They can use media studios to make radio and television spots, and they receive professional assistance on their direct mail. In some states, LCC staff operatives join candidates in the field, essentially running the show. Moreover, the party committees serve as "brokers" (Herrnson 2000). They link candidates with potential contributors and offer discounts for service vendors. Candidates interested in a survey can be put in contact with a top-notch pollster—and receive the benefits of volume pricing. In a kind of matchmaking service, campaign committees bring PAC decision makers and candidates together to see if the relationship will work.

Campaign committees are cold-blooded. Unlike many "leadership PACs," which help candidates friendly to prominent party members, the purpose of campaign committees is to build legislative majorities. They target their efforts on only the most competitive races (Shea 1999). If a candidate's chances are good, significant help might be forthcoming, but a long-shot candidate will get little support beyond basic guidance and a few referrals, if that. As one would-be congressional candidate described his first encounter with the Democratic Congressional Campaign Committee: "All they did . . . was show me a list of PACs and then tell me that the PACs wouldn't talk to me until I was the designated candidate. They promised me nothing. I could count on no help from them at all" (Fowler and McClure 1989, 37). For some candidates, the money game has become one of the most frustrating aspects of new-style campaigning—how does one become competitive without first getting assistance? Fund-raising requires funds. The trip to the campaign committee has become a critical part of a candidate's bid for office.

The Rise of Consultant-Centered Campaigns

Even with this new infusion of party resources, the value of the party label per se is in sharp decline. Fewer candidates overtly link themselves to a party ticket. It is sometimes difficult to discern a candidate's party from his or her campaign ads, and party signifiers have fallen from many campaign posters. Character, not party, is what candidates emphasize, and consultants sometimes advise clients to distance themselves from party leaders. This movement away from party labels was described, as noted earlier, in the political science literature during the 1970s and 1980s as the emergence of "candidate-centered" campaigning. "The candidate, rather than the party," writes Agranoff, "tends to be the chief focus of today's campaign communication" (1972, 4).

This notion does not fit neatly into the context of the new millennium. When the term "candidate-centered" was first coined, the notion reflected changes in presidential elections. During the 1950s, for example, Dwight Eisenhower demonstrated that Democratic voters could be unhitched from their partisan moorings by the sheer personal appeal of the candidate. In 1976, Jimmy Carter ran on honesty, not his Democratic credentials, and in 1980 Ronald Reagan showed strength of character—not just Republican ideals.

The shift was made possible, in part, because the "image makers" began providing their services. Image-based campaigns emerged at the presidential level because survey and marketing experts pushed candidates in that direction. Only after persistent appeals from his new-style advisers did Richard Nixon make the transition from party to image—leading to his success in the 1968 presidential election. It was a two-way street. Consultants required candidates, and candidates required consultants. McGinniss wrote, "[Nixon] would need men of dignity. Who believed in him and shared his vision. But more importantly, men who knew television as a weapon: from broadest concept to most technical detail" (1969, 34). From this symbiotic relationship would emerge the "selling of the president." Years later, Bob Squier, who was once Washington's premier media consultant, could say in passing, "You'll find people in my business tend to use this word 'viewer' and 'voter' almost interchangeably" (Squier 1998).

While McGinniss viewed the use of campaign advertising with a mix of awe and contempt, few serious candidates above the local level try to run a campaign without benefit of professional consultancy services. Professionals measure public opinion, shape candidate appeals, raise funds, and implement the most efficient voter contact methods available. Contemporary campaigns are not party-centered, nor are they strictly candidate-centered—rather, they are consultant-centered.

There is a bit of exaggeration, but also some truth, in Dan Nimmo's claim that campaigns may no longer be battles between candidates but between titans of the campaign industry, working on behalf of those personalities (Nimmo 1970). True, the candidate builds the campaign, hires the consultants, asks for money, and has his or her good name and reputation on the line. In this sense modern elections *are* candidate-centered. But if one looks at the campaign structure beneath the candidate to see who is running the show, one no longer finds a Tammany-style party operative promising government jobs. Campaigns are now staffed by people who know the strategies, tactics, and art of political campaign management—that is, by professionals.

Everything from fund-raising activities, to direct mail, to television advertising, to grassroots activities is now coordinated by well-paid campaign consulting firms. Significantly more people now make their living with campaign consulting firms than political parties, and most party organizations are staffed with the aid of campaign consultants—at least on a part-time or temporary basis. A state LCC will, for example, target a winnable race, hire a consultant, and then send the consultant into the field to run the campaign. Plunkitt of Tammany Hall dismissed academics as party "ornaments," but in recent years the ranks of the campaign committees and the consultancy firms have been filled with alumni from graduate schools like the Bliss Institute of Applied Politics at the University of Akron and the Campaign Management Institute at American University. What would Plunkitt have thought of the American Association of Political Consultants, complete with dues, conferences, industry honors (the "Pollie" awards), and a professional code of ethics?

The recruitment of top consultants has become a campaign issue in itself. Journalists pay attention to the formation of each candidate's consulting team. With a strong corps in place, donors waiting to see who has a real shot at winning may start to open their checkbooks. A professional media consultant knows how to leverage press attention, and a professional fund-raiser knows how to get the most money for the campaign. For a campaign on the move, the hiring of a strong consultancy team becomes something of a self-fulfilling prophecy. Few candidates fail to recognize the skills afforded by these new "wizards of American politics" (Luntz 1988).

ORGANIZATION OF THE BOOK

Each of the following chapters is designed to help students of American politics understand the history and logic of campaigns in this new age of high-tech, consultant-centered campaigning. The focus here is on subpresidential elections. Few consultants get the opportunity to plan media buys, organize direct mail, or raise funds in the higher echelons of a presidential campaign. State and local elections are at issue here. While it is useful to look at presidential elections for guidance—they epitomize campaign strategy, and most students of politics already know the plots and players—for the most part, the book addresses the strategies, tactics, and technologies most appropriate for midlevel elections such as those for Congress, state legislature, county executive, and city council. Chapter 2 provides a glimpse into campaign plans at that level.

Part One investigates campaign context, beginning with Chapter 3, which looks at the mix of factors that defines a particular electoral race. This examination is followed by an extended look at demographic analysis in Chapter 4. Chapter 5 examines opposition research—the collection of detrimental data on candidates.

Part Two looks at elements of strategic thinking. It begins with an overview of electoral targeting in Chapter 6, moving on to survey research in Chapter 7 and general strategy in Chapter 8. Here, the "art" of new-style campaigning can be found.

Part Three looks at voter contact techniques, beginning with campaign fund-raising in Chapter 9, moving forward to communications in Chapter 10 (media strategy) and Chapter 11 (news coverage) and grassroots voter contact techniques in Chapter 12. Finally, in a concluding chapter, the future of campaign organization is explored in light of new data management and voter contact technologies.

Throughout, the book maintains that a critical transformation of American elections is underway. New-style campaigning has taken hold from the presidential level down to town council contests. Political scientists have taken steps toward understanding many of the larger processes, but the details have been elusive. Gerald Pomper noted a quarter century ago that although Americans choose over half a million public officials through the ballot, "elections are a mystery" (1974, 1). The intention of this book is to explain the basic operation of campaigns and hopefully to underscore both the art and the science of professional electioneering.

Chapter Two

The Campaign Plan

Campaign manuals are unanimous on the importance of advance planning. One says, "[T]he need to make a plan and follow that plan is absolutely crucial" (Grey 1999, 96). From another, "A flowchart is an essential tool in any successful campaign. It is helpful for the campaign team because members can see the plan of the whole campaign. Flowcharts keep the campaign organized" (Shaw 2000, 249). Yet another tells its readers, "[D]o not ever go into a campaign without some sort of plan" (Bike 1998, 176). Indeed, "[A] chart can have a calming effect on the candidate and staff because it clearly outlines exactly what needs to be done and when" (Shaw 2000, 249). S.J. Guzzetta talks about the shock of insight that accompanies forward thinking: "As you read this Manual you will notice the relatively high costs and enormous amount of work involved. The immediate reaction generally is, 'Is all this really necessary to win?' The answer is an emphatic YES" (2000, 129).

Planning is critical. In Theodore White's classic book on the 1960 presidential campaign, one sees how John F. Kennedy and his advisers spent three years planning their run for the presidency. A year before the election, a late October strategy session was held to lay out the "final assault plans" (White 1961, 53). In the morning, Senator Kennedy ticked off the general plan for each region, each state, even getting into the details of local political issues and factions. After lunch, with brother Bobby taking the lead, the day turned to "operational" matters, and "assignments were to be distributed and the nation quartered up by the Kennedy staff as if a political general staff were giving each of its combat commanders a specific front of operations" (1961, 56). Thus began one of the hardest-fought presidential campaigns in recent history.

In the early 1960s, Kennedy's brand of discipline was noteworthy. In the new millennium, it is routine. Contemporary campaign manuals offer sample work sheets, basic strategies, and even model campaign calendars to guide readers through the planning process. Every theater of operations presents unique challenges. Campaign planning is not a one-size-fits-all endeavor. But there are some overarching principles. This chapter discusses the main reasons to develop campaign plans and the contents of a typical plan, along with some notes on strategy and timing that often guide the planning process.

THE NEED FOR CAMPAIGN PLANS

Consultants who expect to deal with problems on the fly will likely find themselves wishing that they had planned ahead of time. Open-ended assignments become failed assignments; undefined schedules become wasted time. As noted by one top consultant, "Neil Armstrong could never have reached the moon simply by pointing the rocket" (Sweeney 1995, 15). Campaigns entail details and deadlines, not to mention ever-changing circumstances. Without written plans, campaigns founder, and in competitive races they tend to fail. A campaign plan, it has been said, is meant to "bring order out of that chaos we call the democratic process" (Grey 1999, 95).

A campaign plan defines *what* is to be done, *when* it should be done, *who* should be doing it, and *what* will be needed to finish the job. Good plans divide responsibility, integrate work, and offer a step-by-step blueprint of the election. With agendas and timetables in hand, everyone on the campaign has a job to do. A plan might be flexible; it might change; it might even require fundamental revision at the campaign's midpoint, yet the campaign plan remains a basic management tool for coordinating a diverse, concurrent, mutually dependent series of tasks.

Thoughtful campaign plans minimize campaign uncertainty. A plan helps keep the candidate fixed on strategy, smoothing the impact of opposition attacks and tightening the focus on the endgame. As noted, the very existence of a campaign plan can go a long way toward assuaging the fears of an overly anxious candidate or staff. It is all too easy for volunteers and paid staffers to become fixated on day-to-day assaults, which tempt the campaign team to get off-message and reallocate resources away from mission-critical objectives. A campaign plan can help keep everyone on task and on schedule, or at least it can help maintain big-picture perspective on day-to-day volatility.

Uncertainty is minimized, in part, by weeding out redundancy. Establishing command authority and delegating staff responsibilities, a campaign plan can go a long way toward conserving precious time and money. Canvassing the same neighborhood twice with the same flyer is a waste of resources. In some instances, duplication can be not just profligate, but downright harmful. If more than one staff member is talking to reporters, conflicting messages might appear in the press, leaving the campaign in the embarrassing position of explaining what it was really trying to say. In a world where image tends to become substance, a confused campaign looks irresolute, perhaps too weak for governance.

Plans not only help to guide internal campaign operations but also inspire confidence in potential supporters and the news media. The candidate starts to look like a winner—an invaluable attribute, because one of the most difficult obstacles that a challenger has to overcome is public skepticism. People assume that incumbents are entrenched and that there is almost no point in supporting anyone crazy enough to buck the system. "Sure losers" are given scant attention by reporters and even less help from donors. A strong campaign plan leads influential people to see that the campaign is serious, that it will be conducted in an organized, efficient manner and will not waste resources or miss opportunities. The party faithful, prospective donors, and even the media elites might start to think that there is a way to get to the front of the pack.

ELEMENTS OF A CAMPAIGN PLAN

The contours of a new-style campaign plan vary from candidate to candidate, campaign to campaign, consultant to consultant. There is no single, step-by-step guide. Nevertheless, a core set of elements are addressed by serious campaign organizations. A strong plan lays out contextual information, voter summaries, and strategy and tactics, as well as staffing and resource requirements. A brief listing here illustrates some of the elements that typify a well-written plan.

District Profile. Campaigns must understand the district's geography, industry, housing patterns, community organizations, transportation infrastructure, and other fixed variables. This is the political terrain on which the candidate will maneuver. A campaign operation must chart the territory before the race begins. See Chapter 3.

Demographic Profile. Political professionals understand the close relationship between the characteristics of a voting population and electoral outcomes. For example, districts with a large number of union members tend to vote Democratic—and even a Republican candidate will have to pay attention to labor issues. A demographic profile sketches the characteristics of the voters, often including a narrative description along with maps and summary tables. See Chapter 4.

Candidate and Opposition Profiles. Personal and professional qualifications are almost always highlighted in a campaign plan. Heavy emphasis is placed on a candidate's background, experience, committee posts, bill sponsorship, appointments, and so on. The same goes for the opposition. As new-style campaigns have become increasingly "comparative," even "negative," it has become critical to research one's self and one's opponent. See Chapter 5.

Electoral History. One of the best ways to predict future voter behavior is to look at recent elections. The past truly is prologue. A ward that has voted Republican in the past will likely vote Republican in the future. Even in the Digital Age, campaigns are tied to their geography—candidates are still expected to walk door to door—so it is useful to determine which parts of the district will be most receptive to the candidate's message. See Chapter 6.

Public Opinion. Campaigns have become increasingly reliant on polls. A section of the plan regarding public opinion might contain an overview of voter concerns and topics of interest to voters throughout the district. If a campaign expects to hire a pollster, some thought might be given to the types of information that will be sought—what sorts of questions should be asked and how the data should be used. See Chapter 7.

General Strategy. Candidate positioning is a crucial part of any plan. The campaign must know where the candidate will appear on the political spectrum. A conservative candidate in a middle-of-the-road district might call attention to the moderate aspects of the campaign agenda. A liberal candidate might reword progressive issues in more conservative terms. Often, in an effort to clearly identify what the campaign is all about, a one-page rationale is in order, answering the question, Who will vote for this candidate, and why? See Chapter 8.

Fund Raising Plan. Strategies cost money to implement, and the money has to come from somewhere. This section discusses how the campaign war chest will be filled—who will give the money and when it can be expected to arrive. See Chapter 9.

Communications Strategy. A strategic plan for campaign communications is commonly broken into subsections—one for each medium. There might be separate schedules for radio, television, and a campaign Web site. This section also lays out a strategy for news coverage—press events and meetings with editorial boards, for example. One-page summaries of the candidate's stand on all the expected issues of the race might be included, and a set of more detailed position papers with prepared questions and answers is often developed for rapid-response purposes. See Chapters 10 and 11.

Grassroots. Even as an increasing share of campaign spending is devoted to media outreach, campaigns continue traditional grassroots efforts such as knocking on doors and putting up signs. Particularly important are "get-out-the-vote" drives, which professionals pronounce as "G-O-T-V"—making sure those who have committed themselves to voting for the candidate actually cast a ballot. (See Chapter 12.)

NOTES ON STRATEGY

According to Joseph Napolitan (1986), strategies must fit the candidates who use them. Strategic plans often imply difficult choices. When the candidate is not comfortable with the plan, blunders tend to follow. A candidate who is disappointed with the plan can become hostile, second-guessing staff decisions. No campaign manager wants to hear the candidate ask, "Why am I doing this?" The ideal plan will be so well understood, so strongly documented, and so deeply ingrained in all campaign activities that the reason for every event will be obvious. The alternative is organizational chaos. "One of the worst things that can happen is to have a campaign go off in several different directions simultaneously" (1986, 27). If actions do not occur when and where they should, coordination is lost, resources are wasted, and the wrong message is sent.

Careful attention must be paid to message consistency. Throughout the race, a variety of messages may be put forth, but all must relate to a single core theme.

Many campaigns have a message-of-the-week. For each seven-day period, one aspect of the campaign theme will be hammered home—the expectation being that repetition helps the message break through. To avoid mixed messages, campaign managers insist that policy pronouncements not overlap. If, for instance, the campaign is interested in following a pro-environment track during a given week, all communications during this period should reinforce that theme, and nothing should be said regarding consumer protection. Later, if radio spots are aimed at consumer protection, the direct mailer should be sending the consumer protection letters just as the press secretary tries to get these same issues in the daily paper.

Careful media planning helps a campaign stay on message. One effective strategy is to get the campaign into the news and then use paid advertising to reinforce the news coverage. Before any candidate ran a paid ad touting the 1994 Republican Contract with America, GOP organizers ensured maximum attention on the airwaves. A massive event was held on the steps of the Capitol Building, with rows of GOP candidates pledging their allegiance to Republican principles. It was a show of unity and power. Live shots were beamed to local stations after consulting news directors to find out what they wanted to air (Tron 1996, 50–52). In the months that followed, campaign advertisements bolstered the message of GOP unity planted in the minds of voters by a powerful news event.

Finally, successful campaigns try to think a few moves ahead, figuring out what the opposition will do and then developing options for dealing with the consequences. According to one strategist, "There's nothing more pleasing, from the point of view of a strategist, than to work against an incumbent who runs the same campaign again and again" (Shea and Brooks 1995, 24). Why? Because it is easy to predict what the opposition will do, and far simpler to outmaneuver and disarm it. If the candidate's own record is vulnerable, then responses must be devised ahead of time. If there are weaknesses in some of the planned campaign promises, it is better to know what they are prior to the announcement. As consultant Mark Weaver suggests, the job of a campaign is "to predict the counter-attack and be ready—because it will come" (Shea and Brooks 1995, 29). Like chess, campaign politics is very much a game of predicting and defeating opposition tactics before they come into play. A campaign plan helps bring the future into view.

NOTES ON TIMING

The integration of tactical elements into a unified blueprint is difficult. The timing of each step often hangs on preceding steps. Fund-raising usually comes first, and voter contact might best proceed after the accumulation of survey data. Messages are most effective when they reinforce one another, so campaign ads should complement news coverage (and vice versa). The budgeting process must find a way to match income and outflow. Campaign literature should bear a strong resemblance to campaign signage, both of which are contingent upon the general message of the campaign, which, in turn, depends on the strategic positioning of the candidate, which might not be known until after the opposition party has chosen its candidate. The effort to assemble all the pieces into a consistent whole can be an organizational nightmare.

At the tactical level, some campaigns are urged to map their plans as a flowchart, starting with "about ten feet of butcher paper," and, "by placing colored sticky notes for every function in a campaign, you build a visual representation of the campaign" (Shaw 2000, 250, 51). Butcher paper and sticky notes are giving way to sophisticated project management software—but the basic theory has not changed. Tasks must be divided into their constituent parts, arrayed one after the next, and organized so that everything can be completed by the time the election is held. Election Day being a hard-and-fast deadline, most political strategists think in reverse, starting with the last day of the campaign and moving toward the first. "For example," it is suggested, "you know you will need to repair lawn signs the day after Halloween, so put that on a green note above October 31. Lawn signs go up usually one month before an election, so put that up next" (250). This sort of backward mapping ensures that campaigns will not run out of time at the end of the election cycle.

At the strategic level, some scholars see a three-stage evolution in voter attitudes: "cognition" (awareness of the candidate), "affect" (development of opinions about the candidate), and "evaluation" (the decision itself) (Salmore and Salmore 1989, 13–14). Political professionals think in terms of "name ID" (similar to "cognition"), "persuasion" (bringing people to believe in one's candidate), and "motivation" (getting them to go out and vote). For some voters, each phase follows the next in a matter of seconds. Strongly partisan voters know instantly who will get their votes and that they will, in fact, show up at the polls. For others, the process may take time as the candidates come to their awareness, as impressions are formed, and then as a decision is made—perhaps in the voting booth. Either way, campaign planners must know where the candidate stands at the outset of the campaign (Guzzetta 2000; Salmore and Salmore 1989).

Gordon Smith, an Oregon Republican, showed the value in achieving name recognition in his U.S. Senate race when he flooded the television airways with ads early in his January 1996 special election campaign, even though it temporarily depleted his treasury (Gruenwald 1995). Smith narrowly lost that race but won the race for Oregon's other Senate seat months later, his name ID having been well established. In some campaigns, particularly those for lower-level posts, the first phase is not well achieved until late in the campaign—if at all. Consultants Ron Brown and Nello Giorgetti go so far as to suggest that

> for nine out of ten campaigns for local professional offices, the message is the candidate's name—repeated endlessly as election day draws near. It's more important to place the candidate's name before the voter, than a discussion of the office itself. (Brown and Giorgetti 1992, 51)

In high-profile races, however, where the candidates might already be well known, the shift from cognition to affect can begin early, thereby allowing a discussion of issues and other thematic messages.

Billboards, bumper stickers, and yard signs serve almost no function besides establishing name identification and perhaps party affiliation (if shown). There is some question as to whether the best approach is to get these materials out as early as possible—slowly building momentum as time goes by—or if a last-minute explosion will have greater impact (Shaw 2000, 91–92). In some jurisdictions the choice is dictated by local ordinances regulating the number of days prior to an election that yard signs are allowable. In others, the fact that yard signs are vulnerable to late-campaign vandalism might force a decision to use billboards. In recent years, campaigns have refrained from using bumper stickers because they tend to become collectors' items, never entering the campaign at all.

Campaign themes occupy a prominent place at the planning roundtable as the candidate's strategic positioning is discussed and debated. Should the candidate be presented as a moderate, a liberal, or a right-wing conservative? Political professionals always want to control the positioning of the candidate. Mary Matalin calls it "Cardinal rule 101 of politics: *Never let the other side define you*" (Matalin and Carville 1995, 72). When voters have no information about a candidate, they are believed to be susceptible to the first information that they hear. Research suggests that communications are most likely to be effective in the absence of "a nexus of mediating factors" (Whillock 1991, 9). In other words, people tend to believe the first thing that they hear, and voters pay more attention to messages that reflect their preexisting views (see also Diamond and Bates 1992). Sometimes the opposition is completely unknown and is therefore vulnerable. If the sponge is to be filled, the campaign wants to fill it. In fact, the corollary to cardinal rule 101 might well be, "Always define the opponent early."

Defining candidates requires money and media. Early money allows a campaign to attract more money, and just as importantly, it allows the campaign to get a jump on the opposition in the television air war. Timing is important because television is a limited commodity. Campaigns that fail to buy ad slots early see the best ones sold out from under them. Local affiliates can run out of choice pre–Election Day slots because the opposition has already bought up all available time.

End-of-the-campaign media runs are critical because campaigns are often won and lost during the final week. Scholarly evidence suggests that as much as 15 percent of the electorate makes its decision in the final few days (Shea 1996b). Although 85 percent decides well ahead of Election Day, the undecided voters often determine the election. The final push is critical. When a consultant for Democrat Kathleen Brown's 1994 California gubernatorial campaign failed to keep any cash on hand for the standard end-of-the-cycle media blitz, a fellow professional was quoted as saying the consultant "should be tried for political malpractice" (Wallace 1994). The looming possibility that a campaign will run out of money terrifies campaign planners.

All are agreed that late-cycle ads are a good thing, but is this the only time for attack ads? Many challengers attack from the very beginning. Consultant Gary Nordlinger sees little choice: "When most challengers only have one-fourth the money that the incumbent has, he needs to concentrate on the sleeping giants"

(Shea and Brooks 1995, 25). This, of course, means attacking early and attacking often. Other professionals suggest that a candidate's credibility must be established before the attack begins (Whillock 1991). Without the weight of a valid source behind it, charges may not stick—especially in today's political environment where charges and countercharges are commonplace. Incumbents must make a similar choice. The old rule was that a well-established incumbent should ignore challenger attacks. There is no point in giving them the dignity of a response. But after a series of elections in the 1980s, when several aloof incumbents went down to defeat, the conventional wisdom started to shift. Should incumbents sit idly by, knowing that the attack is coming? Perhaps "[i]ncumbents can no longer ignore attacks" (see Shea and Brooks 1995, 25).

Whether attack ads work best at the beginning or at the end of a campaign cycle, the boundaries of that cycle are becoming blurred. Mail-in ballots and the loosening of absentee ballot rules change the timing of elections by allowing a larger number of people to vote early. Strategists must re-time their tactics to fit the new environment. If Internet voting takes hold, the time frame of the cycle may be rendered even more vague, further complicating the timing of strategic plans.

CONCLUSION

Few battle plans survive intact. Without perfect knowledge, mistakes will be made. "The best laid plans of mice and men," Robert Burns intoned, "gan aft agley"—that is, they "can go awry"—"and leave naught but grief and pain for promised joy." If a campaign plan is not premised on an accurate reading of the past, present, and future, of the candidate and the opponent, of the strengths and weaknesses of both campaign teams, and of the voting public, even the most detailed campaign plan will disappoint.

In 1991, those who planned George Bush Sr.'s reelection effort assumed—quite reasonably—that the economy would pick up, that there would be no opponent in the GOP primaries, that the White House and the campaign organization would work cooperatively, and that the president would not have to hit the hustings in earnest until after the Republican Convention. Events unfolded differently. The economy continued to stagnate, conservative television commentator Pat Buchanan ran hard in the early primaries, coordination between the White House and the campaign operation was in constant disarray, and, because the president chose to govern instead of campaign, he fell so far behind Bill Clinton that recovery became all but impossible. The Bush campaign plan—thoughtful though it may have been—was doomed from the start.

Although this chapter has discussed general considerations used to devise campaign plans, a wise strategist knows that a plan is only as good as its assumptions and that assumptions can be terribly wrong. On one hand, the value of a campaign plan is that it keeps the organization focused in troubled times; on the other hand, however, sticking to a flawed plan extends the agony. Campaign strategists must decide when to cut the rope and when to hang on.

Part One

THE LAY OF THE LAND: UNDERSTANDING THE CAMPAIGN CONTEXT

Chapter Three

The Context of the Race

Reinhold Niebuhr, the American theologian, once wrote a prayer that cautioned against foolish thinking. Support groups of all description would later soften its meaning, but what is now called the "Serenity Prayer" was originally expressed in Old Testament prose. It read,

> God, give us grace to accept with serenity the things that cannot be changed, courage to change the things that should be changed, and the wisdom to distinguish between the two. (Sifton 1998)

The prayer was intended to focus the mind not on quietude but on stern wisdom—drawing attention to the rigors of differentiating the tractable from the intractable.

In a way, Niebuhr was describing an important part of political wisdom—the ability to look at a race, a district, or an opponent and then distinguish what can be changed from what cannot. The difference is not always clear. In some districts, the number of registered voters is something that cannot be modified, while in others, a strong voter registration drive can force a dramatic transformation in the eligible electorate. New-style politics begins with an understanding of campaign context. Political consultants talk about the "the landscape," "the environment," or "the political terrain." What office is in play? What do the demographics look like? Who else will be on the ballot? A discussion of strategy and tactics is meaningless until the context is understood—until the tractable elements are distinguished from the intractable.

The first part of this book deals specifically with campaign context. These are the things that, for the most part, cannot be changed. This chapter lists many of the basic features of a political terrain—the office being sought, incumbency status, multiplayer scenarios, election-year type, national trends, candidates for other offices, geography, and other contextual issues. The next two chapters offer a detailed discussion of demographic and candidate profiles, but this chapter begins with an elementary problem, understanding the electoral nature of the office sought.

THE OFFICE BEING SOUGHT

Successful mayors sometimes fail miserably when they run for Congress. Successful congressional representatives sometimes endure embarrassing defeats when they attempt to move over to the Senate. One reason for this phenomenon is simple: the larger constituency may be different from the smaller ones inside it. The electorate of a city will not be the same as the congressional district in which it is situated. True enough. Another possibility is that voters have different expectations for a mayor, a member of Congress, and a senator. A loud tie and bombastic personality may be loved in local politicians and loathed in higher officials. The formality of an executive might seem pompous in a legislator. Many candidates have learned the hard way that the nature of the office sought affects the fundamentals of the campaign.

What the Voters Expect

In matters as basic as tone, body language, and personal style, distinctions make a difference. Voters might expect a Senate candidate to wear a dark suit but might regard prospective county commissioners in business attire as haughty. A judicial candidate will usually want to sound nonpartisan. Candidates for mayor will be required to know the details of local zoning laws and sewer problems; a candidate for the U.S. House of Representatives, standing before the very same audience, will be forgiven if he or she does not know the nuances of recent tax levies but will likely be expected to speak intelligently on issues of national importance—the federal budget, for example.

How does one discern what types of issues are best addressed in House, Senate, judicial, or mayoral campaigns? There are no clear guidelines. Campaigns look at the political history of the district, paying close attention to the themes of prior successful and unsuccessful candidates. They look at the issues that the current officeholder manages. Well-funded campaigns may commission surveys. Pollsters ask not only about issues but about the kind of official who can best handle these concerns. When people say education is important, they might mean (1) that the state and local government, not federal bureaucrats, should invest more in schools, (2) that the federal government should offer better education funding, or (3) that there is enough money, but parents need to get involved. Matching the right issues to the wrong office can prove costly, as the campaign gets involved in matters that the electorate thinks inappropriate.

Voters seem to match issues to offices, and offices to candidate qualities. Research in this area is not well developed, but, roughly speaking, candidates for executive posts are expected to have leadership skills and the ability to implement programs. Stephen Wayne, the distinguished scholar of presidential elections, conducted a survey to determine what voters most admire in presidents. The Chief Executive was expected to be "strong" and "decisive" and have the "ability to get things done" (1982, 192–95). One would expect to find similar attributes admired in gubernatorial and mayoral candidates, which also involve executive leadership. On the other hand, legislative candidates might need to form a close connection with the average voter. Different candidates have different styles (Fenno 1978), but legislative representation is generally expected to be constituent-focused. Asked whether members of Congress should look after the needs of "their own district" or the "interest of the nation," a Harris survey found that respondents favored the former, 57 to 34 percent (Nelson 1995, 17).

A final element of voter expectation relates to formality of tone. In some districts, voters expect executive and judicial candidates to run serious, issue-based campaigns, but allow legislative candidates free play to go on the attack. In other jurisdictions, all candidates, even prospective judges, can take the partisan offensive. Such expectations change over time. Traditional wisdom holds that candidates for the U.S. Senate should remain stately, but during his successful 1992 bid for the Senate, Russ Feingold ran a television spot featuring Elvis—or perhaps an Elvis impersonator—who had come out of hiding to lend his endorsement. Wisconsin voters gave Feingold a comfortable victory. Gubernatorial candidates should have executive stature, but in 1998 Minnesotans elected former professional wrestler Jesse "The Body" Ventura, whose television ads featured a seemingly naked Ventura as the model for Auguste Rodin's sculpture *The Thinker*.

Ventura used a body double—nudity is still taboo—but the conventions of candidate apparel have been changing. Not long ago, it was believed that candidates should wear business attire in public. They might doff their jackets at barbecues and ice-cream socials, but they should arrive wearing a suit. In some areas this advice still holds true, but at a time when even corporate executives endorse "casual Fridays," business attire tends to connote self-importance. Campaign ads and brochures today often show the candidate talking to citizens with a jacket casually draped over the shoulder. As more and more women have joined the ranks of the elected, bright colors have become acceptable, and during the 2000 presidential primary season, much was made of Vice President Al Gore's decision to switch from dark blue pinstripes to friendlier earth tones. Of course, when a candidate—any candidate, male or female, mayoral or presidential—is photographed with sleeves rolled up, the intended meaning is obvious: it's time to get to work.

Media Relations

The office being sought affects not just voter expectations but also the candidate's relationship with the media. Successfully obtaining news coverage is one of a campaign's most important goals. In order to gain positive press, a strategist must understand what reporters expect from a candidate. To many voters, the line between local, state, and national problems is hazy, but to good reporters it is fairly clear: federal candidates will be expected to have a grasp of national issues, state contestants should know about state issues, and local office-seekers should understand community concerns.

Generally speaking, the higher the office, the greater the scrutiny. Senate candidates are often surprised by the rigorous grilling that they receive from the news media. Candidates caught unprepared are tagged as incompetent or naïve. In 1994, Spencer Abraham defeated Ronna Romney for the GOP Senate nomination in Michigan by suggesting that she did not have a solid grip on the issues. By the end of the campaign, the media agreed. The *Free Press* called Romney "unbelievably shallow" after a poor showing in a debate (Beiler 1994a, 32). Incumbents are not immune. Some incumbents are unlucky enough to be listed among *The Progressive* magazine's "Dimmest Bulbs in Congress." Local papers pick up such stories and run them in their political columns.

Scrutiny of professional and personal shortcomings also varies according to office, with the importance of an infraction increasing with power of an official. A reporter who finds dirt on a state legislative candidate might never report the discovery. Congressional candidates are held to a higher standard. Wes Cooley, an Oregon congressman, was convicted in 1997 for making false statements on a voter guide. He had claimed to be a veteran of the Korean War, when he never actually served in Korea. Cooley later explained, "I shouldn't even have said Korea. . . . I was in the Army. I was in the Special Forces. At that period of time, the Korean conflict was going on" (Egan 1996). The congressman was forced to step down. Previously, when running for a seat in the state Senate, Cooley had apparently "moved a trailer into the district so he could qualify as a resident," although "neighbors said he never lived in the district" (Egan 1996). Cooley got away with a seeming untruth at one level of government—he served as a state senator until his election to Congress—but once in Washington his past became news.

Ironically, the lesser scrutiny to which lower-level offices are held may allow for a greater number of unfair charges. Whereas attacks on House and Senate candidates are often checked for accuracy, charges against state and local candidates are rarely investigated. Reporters are overworked, underpaid, and have a great many demands on their time. They suggest that their job is to report the news, not to referee political fights (Dunn 1995, 117). Rather than track down every charge that one candidate makes against another, journalists concentrate on higher-level races. Since 1992, "ad watch" journalism—emphasizing the disclosure of inaccuracies (Ansolabehere and Iyengar 1995)—has come into its own. Presidential and Senate candidates can expect to see their commercials, speeches, and debate remarks reviewed for content while many state and local candidates are effectively held to a lower standard of accuracy. The task of keeping politicians honest is left to the candidates and their campaigns.

Overall Interest in the Campaign

Political novices sometimes become frustrated that their campaigns rarely make the news—and, in fact, that it may be of little interest to most voters. This is a natural phenomenon. Candidates, party activists, volunteers, and even some professional consultants become deeply involved in their campaigns and come to believe that others should be as well, yet most voters prefer to think about their spouses, children, bills, vacations, hobbies, cars, and jobs. Elections are of marginal concern.

Not all offices are ignored equally, however. There is a hierarchy of interest, starting at the top of the ballot with presidential races and dropping to Senate and House races—with the rest falling a distance below, right down to judicial posts and other offices (e.g., coroner) that few voters care about. One former elected appellate judge entirely dismisses television as a means of communicating with voters: "You can . . . forget about any broadcast coverage of your campaign as a news event. . . . [N]ews divisions are operated as entertainment enterprises, and serious news is often not entertaining" (Grey 1999, 170). Statewide and large-city mayoral races receive a good deal of coverage, but most congressional campaigns are given short shrift. Absent a controversy, a colorful candidate, or a cliff-hanger, the general rule is that city council, county legislative, state legislative, and judicial races will be ignored. There are opportunities for coverage—creativity counts—but no guarantees.

The problem of voter inattention for lower-level candidates can be seen in both the number of votes and amount of money that go to "down-ballot" races. Voters at the polls almost always select a candidate for president, governor, and congressional representative, but many leave the ballot blank for county commissioner. Lower-level offices can suffer more than a 40 percent drop-off from the top of the ballot. The same is true in political fund-raising. Individuals and organizations give money to candidates partly because they are aware of the campaign, maybe even excited by it. Presidents raise millions of dollars; county commissioners raise thousands. If few people are familiar with the race, few contribute. Candidates sometimes feel that they are caught in a vicious cycle: without attention, they cannot get money, and without money, they cannot get attention—and as a result, many voters fail to take the time to look for the candidate's name at the bottom of the ballot.

INCUMBENCY STATUS

No other contextual element has a greater bearing on the outcome of the election than incumbency status. There are three basic types of election: uncontested, contested incumbency, and open-seat. An uncontested race, where the incumbent has no challenger, is obviously the most predictable, since there is literally no opposition, and the winner is a foregone conclusion. Races in which the incumbent is contested usually go to the current officeholder, because, as much as people say they want to "throw the bums out," they usually return their own representatives to office. Most uncertain is an open-seat election. Two well-qualified newcomers running against one another can make for exciting political drama. In rare instances, incumbents are pitted against one another after their districts are merged. In 1992, Republican congressman Bob McEwen defeated fellow Ohio Republican Clarence Miller in a brutal intraparty fight that ultimately led to the election of a Democrat. Redistricting may bring more incumbent-incumbent races in 2002.

Despite occasional twists of fate, incumbency offers candidates a tremendously valuable resource. Officeholders enjoy higher early name recognition than challengers, deeper relations with the news media, more experienced staff, better finances, a broader base of volunteers, and stronger connections with parties and interest groups. Incumbents have usually cultivated their relationship with the electorate through publicly financed mailings, town hall meetings, and scores of receptions and dinners. Furthermore, incumbents, by definition, have at least minimal appeal—they were already elected at least once. Even in the Republican sweep of 1994, renowned for the number of sitting members it pushed out of office, fully 90 percent of incumbents were retained. In 1998, 394 of the 401 incumbents who ran for reelection were approved by the voters—a 98.3 percent victory rate (Abramson, Aldrich, and Rohde 1999, 250). These percentages are lower for executive posts, but they remain above the two-thirds mark for mayors and governors.

If an incumbent is scandal-free and makes no great mistake, the challenger's odds are slim. Most nonincumbents have comparatively little name recognition. Political action committees and major donors are hesitant to back a challenger for fear of antagonizing the incumbent—the person most likely to be making policy after the election. According to congressional election scholar Paul Herrnson, "The typical House incumbent involved in a two-party contested race raised just under $818,000 in cash and party coordinated expenditures in 1998, which is three times more than the sum raised by the typical House challenger" (2000, 151). Incumbents, whose official position carries intrinsic power, can get news releases printed by local papers, while challengers might not get any reporter to cover their announcement speeches. Incumbents nearly always attract more attention and a bigger crowd.

There are exceptions to the rule. Generally speaking, the higher the profile of the race, the weaker the advantage for the incumbent. Presidents, governors, and U.S. senators benefit from better media coverage, especially in the early periods of the race, but these carefully watched races offer significant media coverage to the challenger as well. Often, the challenger is a significant player in his or her own right. Charles Schumer was a powerful member of the House of Representatives when he challenged New York senator Alfonse D'Amato in 1998. Given the profile of the race (all Senate races in New York are high-interest affairs) and given Schumer's long-term position in the House, media coverage was roughly equal for each. The 2000 New York Senate race, which featured first-time candidate, Hillary

Rodham Clinton, wife of the sitting president, received worldwide media attention and more than enough votes to make her a U.S. senator, even though her opponent was a sitting congressman.

Challengers have a few unique tools at their disposal. Many incumbents run the same campaign time after time—a warning sign, according to polling consultant Neil Newhouse, of "incumbentitis," whereby incumbents look upon a past successful campaign as the model for all future campaigns (Shea and Brooks 1995, 24). Moreover, incumbents have a record to defend, while a political novice might have a clean slate—sometimes an enviable possession. Says one columnist, "The most difficult opponent is somebody who's never run for anything" (Persinos 1994, 22). Likewise, although it has traditionally been perceived as undignified for an elected official to go on the offensive, challengers have little to lose. This rule may be changing—incumbents are going on the attack much more often than they did in the 1970s—but the problem of early attacks can still be dicey. To ignore challengers is to refuse them recognition; to attack challengers is to add credence to their candidacy. Few political stories get more coverage than an underdog's catching up to an incumbent who everyone thought would win. In fact, a challenger who persuades reporters of the campaign's viability is laying the basis for a media-ready Horatio Alger story.

Although open-seat elections tend to offer a more even footing than those in which the incumbent wins, they present their own unique challenges. In the recent past, many open seats were considered noncompetitive; the partisan predisposition of the districts was lopsided, giving the candidate of the dominant party a distinct advantage. Today, however, with the decline of party identification, many open seats are considered toss-ups. Pennsylvania's thirteenth congressional district, located in the suburbs of Philadelphia, powerfully illustrated this point. Marjorie Margolies-Mezvinsky cracked a seventy-six-year Republican lock by defeating Jon D. Fox in an open-seat contest. No Democrat had received more than 44 percent since 1968 in this wealthy, Republican enclave (Duncan 1993, 1323). Nevertheless, Margolies-Mezvinsky was able to take the seat with an independent-minded campaign. Unfortunately for Margolies-Mezvinsky, the seat returned to its Republican leanings in 1994, when Jon Fox put the seat back into the Republican column. (Two years later, however, Fox would lose the seat to a moderate Democrat.)

MULTIPLAYER SCENARIOS

Elections are commonly imagined as head-to-head battles, but many races involve more than two major players. Many elections have multicandidate fields, and some even have outside interests playing a large role.

Generally speaking, there are two types of multicandidate fields: (1) party primaries and (2) general elections containing third-party, independent, and write-in candidates. Both are difficult to strategize. In primaries, party members are running against one another, and it is common to see rancorous family infighting. Three, four, five, or more candidates might run in a primary, and figuring out how the vote will swing often becomes a matter of speculation and argumentation. Some primaries, particularly in the South, have a two-step process. If a candidate garners more than 50 percent, the election is won; if, however, no candidate crosses the 50 percent mark, then the top vote-getters are forced into a two-way runoff. In Louisiana all candidates run in one primary, regardless of party. And in some jurisdictions, a handful of "at large" seats will go to the top vote-getters: five candidates might vie for three seats, and the three candidates with the largest number of votes win. At-large races, like runoffs and all other types of contested elections, require a good deal of planning and forethought in order to win.

Increasingly, the strategic problems of primaries are creeping into general election campaigns. With the decline in party identification, voters are beginning to see greater numbers of multicandidate general elections. Billionaire Ross Perot, a populist fiscal conservative, added strategic complexity to the campaigns of Bill Clinton and George Bush, which were forced to determine which aspect of the Perot candidacy had greater pull: (1) Perot's folksy call for reform, which would appeal to Clinton voters, or (2) his demand for deficit reduction, which would appeal to Bush voters. Neither campaign knew for sure. Perhaps the most dramatic example of a third-party candidacy was Jesse Ventura's Reform Party triumph in Minnesota. The Democratic candidate had suffered through a bitter primary campaign; the Republican candidate was a former Democrat who had yet to establish a firm GOP base; with the major party candidates busy attacking one another, Ventura ran up the middle and won the election.

Ventura's victory was anomalous. Third-party candidates rarely win, but they often make a difference. They can erode a major party candidate's base of support, undercut the intended message, and siphon off volunteers. Third-party candidates do not affect incumbents and challengers equally. According to Herrnson, "House members who must defeat both a major-party opponent and significant additional opposition average almost 10 percent fewer votes than those who did not" (1998, 204). One reason for this disparity is that minor party candidates often join the race because they are dissatisfied with the incumbent. It is no accident that Ventura's win came at the expense of two well-known Minnesota officeholders. That was precisely the point of his campaign.

Another new challenge to major party campaigns in the late 1990s was the introduction of interest groups as outside forces. Federal campaign law permits outsiders to run ads promoting or criticizing congressional candidates. If the ads never make a specific pitch for votes—if they never say "*vote* for Senator Smith" and instead restrict the message to something like "*call* the senator and thank him for doing a great job"—then the interest group can make enormous ad buys with minimal restrictions.

A study of "strategic battlegrounds" in the 1998 congressional campaigns found "an important shift from candidate centered campaigns to campaigns with candidates competing with interest groups and parties for control of the election agenda and the attention of voters" (Magleby 2000, 211). The battle over Utah's second congressional district saw heavy spending by a group interested in term limits. Incumbent Merrill Cook, an independent-turned-Republican, faced Democrat Lily

Eskelsen, considered by many a strong contender for Cook's seat. Eskelsen wanted to make the election a referendum on Cook's record, touting education and other issues where Eskelsen seemed to have the advantage. The difficulty, however, was that Americans for Limited Terms put $380,000 into a broad-based, anti-Cook ad campaign (Goodliffe 2000, 171). One observer noted that "while the efforts of the parties largely neutralized each other, the term-limits campaign significantly increased the negativity of the campaign, which ultimately reflected poorly on Lily Eskelsen, whom they were supporting" (171).

THE ELECTION YEAR

Campaign professionals talk about three different kinds of campaign year: "on," "off," and "odd." An "on-year" election occurs when there are presidential candidates on the ballot (e.g., 1996, 2000, 2004). "Off-year" elections also occur every four years, but the off-years are so called because there is no presidential contest (e.g., 1994, 1998, 2002). Finally, "odd-year" elections occur in odd-numbered years (e.g., 1999, 2001, 2003). There are neither presidential nor congressional elections in odd years, except for occasional "special" elections held to fill a prematurely vacated House or Senate seat.

The type of election year is important to campaign planning because the number of people going to the polls varies significantly. Turnout is almost always highest during on-years, due to the attention given presidential campaigns. In addition, the entire House of Representatives, one-third of the Senate, most state legislators, and many governors are elected during on-years. Generally speaking, off-years will have the next highest turnout. Although the president is not on the ballot, House, Senate, and statewide races boost public interest and send people to the polls. Almost all states reserve odd-years for municipal and judicial offices. Without high-profile campaigns, few people go to the polls.

"Special elections" also suffer diminished turnout. They are often held on short notice when an office suddenly becomes vacant, usually due to a resignation or death. In May 1997, Bill Redmond, a New Mexico Republican, took the House seat of outgoing incumbent Bill Richardson, who had been named ambassador to the United Nations. Often, as in Redmond's case, the winning strategy is to target voters with a strong commitment to party. There is less interest in politics during these times, and turnout is generally low. Redmond's campaign team later said that their candidate's "animated campaigning and passionate conservatism energized and mobilized the Republican base to turn out in record numbers" (Wilson and Burita 2000, 99). Instructively, Redmond was one of the few incumbents to lose the 1998 off-year election.

Political professionals also talk about "surge and decline." In nearly every midterm congressional election since the turn of the century, the president's party has lost seats. The election of 1990 provides a clear illustration. It took place just two years after George Bush's impressive victory in the 1988 presidential election. The months leading up to the 1990 midterm, however, had public opinion surveys indicating that voters were fed up with "business as usual" in Washington. Because Democrats controlled both houses of Congress, one might have expected the Republicans to take over, or, at the very least, to pick up a few seats. As it happened, Democrats gained seventeen districts in the House and a state in the Senate. While idiosyncratic factors clearly contributed to the electoral outcome, 1990 was consistent with a long-standing trend. On average, the president's party will lose almost nineteen seats in the first midterm election of the president's term (Abramson, Aldrich, and Rohde 1999, 228). In 1994, two years after the election of President Bill Clinton, Democrats braced for the worst—and the results were catastrophic. Losing fifty-two seats in the House and eight in the Senate, Democrats surrendered legislative control to the Republican victors.

Social scientists have struggled to find the causes of the surge-and-decline phenomenon, but no clear answer has emerged. One possibility is that on-year and off-year elections attract different groups of voters. Many people who vote in presidential elections do not cast ballots in the off-year. These people, generally less partisan and less ideological, are responsible for a president's success, as well as an influx of congressional officeholders of the president's party. During off-year elections, however, the pool of voters shrinks as casual voters drop out. Another possibility is that voters lose their initial excitement for the president. As time goes by, voters become increasingly disillusioned and then cast a ballot for congressional candidates of the other party. A third conjecture is that the type of candidate changes between the two elections. Aggressive candidates, angry with the president, run with steadfast determination, along with money from interest groups opposed to the new administration's policies.

A complete understanding of this phenomenon is elusive, and aberrations make prediction difficult. In 1998, Democrats faced a perilous situation. Historically, the third midterm after a president is elected is especially risky for members of the president's party. In 1986, six years after President Ronald Reagan's election, the GOP suffered a net loss of eight Senate seats and consequently ceded control of the Senate to insurgent Democrats. In 1974, in the months approaching what would have been President Richard Nixon's sixth year (had he remained in office), the Republican Party suffered dramatic losses in the House, losing forty-three seats. Prior to the 1998 elections, the president's party could expect to lose an average of nearly thirty-eight House seats (Abramson, Aldrich, and Rohde 1999, 228). Six years after Clinton won the presidency and in the middle of Clinton's impeachment crisis, one might have thought that the Democrats would lose badly. The outcome, however, was quite different: House Democrats actually picked up five seats, putting the party within striking distance of majority rule.

NATIONAL TRENDS

Saying "all politics is local," Tip O'Neill drew attention to the fact that Americans care little about national and international concerns on Election Day, yet even local politics cannot escape national trends, moods, and obsessions. Each year the national media highlight some concerns and downplay others, as popular perceptions of the "crime issue" show. One legal historian has noted, "Throughout the country, newspapers, movies, and TV spread the word about crime and violence—a misleading word, perhaps, but a powerful one. Even people who live in quiet suburban enclaves, or rural backwaters, are aware of what they consider the crime problem" (Friedman 1993, 452). From a crass, strategic point of view, many candidates find that the difference between perception and reality has little meaning. People believe that crime is rampant, so the discussion of lawless behavior has a definite starting point. Hence, in 1994 Republican George Pataki defeated New York's three-term governor, Mario Cuomo, who had repeatedly vetoed the death penalty by stressing a tough-on-crime platform. In Campaign 2000, even as candidates claimed support for better safeguards in capital punishment cases, most still supported the death penalty, mirroring the nation as a whole.

Like crime, economic trends and presidential popularity are powerful political tides. In the early 1970s, election scholar Edward Tufte found that 98 percent of the variability of congressional elections could be explained by these two factors (1975). Although the argument was found to be a bit overstated, and although scholars have continued to refine the variables, Tufte's point is well taken: voters reward or punish congressional candidates for events that are largely beyond their control.

But events are subject to interpretation. A Republican may believe that the economic recovery that started in the mid-1990s was the belated product of Reagan-era fiscal and monetary policy; a Democrat may conclude that crime is on the decline and therefore should not be featured so prominently on the national agenda. Campaign professionals understand that public perceptions can be altered—for better or worse—but only if prior beliefs are taken into account. Whoever might be responsible for economic recovery and whatever may be the statistical reality of criminal behavior in America, crime and the economy are things that voters can feel in their bones. A campaign that wants to bring people closer to the "truth" must begin with what voters believe, not what they ought to believe.

CANDIDATES FOR OTHER OFFICES

Most people believe that presidents can help elect their friends down the ballot. The belief in "coattails" is deeply ingrained in American electoral politics. Most observers assume that down-ballot candidates can benefit from the popularity of other candidates of the same party higher up the ticket. The popularity of one candidate, it is assumed, will trickle down to others. In 1980, for example, a large class of Republicans was swept into office with Ronald Reagan. Although there is little evidence showing cause and effect, many argue that Republicans won thanks to Reagan's mass appeal.

As logical as the coattails theory may appear, it is hard to find direct supporting evidence. Leading election scholar Gary Jacobson suggests that "[n]ational issues such as the state of the economy or the performance of the president may influence some voters some of the time . . . but for the most part the congressional vote is determined by evaluations of candidates as individuals" (1997, 134). Jacobson's "strategic politician" theory assumes that aspiring politicians want to win and defeat is anathema. As such, smart candidates pay close attention to early polling data, particularly as the information relates to fellow party members. When no member of their party is popular, strategic politicians decide to sit the race out. The party nomination is left to lesser candidates, who, with poor qualifications, scant finances, and minimal name recognition, lose the election. Years later, when it appears that others in the party are once again popular, strategic politicians enter the race. Because they are well qualified and adequately financed, they win. Under this theory, coattails have little effect.

A point of clarification: to say that coattails have no direct effect is not to argue that they are inconsequential. The mere perception that coattails exist may bring strong down-ballot contenders into the race when more prominent candidates lead the way. Better candidates bring increased financial support and media coverage. If others believe that a candidate will get a significant boost from a member of the ticket, they will be more likely to lend a hand. Thus, in some ways, the coattails theory may be self-fulfilling—because people believe that a candidate will win, they jump on board; and the more who jump on board, the greater the likelihood of success.

Campaigns can affect one another without a top-down relationship. As Campaign 2000 got under way, many speculated that the Vice President, who was running for president, and the First Lady, who was running for Senate in New York, would draw from the same group of donors. Fundraising can be a zero-sum game. At the local level, consultants might find that a particularly "hot" race in a nearby county is siphoning off financial supporters and filling up scarce newspaper space. Ballot initiatives can also affect candidates. In 1994, California's Proposition 187, which was designed to curtail state-funded services to illegal aliens, overshadowed even the U.S. Senate and gubernatorial races. The highly emotional issue brought out people who would not otherwise vote, activated a diverse set of volunteers for and against the measure, and drew a massive number of voters and a flood of news coverage. Competition between candidates and initiatives will probably increase in the years to come.

GEOGRAPHY

The geography of a district is important for several reasons. Campaign activities are molded by the physical characteristics of the district. Door-to-door projects are possible for the state Senate seats encompassing San Francisco's east side, and they are more cost-efficient than radio and television advertising. Yet in some downtown areas a campaign may find problems with this type of electioneering because high-rise apartments often forbid entry to nonresidents. Geography helps determine campaign tactics.

Among the most important matters are a district's size, density, and location. While a candidate for Senate in Rhode Island has about 1 million people compacted into a 1,000-square-mile area, a candidate in North Dakota has about

640,000 people spread across nearly 71,000 square miles. Each state demands its own sort of campaign. Some regions are particularly difficult to work. New Jersey, for example, is too big for personal contact in a statewide race. Still, the state is not well situated for broadcast television. New Jersey is dominated by two of the most expensive media markets in the country: New York City and Philadelphia. To reach Camden and Atlantic City, a campaign has to purchase television ads that will be viewed in Wilmington, Delaware. To reach Newark and the rest of northern New Jersey, a candidate has to buy television time that will go to people as far away as Bridgeport, Connecticut. In response, campaigns are now targeting New Jersey voters with cable television, a medium that can be narrowly tailored to each local cable franchise (Friedenberg 1997, 187–88).

The geographic distribution of the district may dictate a candidate's activities. The layout of the district might define travel patterns, which may, in turn, dictate the range of viable campaign activities. Some districts allow a candidate to move from one side to the other with ease, but other districts may demand hours of driving or even frequent plane trips. Some districts are split by high mountains, deep forests, or wide bodies of water. Some have urban density at their center, making the placement of campaign headquarters an obvious decision; others are so spread out that careful calculations must be made, and perhaps two or three headquarters are needed to cover the district adequately.

OTHER CONTEXTUAL ISSUES

Any attempt to detail all the things that a campaign must accept as given would fill volumes. In the following chapters, additional elements are carefully examined: district demographics along with candidate and opposition profiles. For now, a few miscellaneous contextual features are briefly touched upon.

Community Organizations

Many districts have strong organizational traditions, boasting a local union, a chamber of commerce, a Rotary Club, and other such organizations. Politically active groups might provide endorsements and contributions, but the importance of an organization should not be measured solely on its explicitly political nature. Nonpolitical groups are often the center of word-of-mouth communication. In some areas, for example, volunteer fire departments loom large, both in size and stature, and while these organizations are officially nonpartisan, campaigns and elections are a constant topic of conversation.

Elected Officials

Local elected officials can help a campaign attract media attention, contributors, and volunteers, and they can make endorsements as well as introductions to other prominent members of the community. In most states, elected officials can transfer campaign funds to other candidates. That said, rivalries often divide political communities from within, and a candidate who inadvertently lines up on the wrong side of a feud can cause irreparable damage to his or her campaign.

Political Heroes and Villains

Past and present politicians linger in the minds of voters. A political hero can be a powerful electoral force, offering endorsements, organizational assistance, and perhaps a sharing of advice. Not all past politicians are viewed favorably, however. Some depart public life on a bad note. Endorsements and pictures associating a candidate with a political villain can prove harmful. Complicating matters, ex-politicians do not always share their checkered past willingly. Many campaigns have been lured into believing that an endorsement will help, only to discover later the full extent of the public's wrath.

Social and Political Customs

Communities often have unique social and political customs. In some districts, yard signs are welcome. In others, they are considered a form of litter. A city might accept the use of mild profanity on the stump, while neighboring suburbs do not. Are political discussions allowed in church? It depends on the community. Is it polite to call people by their first name? Perhaps, but it is best to find out ahead of time. The rules can get complicated. In some locales, there are Democratic taverns and Republican cocktail lounges—and out-of-town guests are often expected to stay at hotels with a traditional connection to the appropriate party.

Parties and Bosses

Local parties vary in the degree of assistance that they give candidates. In some areas aggressive party organizations are eager to assist aspirants to public office, perhaps offering endorsements during the primary season, while in others they are no help at all. Where party organizations are strong, it is common to find a powerful leader at the helm. Often it is the chair, though sometimes an influential veteran is *really* in charge—and sometimes it is an operative from the neighboring county machine. In a sense, helpful parties and powerful leaders are inextricably linked. Candidates at all levels view local party bosses as a mixed blessing. On one hand, they can be pivotal players, leveraging money and volunteers as no one else can; on the other hand, the party gatekeepers can become difficult to work with. In New Hampshire a Republican presidential candidate who wants to call upon experienced volunteers must first "enlist a poobah, a warlord, a New Hampshire potentate," with accompanying political machinations reminiscent of "the old Kremlin and the Soviet politburo" (Ferguson 1996). This sort of power structure can be found, in varying degrees, across the United States.

The History of the Area

Communities are proud of their heritage. Understanding what a population has endured, recently or in the distant past, can yield valuable insight to an electorate. Natural disasters, social and political turmoil, even high school sporting events can be seen in hindsight as momentous occasions. Team songs, former mascots, and great players of the past are critical bits of knowledge. Again, for most people, politics is only a small part of life. A congressional district encompasses a wide variety of communities, and their traditions form a complex mosaic. In many ways, to know this heritage is to know the district.

Tourism and Recreation

Tourism and recreation are important. At one level, ski resorts and stadiums are often large employers, but also knowing what voters do in their spare time helps a candidate develop a connection with voters. A candidate in northwestern Pennsylvania who knows little about waterfowl might want to go on a hunting trip. An aspirant for office in Houston who cannot name a few Clint Black songs should tune into a country station. In campaigns, little things can make a big difference.

CONCLUSION

This chapter was designed to introduce the importance of contextual information in new-style campaigning. Campaigns are about strategy, but they are also about the terrain on which the strategy operates: a party boss who will not budge, a district so large that the candidate has trouble keeping to a schedule, a national economic trend over which the campaign has no control but under which the campaign must labor, poor candidates at the top of the ticket, third-party spoilers, and an opponent who enjoys the benefits of incumbency. Strategists who cannot accept "the things that cannot be changed" find themselves at a disadvantage. In many ways, the difference between amateurs and professionals in the world of campaigns is measured by the degree to which they come to a realistic understanding of the district and then find a way to work within intractable circumstances.

Chapter Four

Demographic Research: The Theory of Aggregate Inference

In the 1986 film *Power*, Gene Hackman, the aging political campaigner, is confronted by his former protégé, a new-style consultant played by Richard Gere. The two are working on different sides of the same three-way race. Gere has a crack staff, top-level clients, and an 85 percent victory record. Hackman is a recently fired drunk whose best days are behind him. An independent candidate for Senate is his last chance: a college professor who got into the race because he thought that the major party candidates were not addressing the real problems of the nation. The professor-candidate has no chance of winning, but for Hackman, the only real goal is to make his client competitive. Even that would be difficult, however, because Hackman lacks one of the basic tools of the trade. He goes begging to Gere, desperate for help. What does Hackman need? "The demographics, God damn it!"

All campaigns need demographics. To formulate a winning strategy, consultants must know what makes a district tick, and part of the process is understanding a district's demographic profile—its mix of race, ethnicity, consumer preference, and a range of other attributes that define the electorate. Political demographers seek to understand a vast array of characteristics that might affect the electoral outcome. This chapter is designed to acquaint the reader with the importance of demographic understanding, the logic of demographic inference, the basics of demographic profiling, and the process by which campaigns pull the data together into a stable hub for strategic planning and implementation. Gene Hackman needed the demographics. The aim of this chapter is to understand why.

DEMOGRAPHICS AS A CAMPAIGN TOOL

Demographic research is different from opinion polling. With a districtwide poll, for example, reasonably accurate assessments can be made about the overall population. Polling is expensive, so perhaps a sample of only 550 people in a

125,000-person district will be contacted—meaning that the poll will be insensitive to some of the nuances of the district. Consultant Wayne Johnson learned early in his career that polling is not enough:

> From the first surveys we learned things like: 62 percent of voters favor taxing the wealthy. So we would send mailings to all voters telling them that the wealthy need to pay more taxes. The problem was that the positive data (the majority position) was as likely to be a lukewarm opinion as a strongly held opinion. In this case, the wealthy mail recipient was far more likely to react than the middle income person receiving the same mailing. We soon found it was possible to mail on a 70 percent plus issue and still lose by a landslide. (1992, 51)

Voter-by-voter income assessments might have identified the people who would be offended by a class-based message, and a smart campaign would remove wealthy households from the mailing. But there are other, more practical ways to reach approximately the same result.

To avoid backlash, campaigns often combine voter opinion data with demographic research. Instead of using the issue of greatest concern for the greatest number, survey results are compared with demographic information to refine the analysis. No longer does the campaign try to determine what all the voters want but, rather, it focuses on what particular neighborhoods or constituency groups desire. In this way, a campaign can target its message much more precisely.

The approach is time-tested. When Mario Cuomo ran his first campaign for governor of New York in 1982, early surveys found him especially popular among voters of Italian descent. Operatives throughout the state were instructed to spur turnout in Italian American communities. On Election Day they were told to call Democrats; and when this list was exhausted, they simply called voters with Italian surnames. Cuomo won. Likewise, Loretta Sanchez, running a congressional campaign in Orange County, California, took advantage of the ethnic transformation of this once-conservative, once-Anglo district, which over the years had become 50 percent Hispanic. The winning campaign team has written, "Orange County's changing demographics worked in favor of Loretta Sanchez' candidacy. In the spring of 1996, voter registration favored the Democratic Party by 46% to 40%. The appeal of a Latina businesswoman whose platform addressed the needs of working families struck a resonant chord with voters" (Wachob and Kennedy 2000, 102).

Attention to the Hispanic vote, a fast-growing segment of the U.S. population, is greatly increasing. As one measure of this phenomenon, both major party nominees in the 2000 presidential race used Spanish in their campaigns. Al Gore proclaimed, "Si se puede! (Yes, we can)," and George W. Bush ran a television ad touting the governor as "un hombre de familia (a family man)" (Milbank 2000). The reason for this newfound attention to the Hispanic community lay in the demographics of the nation and the structure of the electoral college. According to Democratic pollster Mark Penn, "Hispanics provide a crucial swing vote in some

of the nation's biggest states" (Cisneros 1999, 72). Henry Cisneros, formerly secretary of Housing and Urban Development and later the president of Spanish-
language Univision Communications, wrote, "With 271 electoral votes required to
win the presidency, the country's 11 largest states alone account for 269 electoral
votes (and 18 million registered voters). In 1998, 35 percent of registered voters
within those same 11 states were Hispanic" (Cisneros 1999, 72).

THE LOGIC OF DEMOGRAPHIC RESEARCH

The goal of new-style campaigning is to target the right voters. In districts the
size of a neighborhood, some candidates recognize each voter and know whom to
target by sheer instinct. A larger district presents a more onerous task. Getting to
know the interests of persuadable voters in a large district is a job that hangs on
networks of operatives and activists who know the voters personally. This is how
the old urban machines worked. A candidate who did not know every single voter
went through the party boss, and the party boss, in turn, used his connections to
reach out to neighborhoods in need of conversion. But in the Digital Age, long
after the day when political parties and neighborhood clubs were central to American life, candidates cannot rely upon personal relationships alone. Especially in
districts holding tens or even hundreds of thousands of constituents, political professionals must use demographic research.

"Demography" is the study of populations. Demographers attempt to quantify
a population's size, growth, education, gender, race, ethnicity, income, and other
such features. "Demographics" are the results of research on these features of a
population. "Political demography," therefore, is the study of a population's characteristics with an eye to their political significance. It begins with a few basic
assumptions.

First, populations are heterogeneous. Districts that appear to be uniform might
actually contain a wide variety of voter concerns. A young, white, middle-class
neighborhood in which all the houses look alike gives the impression of Milque-
toast consistency. The residents probably share a large number of interests, concerns, goals, and outlooks. But under the surface might dwell a fair amount of
diversity. Some people would be pro-life, and others would be pro-choice. Some
would be pro-gun, and others would be pro-gun control. All communities, no matter how similar in appearance, are made up of dissimilar elements.

*Second, demographic heterogeneity can be used to divide voters into separate
analytic groups.* The Census Bureau asks people to list their gender, race, age,
marital status, and educational attainment, among other things. Because any one
person can be listed by race, whole populations can also be grouped according to
racial characteristics. While there are some ambiguities—people of multiracial
heritage are not clearly categorized—a political demographer commonly looks for
voting differences between various racial groups. Some categories are not politically significant, and sometimes the political significance of a variable will
change. Before 1980, gender was not a strong variable in presidential elections,

but in subsequent years it would become a powerful predictor of voter preference. Women are much more likely to vote Democratic than are men. One of the tricks to demographic research is figuring out which demographic categories will be politically significant in a given election.

Third, membership in a demographic group suggests shared concerns. Americans like to think of themselves as individuals, acting from their own interests and not those of a larger group. A good demographer, however, can make powerful predictions about individuals based on the groups to which they belong. In the white, middle-class neighborhood mentioned earlier there might live a thirty-two-year-old, married white male of English descent employed as a well-paid accountant. Chances are very good that this person would be a Republican who votes regularly. By no means does this generalization suggest that *every* member of his group has identical interests or that *everyone* agrees on any one item—demographic inference is a business of probabilities, not certainties—but there is a clear correlation between party preference and wealth, geography, marital status, race, and occupation.

For political campaigns, these three assumptions are translated into powerful statistical tools. Demographic research helps a political professional discover electorally relevant groups and target them with the right message. Traditional demographic research is a process of *aggregating* data and then drawing reasoned *inferences* therefrom (Robbin 1989, 107–8). The watchword is efficiency. Instead of compiling information on each voter, the researcher needs only to understand the character of large groups of voters. Married white males tend to vote differently than do unmarried black females. The very act of voting seems to be related to demographic characteristics. Older people vote more regularly than younger people. Wealthier people tend to vote more regularly than poorer people. A new-style campaign aims its message at those whom it can persuade. Good demographic research, therefore, compiles a general understanding of an electorate—its differences as well as its similarities.

DEMOGRAPHIC RESEARCH

In the golden age of parties, what passed for demographic research came from direct contact. Local bosses knew their constituents. George Washington Plunkitt could say, "I know every man, woman, and child in the Fifteenth District, except them that's been born this summer—and I know some of them, too" (Riordon 1995, 25). An exaggeration, probably, but with a core of truth. Operating in a world where new immigrants joined social clubs and political parties, at a time when travel was a luxury that few could afford, neighborhood organizers could know their voters and send political information up the chain of command. By the 1950s, urban flight and the decline of tightly knit communities rendered neighborhood-based assessments problematic. The flow of information and depth of commitment that allowed for Plunkitt-style knowledge were disintegrating. At the same time, primitive data handling was coming into its own. Demographic information could be punched into cards and run through computers. Whereas

Plunkitt drew his picture of the district from his knowledge of individuals, new-style consultants start with a macrolevel view and then parse the data into microlevel understandings.

Finding U.S. Census Data

At the highest level of generality, researchers can examine demographics by looking at the *Statistical Abstract of the United States*. It is among the government's most useful publications, but its mission is to summarize the nation as a whole—not a low-level electoral district.

For most campaigns, the basic source of American demographic data is the U.S. Census. Every ten years the federal government undertakes a massive, constitutionally mandated effort to gauge the country's population. Unlike surveys that rely upon sampling, the Census Bureau attempts to enumerate every person living in the United States. All residents are legally obliged to fill out a questionnaire. There are two versions of the census form, short and long. For Census 2000, the short form asked people about the type of housing they lived in; about their age, sex, ethnicity, and race; and about their relationship to others in the home. The long form, given to roughly one in six people, asked, in addition to the short-form questions, a series of questions relating to marital status, ancestry, household composition, home value, education, family language, veteran status, work experience, religion, transportation, and so on. Those who do not submit their response voluntarily receive a visit from a census worker, and the questions are asked face-to-face.

Census data are not perfect. Some people are missed altogether, some forms are not accurately completed, and some people do not want to publicly divulge personal information. More importantly, researchers cannot study individual unit data—a source of frustration for political demographers. But neither shortcoming renders census information useless. As noted by political communication professor Gary Selnow, statistical averages often are accurate enough for campaign activities, and they may be a lot better than no information at all" (1994, 95).

A wide variety of demographic characteristics is available to a researcher. While local politicos in Plunkitt's day might have been able to say which area is predominantly Polish or Italian or which neighborhood is upper-income and which is lower-income, new-style consultants can go deeper than direct observation. Demographics can show how many people in the area own their homes, how many are headed by a single parent, how many are blue-collar versus white-collar, how many are farmers, and how many are over the age of sixty-five. Census data give a researcher a wide array of options. A demographer can look at the entire nation or a city block. The ability to perform multivariate analyses on a large number of geographic units makes census data far superior to casual estimates.

The Census Bureau refines its data collection techniques, adds and subtracts questions, and generally tries to improve its forecasting techniques—but on the whole, the structure of the data has remained fairly constant. Data delivery, however, has changed dramatically over the past few years. In the 1980s campaigns referenced a hard-copy volume. Research libraries furnished racks of census publications, while local public libraries carried selected titles. Accessing this information was a formidable task, requiring legwork and a great deal of cross-referencing. Beginning with the 1990 census, however, the information became available on computer tape reels, tape cartridges, and CD-ROM disks. Not only were the data more accessible, but they were vastly more manageable. Campaign strategists could carry an impressive quantity of searchable data fully loaded into a laptop computer.

In the new millennium, census information is moving swiftly to the Web. A few clicks from the Census Bureau's homepage (www.census.gov) tells a researcher that in 1990, Baton Rouge, Louisiana, had 219,531 people living in 83,340 households. There were 118,429 Caucasian Americans and 96,348 African Americans. There were 36,917 married women and 2,116 widowed men. Between 7:00 A.M. and 8:00 A.M., 24,022 left home to go to work. Fully 4,139 children aged five years and under were living in poverty in single-mother households. All these data can be requested in HTML format for browsing, but more importantly, they can be downloaded in CODATA and tab-delimited formats and imported into commercial database management software.

The quantity of information offered by the Census Bureau is mind-boggling, and the bureau collects and sells more than just the data collected in the decennial survey. It produces information on business, agriculture, building permits, federal fund transfers, and other sorts of demographic knowledge. A typical CD-ROM is "County Business Patterns, 1996 and 1997" (CD-CBP96/97). For fifty dollars, a researcher can get "data by 2-, 3-, and 4-digit Standard Industrial Classification (SIC) code on total number of establishments, mid-March employment, first quarter and annual payroll, and number of establishments by employment-size classes." With the CD-ROM, a consultant can get a strong sense of what the people in a county do for a living. "Congressional Districts of the United States" (STF 1D/3D) gives summary information for all census categories (right down to "Mortgage status, Vehicles available, Occupancy status, Water source, Plumbing facilities, Year householder moved into unit, Race of householder, Year structure built, [and] Rent").

Census data are provided in two basic formats: "summary data" and "microdata." Summary data sets are based on specific geographic units—states, cities, townships, census tracts, or units that the Census Bureau calls "blocks." Based on the city block, the concept is extended to rural communities by selecting geographically defined areas (using, e.g., roads and railroad tracks) encompassing about seventy people each (Lavin 1996, 178). At the block level, only the condensed short-form data are available. Up the hierarchy from blocks are census tracts and block numbering areas (the rural version of a tract), towns, cities, counties, Metropolitan Statistical Areas, congressional districts, states, and the nation as a whole. For areas larger than the block level, researchers can obtain preformatted data segmented in a variety of ways. (The Baton Rouge information was based on summary data.) In addition, the Census Bureau and individual states have been trying to conform their geographic boundaries. For the sake of convenience, some states have been drawing their voting districts along the lines used by the census, and "the Census Bureau has . . . created district boundary files . . . based on maps provided by state education agencies" (182–83).

Microdata sets are a completely different type of resource. Like summary data, they begin with the answers to census questionnaires, but unlike summary data, microdata can be restructured by the researcher. The Baton Rouge data show the number of married women and the number of people who commuted to work between 7:00 A.M. and 8:00 A.M. If a consultant wants to aim radio advertisements at women on their way to work, it would be useful to reconfigure the data to see not just the number of *people* commuting between 7:00 A.M. and 8:00 A.M. but the number of *women* on their way to work at that time. Summary data do not allow this kind of manipulation. Reconfiguring the data would require that the researcher access individual census forms. Even with identifiers like name and address removed, a researcher could divide and crosscut the data and eventually figure out who is attached to which questionnaire, raising serious privacy concerns.

To maintain confidentiality while allowing demographers to run their own analyses, the Census Bureau has created data sets called Public Use Microdata Samples (PUMS), made up of census form results with multiple safeguards. All identifiers have been removed. Additionally, PUMS data sets are not offered for geographic populations smaller than 100,000 residents, and even then, only a sample of the census form results is provided. Still, microdata sets are extremely useful, allowing the researcher to perform custom queries on individual-level survey results.

Researchers have a number of options in obtaining raw microdata and summary data. PUMS microdata sets can be purchased as 1 percent samples or 5 percent samples. The entire country is covered in seven disks. There is even a special 3 percent PUMS data set covering older Americans.

The data sets cost between $100 and $450, depending on sample size and scope. Summary data sets are available on CD-ROM—data sets for most states cost about $100—but most of the data sets are on-line and fully downloadable. Since the late 1990s, the Census Bureau has been making a strong effort to put its data on the Web, and it will continue to do so in the coming census cycle. Data from Census 2000 began posting in early 2001.

Using Census Data

Raw data sets, however, are only the beginning. The key to using census data is the search for correspondence and specificity. First, census data do not always correspond to the political district in question. If the district is a state, county, city, or congressional district, then researchers can simply start with predefined summary data. If, however, the district is only a portion of a city, or if it snakes across county lines, then researchers will have to piece together the voting district from small units of analysis—government jurisdictions and census blocks—building the district from scratch.

Whether a district as a whole comes ready-made or has to be assembled by hand, intelligent demographers learn how to disaggregate the whole into the smallest unit of analysis. The second key to demographics—building specificity—relies on a researcher's ability to refine macrodistricts into microunits. Looking at 1990 data, for example, Athens County, Ohio, as a whole contained 59,549 residents. Within the boundaries of Athens County is Carthage Township, with 1,360 residents, 17 of whom were listed as African American. Inside this small African American population there were three married-couple families with related children and two without related children, and another two African Americans who lived alone. Summary data can be *very* specific. For political consultants, this is a good thing, because modern political campaigns are judged by the precision of their targeting. Campaigns have become data-driven, but there is a cost. In addition to the money spent developing a database, a campaign must train its operatives in the use of sophisticated database management systems. Furthermore, with each new variable introduced to the database, the number of theoretical groups is multiplied accordingly, and the complexity of the database can become overwhelming.

One answer to the complexity problem emerged in the early 1970s, when the Claritas Corporation pioneered the use of geodemographic clusters. Claritas assumed that people gather into "areas where the resources—physical, economic, and social—will be compatible with their needs" (Robbin 1989, 109). In other words, people create or choose neighborhoods based on their lifestyle choices. These neighborhoods, in turn, have identifiable demographic characteristics. By systematically examining 535 variables for the entire U.S. population, Claritas established forty distinct groupings, which combined to account for 87 percent of American diversity. Each cluster was given a nickname. One was tagged "Share Croppers" because it contained low-income, rural, poorly educated, southern whites. Other groups were "God's Country," "Blue Blood Estates," "Archie Bunker's Neighbors," and "Bohemian Mix." Each unique cluster was thought to comprise like-minded individuals. In a sense, geodemographic clustering moved casual perceptions of neighborhoods toward a more sophisticated understanding of shared geography.

Pundits soon began to find fault with the new approach. Was it a magic bullet, or just smoke and mirrors? Was geodemographic clustering simply an advertising ploy to build a market for Claritas? Consultant Mark Atlas argued that geodemographics did not live up to its billing. First, there did not appear to be any statistical documentation to support claims of improved targeting. In fact, before-and-after evidence provided by the company, when reexamined, showed that the system did little to change the electoral outcomes. The problem might have been simple methodology. Atlas wrote, "Clusters derived from the entire nation's Census data may be very different from clusters that would be generated if each state's data had been clustered individually" (1989, 134). "[T]he allocation of campaign resources," argued Atlas, "is too critical a task to be undertaken when there is substantial uncertainty about the targeting procedure's validity" (135).

Nevertheless, clustering has endured as a form of demographic shorthand. Even though many consultants now believe that clusters derived from a national data set are imprecise and unnecessarily expensive, the lasting impact of geodemographic profiling is the very idea of efficiently identifying targeted groups based on broad sets of characteristics. One of the campaigns in the movie *Power* relied on "Pools and Patios"—upscale couples whose children have left home. The GOP longs to capture "soccer moms." In 2000, some Democrats scoffed at Bill Bradley's supporters, calling them a bunch of "Volvo drivers." Even if such categories reduce whole populations to a caricature, Claritas-style groupings offer a richer understanding of an electorate than the traditional left-right continuum. As one consultant has noted, "Seasoned political operatives generally concede that the geodemographic approach has some merit" (Beiler 1990, 34).

BRINGING THE PIECES TOGETHER

Because most campaigns cannot afford professionally drawn demographic profiles, the task is often left to candidates, consultants, and volunteer research teams. Raw census data can be purchased from the Census Bureau, downloaded from the Web, or perused at major research libraries. Professional reference librarians can be invaluable to novices sorting through census terminology (e.g., the differences between "ethnicity" and "race") and the variety of available data packages (e.g., zip codes, block groups). Guides to census data, such as Michael R. Lavin's *Understanding the Census* (1996) or Congressional Quarterly's *Encyclopedia of the U.S. Census* (2000) also help demystify the statistics.

Once the raw data are gathered, they can be imported into a database as simple as a spreadsheet or as complex as a relational database management system. The advantage of relational databasing is that it allows researchers to link data sets. For example, a campaign may have census data for a county, along with a raft of economic data points. With a relational database, the name of the county can be used to link the table containing census information with the table containing economic information. Using basic demographics as a starting point, a campaign can add raw voter files and other "enhancements." Here, public information data, such as state motor vehicle department information, data from the state fish and game commission, and records provided by the county assessor's office, can be combined into a deep profile of the district (Beiler 1990, 33). A motor vehicle database, if available, can show where people own expensive cars, mobile homes, and recreational vehicles. A list of people with hunting licenses can display high concentrations of hunters, and the appropriate inferences can be drawn therefrom.

One interesting enhancement is name-based ethnicity. Campaigns have been encouraged to pay close attention to an "ethnic targeting program" in which a researcher will "identify what ethnic group an individual or family belongs to primarily by looking at and analyzing the last name" (Dawidziak 1991, 52). A table of surnames is created, and, by using the last name, each voter's ethnicity is recorded: "A last name beginning with O' would be Irish [and a] last name ending with 'ski' would more than likely be Polish" (52). As the campaign moves forward to voter contact, ethnic-based mailings can be sent based upon each ethnic group's presumed interests. The method is not foolproof: "Park" is very commonly a Korean name, but many people with the last name "Park" have no Korean heritage.

Another source of information is a campaign's "in-house" data set. Nearly every campaign maintains lists of voters, contributors, and volunteers. Data might also be compiled from newspaper clippings, letters sent to the candidate, attendance at candidate forums and fund-raising events, and rosters of prior campaign staff, (Selnow 1994, 75). In-house lists might also be garnered from parties, interest groups, and other campaigns. Furthermore, most elected officials have a list of voters who have expressed an interest in one topic or another while serving in office. Many jurisdictions forbid the use of lists acquired during official hours or in the conduct of official business. Furthermore, election laws and privacy statutes regulate the collection and use of some lists. As with all other aspects of a campaign, compliance with legal and ethical codes must be the top priority.

List production is an industry. Vendors offer data sets ranging from zip code sorts, to club membership data, to magazine subscription lists. Such lists can be rented directly from the owner or through a list broker. Entrepreneurs help campaigns search the market for lists that suit the campaign's needs. The brokers acquire the lists, handle the billing, and test the data (Selnow 1994, 80–84). The high cost of brokered lists means that most campaigns restrict their use to fund-raising activities, but some campaigns may want to use the lists for narrowly targeted grassroots efforts.

Many demographic databases are dual-use. Aristotle, a Washington, DC-based firm, maintains a nationwide voter database based on party registration, probable ethnicity, and gender. A client can purchase customized data sets to meet particular strategic goals. For example, a campaign might want to locate middle-income GOP males, especially ethnic renters, who voted in the 1994 and 1998 general election. Specifying these criteria, the campaign can locate names, phone numbers, and street addresses. These data can be combined with other demographic information and then mapped onto district boundaries using proprietary software. On one hand, this sort of database can provide general demographic understanding. On the other hand, because the data set is derived from individual-level information, complete with names, addresses, and sometimes party affiliation, the database can be used as a voter contact tool.

Voter contact works both ways: the campaign talks to the voter and the voter talks to the campaign. Precinct walkers and telephone callers gain voter-specific data. Information on specific voters can be returned to headquarters and entered into the larger data set (W. Johnson 1992). Voter identification is different from polling in that the goal is not statistical inference but, rather, precise information on specific voters.

Attention to detail is time-consuming and resource-intensive. Only affluent campaigns with a lot of volunteers can gather information on more than a fraction of the electorate. Nevertheless, a list of voters and their specific concerns is a powerful targeting device. Campaigns are often won and lost at the margins, and, as one consultant notes, "We are already making direct contact with actual voters. Why shouldn't we be collecting data in the process?" (W. Johnson 1992, 52). By combining individual-level data with demographic information, campaigns can better discern the interests of demographic subgroups. With the increasing use of database technology in political campaigns, demographics have become a routine part of campaign operations.

The looming problem is information overload—and information obsession. If a database is "sliced and diced" too much, it loses meaning. Five census characteristics can be multiplied into 4,000 theoretical groups. With this many groupings, a 125,000-resident population will average about thirty people per theoretical group. The utility of such a narrow cut is suspect from the outset.

Still, there is value in sorting through the numbers. A researcher can get a feel for the district. What is the percentage of blue- versus white-collar workers? How many African Americans live in the district? How many crimes occur each year? Where are they occurring? After looking at the overall statistics, the next step is to examine the data progressively, moving to smaller and smaller geographic divisions. What is the districtwide unemployment rate? What is the unemployment rate for each of the counties and townships in the district? This sort of investigation might be open-ended, intuitive, based principally upon the political goals of the campaign team, but it has a well established place in American electioneering.

An obvious component of this analysis is the electoral history of the district along with any polling that might already have been completed. Where are the Democrats? Where are the Republicans? Perhaps more importantly, where are the Independents? Do they live in precincts with high rates of split-ticket voting? Do most of them live in the same media market? All these characteristics can be summarized in a demographic profile. Together, demographic research, survey data, and prior electoral data merge to form a powerful implement of political combat.

Some consultants pay to have the work done for them. The campaign team simply provides researchers with a voter list, and names are matched with a master file. CSS Direct, a marketing demographics firm, matches voter files with scores of consumer and business listings. Database companies provide speed and accuracy. Many firms produce mailing labels, preprinted envelopes, even entire mailing packages, transforming the once-onerous voter-contact process, which relied on volunteer labor, into an outsourced operation that can be handled via email. The disadvantage of outsourcing is primarily cost, but also the loss of hands-on control. Although database companies can provide information on short order, a great deal of campaigning takes place late at night and over the weekends. Having this targeting data at a campaign's immediate disposal can be worthwhile. Perhaps more importantly, the very act of compiling and configuring the data is a learning experience. Creating a database from scratch helps a campaign come to grips with the district by familiarizing team members with the details of the district.

CONCLUSION

New-style campaign consultants understand Gene Hackman's desperation for "the demographics." Aggregate data improve a campaign's ability to convey an appropriate message to each voter. Understanding that a district's "bedroom community" is where all the Independents live tells a campaign that it should pay attention to train stops, bus depots, and other places where commuters assemble, perhaps suggesting that the campaign should use billboards visible from the main commuter lines. Demographics add wisdom.While imperfect and sometimes difficult to manage, the value of demographic research lies in the way that it helps a campaign reach informed decisions at a relatively low cost, adding to a campaign's strategic vision.

Chapter Five

Candidate and Opposition Profiles: Looking at the Record

Democrat William MaGee's 1990 campaign for New York's heavily Republican 111th State Assembly District paid careful attention to demographics. MaGee operatives knew their voters, and their adversary. MaGee had painstakingly compiled large stacks of information on Republican Jack McCann. Having served twenty-five years in public life, McCann had amassed a long public record. MaGee's campaign team used it to assemble a damaging profile of their opposition.

MaGee's line of attack would take advantage of the upstate–downstate split in New York politics. In many ways, New York is really two states in one: the greater New York City area is "downstate," and everything north of Westchester County is "upstate." Downstate is heavily Democratic, as are most members of the assembly from the area. Conversely, most elected officials from upstate are Republican. Political and cultural animosity between the two regions is sharp, stretching back to early American history. Among the worst insults that one can hurl at upstate politicians is to call them pawns of downstate interests, and vice versa.

In the state assembly, the Democratic Party has held the majority for decades. Accordingly, Democrats control the flow of legislation, budget appropriations, committee assignments, office space, and pork-barrel allocations. Republicans are left to nip at the edges and stall the process. Parliamentary games are played out during each legislative term when both sides posture, harass, and embarrass each other. While the Democrats have nearly complete control over the budget process, the Republicans can stonewall by offering amendments. Many tactical measures are intended to embarrass the Democrats. For example, Republicans might suggest adding money for law enforcement, leaving Democrats to vote against the amendment because a budget agreement had already been struck with the state Senate and the governor. Republicans would then claim that Democrats were "soft on crime." Republican candidates could tell voters, "You see, we tried to get more money to put criminals behind bars—because we know you're concerned about it—but the Democrats voted us down!"

One year, the Republicans made a pledge to vote as a team. A few of the Republicans were from downstate—Long Island, mostly. These members, like the rest of the minority, offered amendments seeking funds for roads, bridges, rail stations, parking lots, ferry ports, and other projects helpful to downstate residents. McCann was a team player, so he voted for these amendments, even though his district was 200 miles to the north. Here the MaGee campaign found a silver bullet. Why was McCann voting for downstate projects?

The campaign assembled a direct-mail piece with a large picture of then-New York City mayor Ed Koch on the outside and a caption asking, "What Do Ed Koch and Jack McCann Have in Common?" Upon opening the mailer, the reader saw, "They Both Work for New York City!" Below was a list of downstate projects for which McCann had voted, including some staggering legislative price tags. At the bottom, the costs were summed up, and a final caption read, "At a time when *our* roads, bridges, and schools are falling apart, Jack McCann is pushing for over $1 billion for New York City. Who is he working for, Ed Koch or us?" The mailing caused an uproar. Newspapers throughout the district picked up the story, as did many television and radio news programs. The notion that McCann was a "pawn of downstate interests" quickly spread. McCann was forced to defend his tactical votes, distracting attention from his accomplishments. This one mailing, sent early in the campaign, turned a long-shot venture into a neck-and-neck race that MaGee eventually won.

MaGee's victory was made possible by meticulous research. Only twenty years ago, aggressive ôpposition research—termed "oppo" in the trade, or simply, "O-R"—was viewed as a novelty. Few knew how to compile and organize this information, and even fewer knew how to use it well. Today, new-style campaigners agree that O-R plays a lead role in nearly every campaign. This chapter is designed to acquaint the reader with opposition research. It discusses some of the ethical considerations surrounding oppo, the reasons for its effectiveness, the need for researching one's own candidate, several different types of profile data, where the information can be found, and the efficient management of opposition and counteropposition research data.

ETHICAL ISSUES IN OPPOSITION RESEARCH

Aggressive O-R is a mainstay of American politics. During the presidential election of 1800, Federalist operatives dug up information that Thomas Jefferson might have had several slave mistresses and may have fathered a child with one of them. (Scientific research performed in the 1990s suggested that the Federalists were right.) Years later, in the election of 1884, Grover Cleveland was charged with fathering a child out of wedlock with a woman named Maria Halpin. Supporters of James G. Blaine chanted: "Ma, Ma, where's my Pa? Gone to the White House, ha, ha, ha." The Cleveland team retaliated by disclosing that Blaine had used his congressional office for financial gain. Democrats returned fire: "Blaine, Blaine, Jay Gould Blaine! The Contentional Liar from the state of Maine." Cleveland won the election. On election night, Cleveland supporters shouted: "Hurrah for Maria, Hurrah for the Kid. I voted for Cleveland, and I'm damned glad I did!" (Johnson-Cartee and Copeland 1991, 6–7).

In the recent past, oppo was conducted by college students or by the candidate's spouse at the kitchen table, and paid professionals were considered an extravagance. Today, scores of consulting firms specialize in this field, and the resources available to opposition researchers have increased immeasurably. New-style campaigns have incorporated opposition research into their operations for a variety of reasons.

First, the digital revolution has drastically altered the means of collecting, organizing, and distributing campaign-related data. One consultant writes, "prior to the popularization of the Internet, [a campaign's] examination of the public record had to be done on-site, by hand." A public record spanning twenty-five years "took five people six months to complete. In addition to being slow and time-consuming, the cost to the client was staggering" (Bovee 1998, 48). In the Digital Age, opposition research is typified by "someone sitting in front of a computer examining everything from newspaper articles, to property records, to civil and criminal court records" (48). Online services, such as Lexis-Nexis, Facts.com, and NewsBank, allow for swift candidate research. The Federal Election Commission has most of its raw data posted on the Web. With local papers joining the online community, it seems as though every published word, every vote, every financial transaction can be located in moments. Furthermore, with the digital storage of oppo, rapid response has become its own art form. Factsheets correcting the record after the Clinton–Dole debates were issued at about the same moment that the two candidates left the stage. What was extraordinary in 1996 is becoming commonplace in the new millennium. There is simply nowhere left for a candidate to hide.

Second, it has been suggested that the demand for O-R stems from the laziness of some reporters. One consultant notes that policy issues are complex and that politicians are therefore able to spoon-feed reporters with the results of campaign research (Persinos 1994, 21). Some suggest that Watergate brought the rise of investigative journalism and that the news media have thereafter become fixated on "character" (Sabato, Stencel, and Lichter 2000, 37–38)—feeding into the hands of campaigns that are ready and willing to push these sorts of stories. At the same time campaigns must be wary of oppo overload, and must use derogatory data with discretion. "There appears to be a public suspicion that the press . . . has intruded into private territory," wrote Kathleen Hall Jamieson at the height of the Lewinsky scandal. "What some in the press regard as investigative journalism seems to many to be simple voyeurism" (1998).

Finally, even if lurid details cross the line of decency, the increasing use of opposition research may be a function of its unmistakable effectiveness. Oppo is used because new-style consultants understand how to employ it effectively. As media consultant Bob Squier once noted, "I love to do negatives. It is one of those opportunities in a campaign where you can take the truth and use it like a knife to slice right through the opponent" (Luntz 1988, 72). O-R has become a fundamental piece of modern campaigning because it works.

But is it appropriate? One researcher has said frankly, "If [candidates] are not willing to have their backgrounds checked out—particularly their financial backgrounds—they shouldn't be running for public office in the first place" (Robberson 1996). Still, there are broad gray areas. Is it right, for example, to tell the voters about something that happened ten, twenty, or thirty years ago? George W. Bush's 1975 drunk-driving arrest offers a case in point. Is all public information fair game? What about the private lives of candidates? After the release of President Clinton's deposition in the Lewinsky case, does any zone of privacy remain?

Many professionals argue that opposition research is good for the democratic process. It moves campaigns away from style and imagery and pushes them toward political issues. Elected officials and candidates are accountable for their actions. In other words, it keeps politicians in line. From this point of view, oppo ultimately leads to a cleaner, more responsible system. When Squier, working for Bill Clinton's 1996 campaign, saw video footage of Bob Dole boasting that he had voted against Medicare, Squier shared this policy fact with the electorate. He suffered no pang of conscience. Comparative campaigning serves a watchdog function. "This is particularly true," writes scholar Linda Fowler, "when one considers how difficult it is to monitor and evaluate the performance of politicians in office" (1995, 203). So long as the public demands this sort of information, campaigns will supply it.

Others say that aggressive O-R creates mean-spirited politics (Persinos 1994, 20). While there is certainly nothing wrong with disclosing factual information about an opponent's official duties, it is quite another issue to resurrect decades-old personal issues with little relevance to the responsibilities of office. By making everything fair game, sometimes even family problems, modern campaigning might drive good people from seeking public office. Ethics charges, even if trumped-up—even if proven wrong—can seriously damage a person's reputation. Moreover, personal attacks and the misrepresentation of policy commitments might alienate voters. Opponents of oppo argue that the steady decline of voting is linked to the malicious nature of modern politics.

At least one observer believes that oppo should be allowed to cover "[a]nything that's honest, legal and relevant to the race" (Persinos 1994, 22). At the end of the day, however, it matters little where scholars, pundits, consultants, or candidates mark the ethical boundaries of opposition research. The real question is how the findings of O-R will affect the campaign. As a practical matter, the news that gets through to the public is filtered through the prism of the journalistic community and then the public's perception of truthfulness, relevance, and fairness. If the press declines to run with negative information, it has little or no value. If the campaign does an end run around reporters and airs its charges through paid advertising, the campaign risks backlash. The 1992 Bush campaign deliberately avoided talking to reporters about allegations of marital infidelity by Governor Clinton out of fear that Bush would pay a price for raising the issue. During the 1996 campaign, many established news outlets made a conscious decision not to run salacious stories about Bob Dole. According to a close analysis of recent political scandals, "[M]ajor national publications initially refrained from publishing stories about an extramarital affair in the candidate's past. Yet the eventual coverage of Dole's long-ago affair also shows how competitive forces can effectively override good editorial decisions" (Sabato, Stencel, and Lichter 2000, 101). The rise of amateur reporting on the Internet further threatens to undermine professional journalistic standards.

Scandal is a powerful persuader. One of the biggest upsets in New Jersey's 1992 state Senate election was the defeat of the Republican majority leader, John Dorsey, who had held the post for eighteen years. The news media uncovered, among other things, the fact that "Dorsey had been retained as an attorney by four local governments, and that his billings to them had totaled more than a million dollars in the previous year—fully 6,000 hours of claimed work" (Beiler 1994c, 45). An editorial in a lead paper noted:

> While Dorsey gets rich off his political friends, he uses his position to ruin political enemies. After 18 years in the Senate, Dorsey acts like he owns the place. He is a walking argument for term limits. (Beiler 1994c, 61, citing *The Daily Record*, October 24, 1992)

Dorsey lost because the problems went to his own record, but scandal sometimes paints candidates with a broad brush. The 1991 "check-bouncing" scandal in the House of Representatives centered on a long-standing privilege allowing members to write penalty-free overdrafts on a huge, Congress-wide joint checking account. Taxpayers' money was not used to cover the checks but many people were enraged over the "abuse." When a list of overdrafts was published, members who had written large numbers of bad checks had to explain themselves. Some retired voluntarily; others were forced into retirement. The affair helped foment the anti-incumbent sentiment prevalent in the early 1990s. The exact effect of the check-bouncing affair is difficult to discern; there are conflicting arguments among social scientists (Ahuja et al. 1993; Alford et al. 1994; Dimock and Jacobson 1995), especially since a large number of members who had bounced checks were reelected anyway. In any event, the issue made 1994 a much more difficult year for incumbent campaigns.

While the standards set by the press and public are sometimes cryptic, there are some reasonably clear guidelines in political news that wise campaigns must follow.

Truthfulness

Professional reporters are concerned that their stories are both newsworthy and accurate. Rumors are rampant in the political community, but most are not reported because the hearsay cannot be verified. Without verification, a reporter who runs a rumor-based story violates a key tenet of the profession. Worse, elections sometimes turn on false information. There are few filters when the reporters are cut out of the process. In Georgia Republican nominee Guy Millner ran television ads accusing his opponent, Roy Barnes, of voting to allow parole for murderers and rapists. "The only problem," according to the *Atlanta Constitution*, which tamped the story down, was that "Barnes actually voted for the only amendment put before the House [in 1998] that specifically named those crimes and 10 other violent offenses as ineligible for parole" (Helton and Pruitt 1998). The ad was soon pulled from the air. But journalists are not perfect. One analyst suggests that erroneous opposition research, passed to journalists, may have changed the course of the 1991 mayoral race in Houston (Frantz 1999).

Two subsets of the truthfulness criterion are that the information must have been gained from a legitimate source—one that is both legal and appropriate—and that the information must be independently verifiable. Examples of stories being spiked because the sources were illegitimate are scarce for an obvious reason: they were never run. Those few that have gotten out have made news, though not always in the way that the campaign would have liked. When reports emerged in 1992 that Bush administration officials had pulled Bill Clinton's passport file, the result was short-lived anger in the Clinton campaign and a federal investigation of the State Department employees that led to serious legal proceedings. In addition, some lawful and ethical information is withheld because it cannot be confirmed through independent sources. At about the same time as the passport file incident, the Clinton campaign was given a foreign news report that Bush campaign materials were being produced in Brazil, but the Clinton campaign was unable to get the U.S. media to air the story because no one could find independent verification that the Bush campaign actually knew that its materials were being manufactured abroad. The story could not be authenticated, and therefore it could not be run.

Relevance

A candidate's official actions are automatically considered relevant. Negative information is newsworthy. The difficulty comes in the sometimes-vague distinction between official conduct and personal behavior. Larry Sabato, Mark Stencel, and S. Robert Lichter have offered a standard that draws a line between reportable news and unreportable news according to relevance (2000). A candidate's personal life becomes news only when it affects public business, and thus, for example, extramarital affairs are usually out of bounds, but if the relationship is with a lobbyist, the news is reportable because in that case "there is a clear intersection between an official's public and private roles" (8). In general terms, the public has a right to know when the public might be affected by otherwise private behavior.

Fairness

Fairness is closely related to truthfulness and relevance, but it has a unique quality that campaigns sometimes misunderstand. The guiding question will be, Is it fair to single out one candidate for criticism when all are guilty of the same misdeed? More to the point, campaigns that level a charge must be sure that their own candidate is clean. In 1998, New York senator Al D'Amato's campaign accused opponent Chuck Schumer with having missed critical votes while he was out campaigning. The only problem was that D'Amato himself had missed a number of votes when he was running for Senate in 1980. Although D'Amato originally gained a lot of traction against Schumer, the missed votes argument turned into an embarrassment for the D'Amato campaign. Not only did the campaign lose whatever advantage it once had with the issue, but lethal questions of hypocrisy and incompetence were added to the mix.

Opposition research is largely unregulated. A consultant might suffer the scorn of associates, but there are few ways of officially condemning a consultant's misuse of opposition data. In January 1994, the American Association of Political Consultants (AAPC) passed a "Code of Ethics." Members pledge, among other things, to "document accurately and fully any criticism of an opponent or his or her record." Still, there is no strong disciplinary mechanism enforcing the code, and those running campaigns need not belong to the AAPC, as there exist no licensing requirements for campaign consultants.

Several states have adopted "tell-a-lie, lose-your-job" statutes, designed to take the profit out of dishonest campaigning. A 1984 California law, for instance, strips a politician from office if a jury finds that deceptive claims were the major cause of victory. It applies to all local, state, and federal offices (except the presidency). Unfortunately, these laws have, for the most part, proved hollow—it is exceedingly difficult to prove that a deliberate distortion was the reason for success. A notable exception is the case of Wes Cooley, who was forced to retire from Congress and later convicted in Oregon for having lied on a voter information pamphlet. Regulations have been proposed that would mandate that candidates appear in all attack ads, that state or federal funding be made available to candidates who are unfairly attacked, that free media time be given to respond to attacks, and that bipartisan commissions be created to review the truthfulness of all charges. None of these reforms seem imminent.

THE FUNCTION OF OPPOSITION DATA

Students of the political arts talk about *prospective* and *retrospective* evaluation. Prospective evaluations are based upon anticipatory assumptions. The voter looks at the candidate—qualifications, party label, personality, and campaign promises—and then guesses what kind of job the candidate will do in office. When Bill Clinton promised a "bridge to the twenty-first century," he was asking voters to view his campaign prospectively. Retrospective evaluations look in the opposite direction. Past actions are weighed in order to judge a candidate's future behavior. When Ronald Reagan asked, "Are you better off now than you were four years ago?" he was inviting citizens to think about the problems of the Carter administration. The consensus is that retrospective evaluations are the dominant mode of decision making because (1) prospective evaluations require voters to study campaign plans, and (2) all else being equal, the past is considered a strong predictor of the future.

Opposition research taps into the process of retrospective evaluation. It is an attempt to convey the perils of selecting the opponent by pointing out the shortcomings of past behavior (see Fiorina 1981). In a sense, voters are confronted with a choice: either look at each candidate's plans for the future (a speculative, time-consuming chore) or examine what the candidates have done in the past (a quick, "factual" process). If the backward-looking clues are unflattering, the evaluation of the candidate will be likewise. The power of this process carries an obvious appeal to candidates. As more and more contenders use the technique, voters become accustomed to it, and they may be starting to depend on it even while they decry negative campaigns. Hence, opposition research has become an important specialization in the campaign profession.

COUNTEROPPOSITION RESEARCH

An important caveat must be mentioned. Opposition research cannot focus exclusively on the opponent. It is a nearly universal philosophical principle—from existentialism, to Christianity, to military theory—that one must look at one's own behavior before attacking others. To the extent that O-R is a search for comparative advantage, both sides of the equation have to be known. After all, opponents conduct research, too. The only way to be prepared for negative attacks is to know what the opposition might have. Missed votes need to be accounted for, along with defaulted loans, off-color comments, and difficult votes. As D'Amato learned, campaigns must avoid charging the opposition with misdeeds that the candidate has also committed.

Just as any job seeker must assemble a résumé, prospective candidates must develop a scrupulous account of their past work experience, political affiliations, memberships, outside activities, and the like. This sort of information is generally distributed in the form of a one-page biography, but files are kept to back up any question—positive or negative—about the candidate's background. Particularly since the 1970s, when journalists began writing investigative profiles of public officials, political campaigns have kept records on even the most trivial bits of information. A documented fact can stop a rumor before it starts, but exculpatory facts that cannot be authenticated might just as well not exist. Politics can be a rough game.

A good campaign team will not assume that its candidate has perfect memory and candor. Problems can be painful; memories can be selective. The only way to understand a candidate's strengths and weaknesses is via thorough research. Even private information leaks into electoral campaigns. All the candidate's writings, tax records, school transcripts, court cases, tax forms, investment documents, vehicle registrations, medical histories, and so forth should be retrievable at a moment's notice. It can be a difficult chore. Most people dislike taking stock of themselves. Layers of pride, shame, and forgetfulness tend to make self-portraits difficult to render accurately. Listing simple biographical information can be difficult enough. Given the scrutiny that attaches to contemporary candidates, it is important to record exact titles and job descriptions, but determining whether or not a candidate upholds the highest ethical standards can become an uncomfortable journey. Some consultants may begin to think that Dostoyevsky was right: "Lying to ourselves is more deeply ingrained than lying to others."

TYPES OF PROFILE DATA

The point of counteropposition research is to help a candidate know himself or herself better than anyone else ever could, because only then can the campaign respond to attacks. As campaigning becomes more and more aggressive, opposition research will continue to be an integral part of new-style campaigns. It is therefore important to know how oppo works. In this sense, the information involved in opposition research can be separated into four different types of information: (1) political, (2) campaign finance, (3) career, and (4) personal.

Political Information

Political information is that which pertains to activities undertaken by a candidate while in an elected or appointed public position or to statements the candidate has made while seeking public office. Many of these activities will have been overt—made for public consumption—and others will have been made behind closed doors. No matter how thoughtful, careful, and attentive to the public's needs an official might be, a candidate's record always seems to hold something damaging. The task of the opposition researcher is to find words, deeds, and works that will disappoint swing voters.

Voting Record. The 1994 midterm election was a disaster for Democrats, as myriad gubernatorial, state legislative, and U.S. Senate and congressional candidates went down to defeat. Bob Barr knocked off ten-year incumbent Buddy Darden of Georgia because Darden was perceived to be out of touch with the district (Shea 1996b). Among the votes highlighted by Barr was his support of the 1994 crime bill. Even though the bill sought to increase funding for prisons and police protection, one section banned the sale of assault rifles. This part of the bill became the rallying call for gun advocates throughout the district. Darden had also voted for Clinton's budget bill in 1993, which raised taxes on gasoline and upper-income taxpayers. In the end, Darden found himself dubbed a "liberal" in conservative Georgia. His defeat shocked political observers around the country. Ironically, had Darden voted against the 1994 crime bill, he might have been labeled "soft on crime."

Congress, as well as most city councils, county legislatures, and state legislatures, confronts literally thousands of measures each session. Many of these bills are technical and may be of little importance to the voters, but a few are hotly debated. Research teams find it imperative to record all these votes, no matter how insignificant some might seem, spanning the opposition official's entire career—including both floor votes and committee votes. Which votes matter? Campaigns often consult lobbyists and legislative staffers familiar with the legislation on the technicalities, as well as the best ways to word the significance of "bad votes" in plain language. Surveys and focus groups can also be helpful.

One readily understood "bad vote" is the "flip-flop," in which an official's position changes from one time to another. The 1992 Clinton campaign charged that George Bush had "four different positions on civil rights," while the Bush campaign stressed Clinton's reputation as a "slick" politician. Highlighting a flip-flop is effective. First, the switch might offend people on both sides of the issue. If a candidate is shown to have changed positions on abortion from pro-life to pro-choice, the pro-choice voters may doubt the candidate's sincerity, and pro-life voters are reminded of the candidate's present views. Second, a flip-flop goes to the question of trust. Politicians who changed their votes in the past may well do so in the future. Indeed, some will ask whether the new-found convictions were planted for no other reason than electoral politics.

Absenteeism. Missed votes suggest dereliction of duty. Some absences are understandable, of course. Family and health concerns will be excused, but a sure way to intimate that an official is not "working for the people" is to point out chronic absenteeism. In the 1984 Kentucky U.S. Senate race, Republican challenger Mitch McConnell was able to unseat incumbent Democrat Dee Huddleston by highlighting the senator's missed votes. In a now-legendary television spot, a man led by four bloodhounds frantically searched for signs of Huddleston—in his Washington office, back home in Kentucky—but Huddleston was nowhere to be found. According to the ad, Huddleston missed important votes while collecting money for speeches in California and Puerto Rico. Sometimes, a single vote makes all the difference. Democrat Harley O. Staggers was defeated in 1992, in part because he missed a key vote funding a new FBI center in his West Virginia district. Voters expect their representatives to be there for every vote—even every committee vote—a point that opposition researchers stand ready to exploit.

Bill Sponsorship. Another aspect of an official's record is an incumbent's bill sponsorships. Some bills have only a single sponsor, others have two or three, and a few popular measures see dozens of members "sign on." Members are not always careful in screening their colleague's bills, and there are several methods of using this information. First, if the legislator fails to sponsor legislation important to the voters, he or she can be attacked for this neglect. Second, if the legislator sponsored a bill that did not become law, he or she can be charged with ineffectiveness. Third, when the member has a tendency to cosponsor many bills, it might be fruitful to ask whether their combined weight would have busted the budget. (The National Taxpayers Union scores members of Congress in just this way.) Finally, campaigns examine the relationship between bill sponsorship and voting records. Occasionally, legislators vote against measures nearly identical to ones that they are sponsoring—an act that can be portrayed by a skillful campaign as a legislative flip-flop.

Committee and Leadership Assignments. Committees and subcommittees have jurisdiction over only a limited set of issues. An official's committee assignments, therefore, tend to reflect on the legislator's priorities. Some committees are more prestigious than others; some tackle problems relevant to the candidate's district; and some are neither prestigious nor helpful to the people back home. Leadership responsibilities also speak to an official's status and effectiveness. A failure to move up the leadership ladder might be seen to indicate a host of problems, namely, ineffectiveness or simple apathy.

Bill MaGee used Jack McCann's leadership in committee to great effect. McCann served on the Agriculture Committee during much of his tenure. This made sense because his mostly rural district boasts many family farms. A year prior to the election, however, he was bumped from his position as Republican leader of the Agriculture Committee to become the Republican leader of the Racing and Wagering Committee. Not only was this new assignment less prestigious, but there were no racetracks in McCann's district. MaGee spread the word that McCann was more interested in gambling than the survival of family farms.

Pork. A mainstay of incumbency reelection is the procurement of "pork-barrel." Each year, city, county, state, and federal budgets are carved up for specific projects—military contracts, environmental remediation, highways, and the like. These projects, called "particularized benefits" by one scholar (Mayhew 1974b), allow public officials to get credit for actions performed in the Capitol, the courthouse, or city hall. Officials report their success in the media and the mail, leading voters to believe that they are represented by effective legislators. The issue can cut either way. First, the quest for high-grade pork can be viewed as a propensity toward profligate spending—a possible problem for a fiscal conservative. More commonly, however, a legislator will be punished for failing to take care of the district, as Harley Staggers' problem with the FBI Center makes clear.

Official Mailings. Many public officials have the ability to use official mailings to keep the voters informed. The privilege is called "franking," and it originated with congressmen and senators being allowed to substitute stamps with handwritten signatures. Later, printed signatures were deemed acceptable. The upside for incumbents is that they can stay in touch with the district. The downside is that an overly ambitious mail program can lead to charges of misusing public funds. In the 1990 Indiana U.S. Senate race, Democrat Barron Hill gained ground against incumbent Republican Dan Coats by highlighting Coats' ambitious franking. In a television spot, a homeowner stood in front of his open roadside mailbox watching a gusher of letters spray out. The flow continued as the announcer said, "Dan Coats has dumped 13.1 million pieces of junk mail on Indiana." The message: Coats was wasting taxpayer money.

There are legal and ethical issues as well. In the House of Representatives, for example, the words that go into franked mass mailings are tightly regulated. No express call for votes can be made, for example, and the word "I" cannot be used in reference to the congressional representative more than eight times. Mailings contrary to the rules are rejected. In the current political environment, however, even an approved mass mailing can be used against a candidate. In May 2000, Nebraska Republican Lee Terry was accused by the Nebraska Democratic Party of sending out a franked message that looked more political than informational. The legality of the mailing—a case strongly argued by Terry's senior staff—seemed a weak defense.

Office Staffing and Expenses. Perhaps the only thing that voters despise more than a public official wasting money on unnecessary projects is a public official wasting taxpayer money on him- or herself. Democratic Ways and Means Committee chairman Dan Rostenkowski's fall in 1994 can be attributed, in part, to allegations that he had kept ghost employees on the payroll, had converted office stamps into cash, and had used taxpayer money to buy a variety of expensive chairs and other "gifts." Opposition researchers look at an opponent's office expenses and compare them to those of the opponent's colleagues. Incumbents who seem to waste taxpayer money can find themselves in trouble with the voters.

Official Travel Information. Wise campaigns pay special attention to the opponent's travel records. Elected officials often conduct business on the road. These trips, often called "junkets" by political opponents, can be a rich source of embarrassing information. Members can often be found to have traveled with their spouses to conferences, seminars, study sessions, and the like—sometimes held in exotic, sunny places. Any travel can be made to look bad, particularly if the press fallout is not handled well. In 1999, Congressman Brian Bilbray of San Diego, California, traveled to Australia, where he attended a conference on U.S.–Australian relations, saw the Chargers and Broncos play an exhibition game, and took a couple weeks of personal time. The costs were borne by an Australian province. Playing defense, the congressman's chief of staff responded to press inquiries by saying that Bilbray "only missed one week of votes for this, none of which were determined by one vote" (Braun 1999). The *San Diego Union-Tribune* reported, "Bilbray, who has not returned from Australia, could not be reached for comment" (Braun 1999). Bilbray lost in 2000.

Gaffes. Almost everyone says something inappropriate, at one time or another, and candidates are no exception. New York's 1992 U.S. Senate race, which Linda Fowler called "one of the nastiest campaigns ever visited on the state" (1995, 206), offers a good example. In the waning days of the general election, Democratic challenger Robert Abrams was campaigning in a small upstate city when, in the heat of a rally, he called his Republican opponent, Al D'Amato, a "fascist." Little was made of the comment at first, but, as the story made its way across the wires, more and more news outlets carried it. Though the campaign had been hard fought all along, Abrams' choice of words was considered excessive—a shallow attempt by him, a Jew, to play the religious/ethnic card, implicitly linking D'Amato, an Italian American, with 1940s European fascism. The attack didn't work; D'Amato won.

Contradictions. In addition to verbal gaffes, a campaign can compare the words of an opposition candidate with his or her deeds. In many instances, candidates and elected officials make remarks that contradict a prior speech, vote, or bill sponsorship. Often, holders of lower-level posts pledge to serve the full term only to find opportunities for higher office before the term ends. Others are dogged by term-limits pledges made in earlier years. Taxes are another problematic area. In 1988, George Bush, in a dramatic display of resolve, pledged: "Read my lips: No new taxes." After the president joined with Democrats in raising taxes to lower the deficit, the 1992 Clinton campaign had a ready-made campaign issue.

Campaign Finance Information

A second type of oppo looks at campaign finances. Federal candidates make detailed reports to the Federal Election Commission listing, among other things, all the individuals and Political Action Committees (PACs) that contributed more than $100 to their campaign. Nearly all states have similar disclosure requirements. Opposition researchers scour these data for irregularities. For example, if four people with the same last name and address give the maximum allowable contribution, and if two of the contributors list their occupation as "student," then some might wonder if the head of the household was actually augmenting a personal donation by funneling disallowed contributions through family members. Also, extremist groups or very unpopular individuals can sometimes be found backing the opponent. Martin Luther King III was hurt in his race for the Fulton County, Georgia, Commission chair by the discovery that one of his contributors was suspected in a murder case. Money is always needed, and in the hurry to fill war chests, many candidates pay inadequate attention to who is giving it.

Moreover, well-funded campaigns can be accused of "buying" the district. In California exorbitant personal spending is an emerging tradition. Michael Huffington spent $27 million of his own money in 1994 on a Senate seat. He lost. Darrell Issa spent $11 million of his own money for the other Senate seat in the 1998 GOP primary. He lost, too. Al Checchi, who spent $40 million in the 1998 gubernatorial primary, lost with an embarrassing 13 percent of the vote. According to one analysis, "Despite all the popularity in recent years of anti-establishment, 'outsider' candidates such as Perot, voters ultimately have chosen candidates who paid their dues by serving first on school boards or city councils, volunteering in community organizations, or attending countless political meetings and conventions to help other candidates or the party" (Westneat and Brown 1998). If that is what voters ultimately choose, then charges of excessive candidate spending would seem to cut deeply.

Career Information

Public service is not the only way that a candidate can amass a record. Prior business activities and other career information can provide a powerful stockpile of inauspicious material. This information can be grouped into three broad areas: résumé inflation, questionable practices, and dubious associates.

Resume Inflation. Many voters stretch the bounds of honesty when they write their résumés, but this sort of behavior is not tolerated in candidates for public office. Wes Cooley paid a price for puffing up his credentials, as noted earlier. Democrat Ken Bentsen's 1994 upset victory over Republican Eugene Fontenot in Texas' twenty-fifth congressional district also illustrates the perils of résumé inflation. Fontenot had billed himself as a physician and a lawyer, but he was forced to admit that he had not practiced medicine in a decade and had never practiced law. The candidate's collapse did not end there. As consultant Craig Varoga notes:

> Prompted by Bentsen's TV and mail showing $3 million in IRS tax liens against Fontenot's hospital, Fontenot said he hadn't run the hospital during the years in question—contradicting his official biography. (1995, 35)

Bentsen successfully defined his opponent, essentially stripping Fontenot of his ability to stress professionalism and character.

Questionable Practices. A candidate's professional years can be important. In the race for the 1994 Ohio state attorney general's office, Betty Montgomery continually reminded voters that her opponent had never prosecuted a criminal case—even though he was the incumbent attorney general. She argued that he lacked courtroom experience. The voters gave the seat to Montgomery. Financial investments can become particularly problematic. In 1995, Republican presidential hopeful Phil Gramm of Texas found that some of his investment money had gone to the production of pornographic films. Even though Gramm had no knowledge of, or role in, its activities, the investment was deemed by many conservative voters to be a serious misjudgment.

Dubious Associates. Guilt by association may be considered unsporting in many arenas, but it remains fair game in politics. Former senator Carol Moseley-Braun's boyfriend, who also served as her campaign manager, was accused of sexually harassing female campaign workers, leading to charges that the senator was ignoring the situation. In recent years, membership in clubs that exclude people based on race, creed, color, or religion has been considered a violation of public ethics. Sometimes the matter is a mix of personal and political association, as in Moseley-Braun's case, and sometimes the association in question is expressly political, going straight to ideology. In 1996 Montana senator Max Baucus endured claims that he "votes like Ted Kennedy." A strong record of support for the National Rifle Association's agenda is sometimes seen as an electoral liability among moderate swing voters.

Personal Information

A last broad classification of O-R is personal information. It is widely considered unethical to find or use information that is either (1) untruthful or (2) not readily available to everyone. In other words, it is generally considered unscrupulous to hide in the bushes with a camera or to present gossip as if it were fact—or to hire a private investigator to do the dirty work on the campaign's behalf. Indeed, an investigator is rarely needed. A good deal of personal information can be obtained from the media, court records, the local recorder of deeds, liens, and taxes, professional associations, the board of elections, and the candidate himself or herself. Still, even if the information is available to the public, a campaign must proceed carefully with personal information, as the news media is wary of low-blow attacks.

The current news environment can be traced to an episode of drunk driving by Chairman Wilbur Mills of Arkansas, who led the powerful House Committee on Ways and Means. In the 1960s, the private lives of politicians were largely considered out of bounds. Reporters would overlook personal indiscretions so long as there was no gross interference with a candidate's public duties. But with the onset of journalistic distrust of government that accompanied Vietnam and Watergate, a more skeptical approach came into vogue. In 1974, Mills was pulled over for speeding at night without headlights, at which point a stripper jumped out of his car and into the Tidal Basin. While reporters had known about Mills' problems with alcohol for some time—one even engaged in a detective-style stakeout (Sabato 1991, 47)—the chairman's drinking did not become an issue until his run-in with the police. After Mills, the floodgates were opened. Ohio Democrat Wayne Hays, chairman of the House Administration Committee, employed a secretary, Elizabeth Ray, a former beauty pageant contestant who admitted, "I can't type." After that, Utah Democrat Alan Howe was arrested for soliciting police officers who were posing as prostitutes and was thereafter disavowed by his own party. (The party launched a write-in campaign for an alternative candidate.) Mills, Hays, and Howe all saw their congressional careers cut short.

While a candidate's extramarital affair may become a campaign issue, a simple divorce raises few eyebrows—but slowness of child support payments draws interest. Bill Yellowtail Jr., a Montana Democrat vying for the state's at-large congressional seat in 1996, was reported to have been long delinquent in this regard. The story hit the papers on Mother's Day. Yellowtail lost the election by five points.

A good deal of research suggests that, as party identification becomes less meaningful, voters look to personalities. As they do, candidates will be more inclined to use character-based attacks, painting their opponents as morally corrupt. Playing the character card can be quite effective—but risky. Even though voters use personality-based information to help make up their minds, they are also sensitive to overly hostile or clearly undocumented charges. Wise campaigns proceed thoughtfully before using this type of O-R.

LOCATING PROFILE DATA

With the onset of digital capabilities, opposition research has come to be divided between old information and new information. Generally speaking, newer information from national and regional sources can be retrieved in data

form; older, more local information is still on hard copy. Even though some research must still be done on site, more and more data are available on the World
Wide Web.

Public Records

There is a method to researching public records. *The Guide to Background Investigations* (1998) gives detailed instructions for searching state, federal, and educational records. Some of the procedures are suited only to a researcher's own
candidate—educational institutions require permission before a transcript can be
released—but public records are, by definition, available to everyone. Companies
like knowx.com, a fee-based public records researcher, put many of these tools on
the researcher's desktop. Writes one consultant, "[I]f there is something you are
looking for—Social Security numbers, DMV [Department of Motor Vehicles]
records, credit reports—chances are there is some data company that sells it"
(Bovee 1998, 52). But at this point the question starts getting into legal and ethical
issues—of which there are many—as well as matters of political wisdom. The
very fact that a campaign sought an opponent's Social Security number can become a campaign issue in itself. Inappropriate opposition research reflects poorly
on a candidate.

That said, almost every government agency, branch, or office provides public
information about its members. Government "blue books" and "red books" are official reference manuals providing everything from government structure and
process, to office telephone numbers, to official biographies for sitting government officials. Commercial "yellow books" offer much the same information,
often in a more useful format. All of these are available at good libraries.

In the past few years, however, a great deal of this information has been made
available on the Web. Legislators and executive officers are now on-line. Agencies and legislative bodies offer data on budget actions, vetoes, measures signed
into law, agency orders, staffing, and so on. Off-line, nearly all legislatures have
some sort of public information office. These offices archive the actions of the
entire legislature and of each member. They provide information on bill sponsorship, amendment referrals, voting records, committee assignments, and committee actions. Many incumbents and senior government officials are required to
submit financial disclosure forms. In Congress, records of each member's mail
account are kept by the secretary of the Senate and the House clerk, allowing for
public inspection. For state and local candidates, these records are kept by the
secretary of state and a variety of local governmental offices. Research may require sending letters, paying for copies, and waiting, but vigilance and patience
should prevail.

Thorough research often demands legwork. Local libraries often maintain files
devoted to the city, county, and state governments. Privately operated data services, which monitor the actions of the executive or legislature, can also be used.

StateNet, for example, provides a comprehensive database of state legislative actions nationwide, including bills, sponsors' memos, members' voting records, campaign contribution reports, and a host of additional information on state legislative actions. Many states have put legislative data online, and those that have not can provide the information for a fee. In fact, many online resources might not go as far back as an opposition researcher would hope. Hard-copy reports are still part of the process. At the congressional level, virtually all the information that a researcher would desire can be retrieved from the Congressional Universe of Lexis-Nexis, and recent actions are searchable on the official Web sites of the House and Senate. To learn what a bill in the U.S. Senate was all about, a campaign can turn to official reports of the Congressional Research Service (a branch of the Library of Congress) available online at major libraries. Many states have similar legislative study agencies.

As surprising as it might seem, another source of information is the opponent's office. By simply requesting information on bill sponsorships or committee assignments, for example, detailed information can sometimes be obtained. The same is true for local projects—pork, that is. If a researcher is interested in the amount of money that an official secured for various projects, the incumbent's office might be helpful. Public officials realize the importance of keeping in touch with concerned citizens, and those requesting information are given prompt consideration. But opposition researchers should understand the ethical problems with contacting an incumbent's office under any sort of false pretense.

For campaign-related information, the best place to start is the local media outlets and online databases. The library may keep past campaign literature. Local parties collect radio and television spots. It is unlikely that the stations themselves will have saved the ads and even more doubtful that broadcasters would provide tapes or transcripts. Another resource for campaigns ads might be a friendly political scientist or communications professor at the local college or university. Contribution and expenditure information on federal candidates is provided by the Federal Election Commission (FEC). Official records are located in Washington, DC, but FEC data are now posted on the Web at the commission's own Web site, as well as the Web sites of "good government" groups. The Center for Responsive Politics maintains a comprehensive online database of campaign finance information.

Data on property liens, which can show whether a business failed to pay its taxes on time, can be useful. The researcher may have to check a variety of sources for this information, including the local recorder of deeds, the district courts, or the county or city courthouse. If the candidate has run a business regulated by a state or county agency, the agency likely has public information related to licensing and enforcement activities. Likewise, states have employment offices, chambers of commerce, and professional organizations that track industries, companies, and professions. Legal proceedings are available from civil courts, criminal courts, family courts, and appellate courts. Each has its own defendant index. Local boards of election are usually checked to see whether the opponent has voted in past elections. This information can also suggest how long he or she has lived in the area prior to the campaign.

News Media

With ever-narrowing profit margins, newspapers have become less accommodating to requests for old articles—many newspapers still index stories and provide copies for a fee, as do many local television and radio stations—but new restrictions are accompanied by a great increase in the availability of news on the Web. The old ways of research had campaign operatives leafing through yellowed clippings at the library, in the offices of interest groups, or at party headquarters. Political professionals might still take advantage of these resources, partly because the strategy brings one in contact with knowledgeable librarians, lobbyists, and party chairs. Increasingly, however, the research is done on desktop computers, where an abundance of information can be retrieved in short order.

Rapid news delivery is one of the great, if imperfect, boons of the Digital Age. Databases such as Lexis-Nexis and NewsBank offer a great deal of assistance. Lexis-Nexis offers national, regional, and major city papers, along with news wires, magazines, newsletters, statistics, and legislative data. NewsBank is particularly helpful for researching local papers. A researcher using NewsBank to look at a candidate from Elkton, Maryland, can search both the *Cecil Business Ledger* and the *Cecil Whig*. For an extensive listing of press outlets from major daily newspapers to weekly shoppers and niche publications, a researcher will look to industry reference materials such as Editor & Publisher's *International Yearbook* and the *Gale Directory of Publications and Broadcast Media*. Lexis-Nexis and NewsBank carry the full text of many articles, but for research that goes back more than a decade, particularly where small-circulation publications are involved, operatives may need to make a personal library visit. Publications can be located by searching World-Cat at a college or research library. The *Cecil Whig*, it seems, is carried by a dozen libraries, including the General Libraries at the University of Texas, Austin. For many obscure sources, a researcher may be disappointed to find that the publication is not searchable and not indexed. Still, local libraries and historical societies commonly maintain clip files on public officials, so all is not yet lost.

There are a growing number of options for collecting business-related opposition data. A starting point would again be an online service. This time, instead of just searching under the opponent's name, the candidate's business or organizational affiliations would be scanned. A search might begin with Lexis-Nexis and Business NewsBank, but a number of other publications can also prove helpful, including trade journals, regional business publications, chamber of commerce reports, biographical directories, and corporate annual reports. Local newspapers and community libraries may have files on the opponent's business.

Researchers pay particular attention to the partisan press. In Washington, DC, for example, the *Washington Times* serves as a conservative national newspaper. It keeps a close eye on scandals involving liberal officials. Also in DC is the *City Paper*, an urban alternative weekly that, like many such papers, tends to run scandal stories. Researchers want to bear in mind that the mainstream press tends to be suspicious of partisan and alternative news sources, but campaigns should also note the increasing speed with which nonmainstream stories are making their way into the dominant media.

DATA STORAGE AND RETRIEVAL

Once a mountain of information has been compiled, the next step is to organize it for rapid response. In the 1970s, filing cabinets were filled with folders. There might be, for instance, one thick file of news clippings and another of campaign finance reports. As questions arose during the course of the campaign, different files would be pulled and sorted to find the counterattack. Carefully segmented hard-copy information was seen as the cutting edge—the best new thing. Once again, computer technology has changed all.

Like many other new-style campaign technologies, computerized opposition research was pioneered by the Republicans during a presidential contest. In 1984 the Republican National Committee spent $1.1 million to create the Opposition Research Group. Its first task was to collect detailed information about each of the eight Democratic candidates running for president. The group pulled together a mountain of facts, using over 2,000 sources and 400,000 documents. Next, a staff of readers sifted through the material looking for direct quotes, statements attributed to the candidates, and comments about the candidates by others. The information was coded and entered into a massive computerized database. In the end, the system contained approximately 75,000 items and 45,000 quotes (Bayer and Rodota 1989).

When Democrats nominated Walter Mondale, the Republicans were ready. They produced "Vice President Malaise," a 200-page analysis of the Mondale record, and sent it to every party official in the nation. Each time that Mondale spoke, Republicans were ready to point out problematic actions or comments. As Mondale campaigned from location to location, Republicans told voters about his positions and statements harmful to the community. The database was later instrumental in preparing Ronald Reagan for debates. When all was said and done, the project was viewed as the "secret weapon" of the race (Bayer and Rodota 1989, 25). In the new millennium, some sort of opposition database is considered essential in any midlevel race.

But even with digitalization, one of the most important resources that a campaign can tap is the knowledge of experienced operatives. There may be someone in the community who collects political mailings and past party chairs who can recall the details of ancient races. Aspiring candidates are advised to call on an "old hand" who has been through the process before (Grey 1999, 53). It helps with strategy, and it helps with candidate profiles as well. Those who have seen candidates come and go remember old scandals and how they played out. A new-style campaign listens to war stories, first to get information about the foibles of past candidates but also to learn the sensibilities of the district. In some areas, a certain amount of scandal is written off as a cost of doing business, while in others, absolute adherence to moral and ethical codes is paramount—and even opposition research is considered unscrupulous.

CONCLUSION

The collection and organization of opposition research have come a long way since Grover Cleveland was accused of fathering a child out of wedlock. In a sense, however, it is the same as it ever was. Opposition research is a way to learn the strengths and weaknesses of an opponent. If properly used, O-R can change the course of a race, and with the increasing depth and variety of online data, there is little reason to expect that oppo will fade away. Whether the movement toward fast-paced O-R helps democratic accountability or decreases campaign civility, new-style consultants pay close attention to these new information resources—and opposition research will continue to grow in importance.

Part Two

STRATEGIC THINKING

Chapter Six

Prior Electoral Targeting

In the early days of the 1960 presidential campaign, Vice President Richard M. Nixon promised to visit every state in the Union. It was a sensible pronouncement. After all, the president serves the entire nation. Nixon's vow even makes some strategic sense, because many of the smaller states have important media markets beyond their borders. Toward the end of the campaign, however, several states had yet to receive their visit. Reminded of his pledge, Nixon was forced to spend critical days in the final stretch traveling to electorally insignificant parts of the country. Some of the states that Nixon called upon were already in his back pocket, and others could never have been won. The promise ended up sending Nixon to far-off Alaska, robbing precious time from the vice president's endgame schedule. Nixon was defeated that November by a razor-thin margin.

Compare Nixon's 1960 campaign with Bill Clinton's 1996 effort. In the last presidential race of the millennium, political consultants Mark Penn and Douglas Schoen created multilayered, computer-generated maps to locate the most opportune segments of the electorate. It was not enough to say that single mothers were predisposed to favor the Clinton–Gore ticket. Instead, concentrations of single mothers were pinpointed according to their state of residence and local media market, with particular attention paid to states within striking distance of a 50 percent presidential support rating. General demographics were augmented with the results of telephone polling, focus groups, and mall surveys. As each layer of information was affixed to the map—a different color indicating each new factor—a strategic picture of the United States emerged. It became obvious where commercials should be run and where the candidates should be sent. All attention was focused on ground worth fighting for. The result? Little wasted motion—a steady bead on the most valuable targets.

Sophisticated polling and computer mapping are expensive—beyond the reach of most local organizations—but the same general theory of electioneering applies to campaigns at all levels: visualize the district strategically. Political professionals seek a lucid understanding of the district. Resources are concentrated accordingly. Much strategic information can be gleaned from electoral history—inexpensive, publicly available information that says a lot about a district. Again, neighbors tend to vote like one another. Communities are not homogeneous, but a precinct that voted two-thirds Republican in 2000 will probably vote two-thirds Republican in 2004. This theory helps campaign professionals see which precincts have a highly partisan vote and which fluctuate between Republicans and Democrats. Simple arithmetic can demonstrate with a fair degree of accuracy the number of votes needed to win and even where those votes can be found.

Prior electoral data offer critical information to help a campaign allocate resources efficiently. Nixon's team committed a grave error in 1960. Many believe that his well-intentioned pledge changed the career of a rising politician and altered the history of American politics. New-style consultants avoid Nixon's blunder. This chapter reviews the logic behind electoral targeting, the elementary calculations needed to understand historical data, and the manner in which electoral analysis helps campaign professionals develop precinct-by-precinct campaign strategies.

UNDERSTANDING THE DISTRICT

In the study of campaigns and elections, one finds an important distinction between *individual-level behavior* and *aggregate-level behavior*. Individual-level behavior is encrypted in the habits of daily life. Scholars have long struggled with the question, What makes a person vote for a particular candidate? Party politics, of course, but there are other forces—ideology, candidate imagery, a sense of belonging, and so forth. Some voters surely base judgments on the cleverness of a candidate's campaign commercials, others may cast their lot this way or that because they are trying to impress a friend, and still others assume that short people cannot lead the country. Students of politics will always be frustrated by the eccentricities of individual decision making, but aggregate-level campaign statistics look at the big picture, examining the behavior of large blocs of voters.

At the aggregate level, myriad individual actions combine into voting districts, states, and the nation as a whole. Eccentricities are dampened by the sheer weight of numbers. Some districts go Republican by roughly the same percentage every single year. Some states are more favorable than others to third-party candidates. In fact, while Americans are constantly moving from house to house—the Census Bureau estimates that one in five people moves to a new address each year—the predisposition of voters in any given neighborhood remains roughly constant. A city with a high turnout in one year will presumably show a high turnout again eight years later, even though many of the earlier residents have long since moved out of town. The individuals change, but the community remains the same.

A common voting configuration is illustrated in Figure 6.1, which represents a district that generally splits its vote 50–50 between Democrats and Republicans

Figure 6.1
Diagramming an Electorate

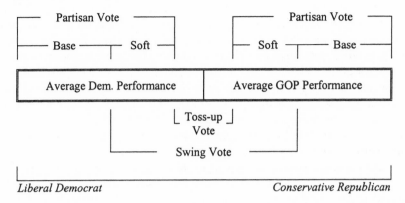

(the average party performance). About 16 percent of the vote (the toss-up) is up for grabs, and another 17 percent on each side (the soft-partisan vote) can usually be depended upon by each party, though not always. Finally, some 25 percent of the electorate (the base-partisan vote) goes with even the worst Democratic candidates, and the same is true on the Republican side.

This model illustrates an important political truth: competitive elections are usually decided by small groups of people. If 25 percent of the electorate always votes Democratic, and another 25 percent always votes Republican, the remaining 50 percent will decide the winner. Only half of the electorate is persuadable. If another 17 percent votes for barely acceptable Democratic candidates, and yet another 17 percent votes the same way for Republicans, then 84 percent of the electorate is off the table in a competitive race. Only 16 percent—the "toss-up" vote—remains in play. Winning requires a bare majority of the toss-up, just over 8 percent. And because turnout is commonly less than 50 percent of those qualified, the key to victory is held by little more than 4 percent of the eligible electorate! Of course, the problem facing campaign professionals is that of finding the (sometimes elusive) middle ground. Electoral targeting is the quest for the deciding vote.

Running the Numbers

Targeting begins with an understanding of the most important single characteristic of a district: the number of potential voters it holds. It is easy to determine the overall population of a district—census data offer a close approximation—but a campaign professional is not interested in *total* population nearly so much as *voting* population. How many people are registered? Usually up to 70 percent, but not much more. How many of the eligible voters actually vote on Election Day? This figure generally ranges between 35 percent and 65 percent, depending on the district, election year, and the kind of offices on the ballot. A county that boasts 130,000 voting-age people may have only 100,000 registered voters, of whom only 75,000 might actually vote in a presidential election year. Moreover, while almost everyone who enters the voting booth selects a candidate for president, people tend to suffer from "voter fatigue" as they work their way down the list toward the judges and county officials. Often constituents choose not to vote for "down-ballot" offices. (See Figure 6.2.) This phenomenon, whereby voters cast their ballots for candidates at the top of the ballot but not at the bottom, is called "fall-off." To figure out how many people will actually vote in an election, a researcher preparing a county-level campaign should look not at the county's whole population or even its registered voting population but at the way that the electorate has traditionally voted for the office in question.

The most obvious source of aggregate statistics is local newspapers and general reference works. Municipal libraries normally have files on recent elections, and newspapers are making back issues available on-line. In addition, Lexis-Nexis and NewsBank give access to a wide variety of journalistic sources. For congressional and statewide races, most libraries carry *America Votes* (Congressional Quarterly Press), *The Election Data Book* (Bernan Press), *America at the Polls* (Congressional Quarterly Press), *Congressional Quarterly's Guide to U.S. Elections* (Congressional Quarterly Press), and other reference works. These books focus on presidential, U.S. Senate, House, and gubernatorial election outcomes. While such volumes can be helpful—some, for instance, provide maps

Figure 6.2
Turnout and Falloff

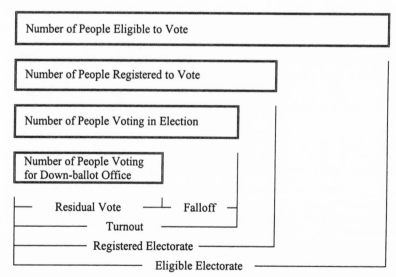

and election overlays with demographic data—they do not supply much information on smaller geographic units.

More refined electoral data is available from the government agencies responsible for compiling them. In some jurisdictions one goes to the local board of elections; in others one goes to the office of the secretary of state or the county or town clerk. Prior election data can be requested over the telephone or by mail, but often these requests are put at the bottom of a pile. Many researchers find it more useful to go to the office and ask for the data personally, partly because the agency might offer a number of data options that cannot be easily described in a brief telephone conversation. The board of elections might offer several precompiled tabular reports (e.g., "2000 Congressional Election Results by Ward"), or it might offer the raw data in a variety of database formats. It may offer to include percentage results in addition to the raw numbers, party registration, turnout scores, and other valuable information. Political professionals ask what is available. Ohio, Texas, and Illinois, for example, were early providers of computer-accessible data. Tennessee emails data files to those who request in-depth statistics. The state of Washington mails floppy disks. Still, although states are beginning to compile results in data form, past races often remain on hard copy only. Party organizations often keep this information on file. Well-heeled campaigns have yet another option. Professional voter contact services compile data sets and provide them in database format, often with the added value of cross-referenced census, voter, and party registration, as well as general demographic information—even home phone numbers. While government agencies charge little or nothing, professional service providers tend to be expensive.

Smith County, USA

Whatever the source, a campaign amasses these data to gain a general sense of the district and the ways in which past elections have been won and lost and, more importantly, to figure out what must be done the next time. There are a number of generally recognized scores and factors used in the analysis of voting districts. Although politics goes beyond simple numbers—researchers need to know about the social, economic, and political cultures of the district that they are mapping—statistical analysis helps manage large quantities of data in an efficient, often thought-provoking manner. The general sense that one gains in crunching the numbers from past elections helps the researcher develop a strategic understanding of the district; a strategic understanding of the district, in turn, helps a researcher determine how the data should be examined. Calculations might be adjusted to fit the local landscape, recent history, and the tactics under formulation. No single statistic can describe a district. Political wisdom is needed, not just under the hot lights of a press conference or television debate but also in the cold calculation of electoral statistics.

To illustrate the calculation of historical performance, it is useful to look at a hypothetical district, Smith County, examining six electoral contests in preparation for a year 2002 run for the auditor's seat. The balance of this chapter is devoted to the mechanics of campaign mathematics, showing how a Republican consultant might dissect a heavily Democratic county in order to strategize a GOP triumph in the auditor's race.

First, the basics. Assume that the election is a competitive two-way, open-seat, general election race between a Republican and a Democrat, where the retiring GOP incumbent has endorsed her successor (thereby avoiding intraparty struggles). The fact that this is a two-way general election simplifies matters. Three-way races are far more complicated to project. Not only does the researcher have to figure out the number of votes the third candidate will take (and which major party will suffer the greatest loss), but the calculation must often be made without benefit of electoral precedent. Relatedly, third-party candidates tend to attract people who do not usually vote, and their voting behavior is therefore not well known. These same problems crop up in party primaries. Sometimes primaries catapult three, four, five, or more candidates into the field. It becomes difficult to figure out from electoral history alone where the voters will turn. A wise student of campaigns will spend a good deal of time learning the statistics of two-way elections before trying to evaluate a multicandidate primary race.

That said, Table 6.1 contains raw voting data for the hypothetical Smith County, an older, heavily unionized electorate in the Midwest. Assume that it has a rusting city at the core of several residential neighborhoods, all of which is surrounded by farms and agriculture-related industry. The numbers offer a preliminary understanding of the county's voting behavior. Turnout is generally greatest in presidential election years. No surprise there. Democrats do much better than Republicans, but Republicans can still win. More people vote for president than vote for auditor. Fall-off is a real issue. Perhaps just as importantly, the consistency of the numbers across time suggests that elections in Smith County are roughly predictable.

Strategizing a Republican's bid for auditor in the year 2002 is a daunting task but one that can be managed by breaking it into smaller steps. The first job is to project the number of votes that will be cast. Year-type is important. The race will occur during an off-year: voters will not choose a president, so many on-year voters will stay home. The appropriate points of departure might be the two recent off-year elections, 1994 and 1998. The most elementary procedure for finding the size of the electorate is to take the number of votes cast for auditor in 1994 and 1998, add them together, and divide the sum by the number of elections under consideration. In this case, 68,234 votes were cast for auditor in 1994, and 63,694 were cast in 1998. Add the two figures together for a sum of 131,928. Divide the sum by 2, the number of elections considered, and the result is an average vote total of 65,964. This last figure is a good prediction of the number of votes that will be cast in 2002.

Note that projections for Campaign 2000 would have been problematic using this method because recent on-year elections have had idiosyncratic features. The 1992 election seems to have had a three-way race for auditor, and 1996 had a Republican running without opposition. These quirks distort the calculation. The

Table 6.1
Smith County, General Elections, 1990–2000

	1990	1992	1994	1996	1998	2000
Eligible Voters	142,651	138,455	127,984	128,301	130,682	130,512
Registered Voters	106,762	103,132	99,678	101,874	101,904	101,803
Democratic	25,658	26,674	24,865	24,659	24,568	24,468
Republican	20,586	19,458	20,485	20,467	19,437	19,734
Actual Voters	75,512	87,085	75,490	75,250	68,080	77,692
Votes for Candidate (by Party)						
President		87,034		75,234		77,608
Democratic		38,453		36,647		36,505
Republican		35,379		32,576		32,959
Other		13,202		6,011		8,144
U.S. Senate	75,478	86,823		75,042	68,046	
Democratic	56,582	44,509		51,524	35,709	
Republican	18,528	41,444		23,069	32,137	
Other	368	870		449	200	
Governor	75,489		75,457		69,354	
Democratic	38,674		40,967		38,549	
Republican	36,495		34,282		30,615	
Other	320		208		190	
U.S. House	75,204	86,579	75,452	74,893	67,843	72,415
Democratic	44,854	46,935	23,582	42,783	40,012	47,043
Republican	30,111	38,844	51,626	31,705	27,643	25,273
Other	239	800	244	405	188	99
Auditor	72,372	86,001	68,234	60,053	63,694	67,285
Democratic	37,675	42,785	32,411	0	28,701	29,503
Republican	34,515	28,574	35,596	58,785	34,823	37,573
Other	182	14,642	227	1,268	170	209

elections would render a mathematical "average," but not a good prediction. One way to make up for these sorts of idiosyncrasies is to use surrogate races. Swapping a state Senate race for a problematic state House race might work. Trading a gubernatorial election for a U.S. Senate race would help even out calculations. For auditor, a county commissioner's seat might have been used as the point of reference. Even this approach is not without hazard, however. In 1992 there was a great deal of excitement among voters, owing largely to the presidential race. The year 1996, by contrast, was considered fairly dull, as illustrated by low voter turnout across the board. A review of past auditor's elections might reveal that at various times the auditor's race was subject to intraparty conflicts, hapless candidates, and brilliant campaign tactics. Taking a simple average downplays the variations, but it does so ham-handedly.

A second method of determining electorate size tries to compensate for such problems by looking at the place of the auditor's race in the larger scheme of things—average turnout, fall-off, and registration. (See Figure 6.3.) Political judgment is involved at each step. For example, what exactly is meant by "turnout"? Is it the total number of *eligible* voters? Or is it the total number of *registered* voters? The choice is critical. A district with high voter registration and only a few people moving in or out probably merits the use of registered voters because that number probably will not change over the course of an election. A district with low voter registration and a lot of people on the move might require some combination of registered voters and eligible voters in an effort to anticipate preelection registration drives. For the purposes of understanding Smith County, assume a stable district with reasonably high registration. In such a case, registration, not eligible population, should be the baseline.

To determine the number of people who cast a ballot, it is not enough to look at the number of people who voted for auditor, because there is apt to be fall-off. Then again, it may not even be enough to look at the number of people who voted for president, because some ballots will likely be spoiled, as Florida's problems with the 2000 presidential election amply demonstrate. Furthermore, precompiled data often neglects votes that went to insignificant candidates and write-ins. Raw data printouts leave this information intact. If, for some reason, the total number of votes cast is not available, researchers can use the data from the office that received the highest number of votes.

The turnouts for 1994 and 1998 are gauged by dividing the number of people who actually voted by the number of people registered to vote. Once again, off-year elections are used because turnout varies drastically between on-year and off-year elections. Smith County shows a significant drop between 1996 and 1998. Municipal elections in odd-numbered years can render exceptionally low turnout scores. Choosing similar years is important because the sorts of people who turn out for an on-year election might be very different from the sorts of people who show up in an off-year. Those who take the trouble to vote in an odd-year primary are probably die-hard partisans, not casual voters who go to the polls once every four years to vote for president—hence, the use of 1994 and 1998.

In Smith County in 1994, a total of 75,490 people voted in the election out of 99,678 people registered. Dividing 75,490 by 99,678 gives a rounded turnout score of 0.757, which is 75.7 percent. (Turnout calculated as a percentage of the 127,984 *eligible* voters is a weaker 59 percent—still quite strong by national stan-

Figure 6.3
Projecting the Size of the Electorate

Method 1: Averaging Two Similar Years

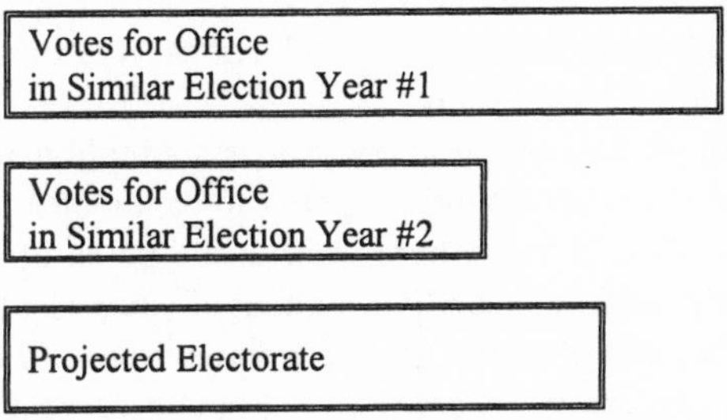

Votes for Office
in Similar Election Year #1

Votes for Office
in Similar Election Year #2

Projected Electorate

Proj. electorate = ((votes in year #1) + (votes in year #2)) / 2

Method 2: Multiplying Registration, Turnout, and Residual Vote

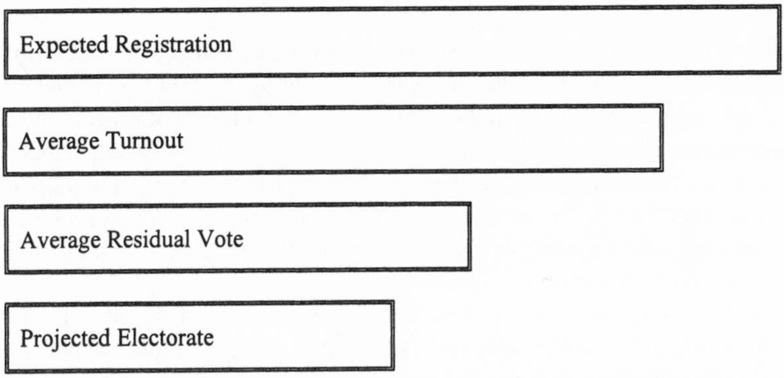

Expected Registration

Average Turnout

Average Residual Vote

Projected Electorate

Proj. electorate = (exp. registration) x (ave. turnout) x (ave. residual vote)

dards.) Repeating the process for 1998 yields a turnout score for registered voters of 0.668. Next, the average is found by adding the individual turnout scores together and dividing the sum by the number of elections considered, which in this case was two. The sum of the 1994 and 1998 scores is 1.425, which divided by 2 leaves 0.7125. Rounding to 0.713, the average turnout in off-year elections is 71.3 percent.

Knowing the percentage of the electorate that will show up to vote is important, but not all voters cast a vote for auditor. It becomes necessary to calculate fall-off or better yet, the portion of the electorate that does *not* fall off—in other words, the residual share that will vote in down-ballot races. The equation for calculating this residual vote is similar to the one used for determining turnout, except that it looks at *all* the years during which the office in question was on the ballot. (The conjecture is that falloff remains stable regardless of year-type.) In this case, the years under consideration would be all of the elections, on- and off-year, 1990 through 2000. Again, political judgment should guide the analysis. If a data set shows one pattern for on-year elections and another for off-year elections, it is unwise to combine the two types of years into a single score.

Calculating the residual vote for any single given year is a simple matter of finding the portion of the total vote that wound up going to candidates for the lower office. For example, in 1990, 75,512 voters went to the polls, of whom 72,372 voted for candidates in the auditor's race. The number of votes cast for auditor divided by the total number of votes cast gives a rounded score of 0.958. Falloff is often expressed as a percentage—here it would be 4.2 percent—but, more importantly is the number of people who persevered. A score of 0.958 means that 95.8 percent of those who voted in the 1990 election voted in the auditor's race. Residual vote scores can be determined for each subsequent election year, 1992 through 2000, and then calculated as an average for all years. The average residual vote score for the auditor's office is thus found to be 0.908, or 90.8 percent. (Average fall-off is 9.2 percent.)

With this statistic in hand, the expected number of voters can be determined. It is found by multiplying the average residual vote by the average turnout and then multiplying the product of that calculation by the number of voters who will be registered on Election Day. The first step (multiplying the average residual vote by the average turnout) figures the portion of the registered voter population that will actually vote for auditor. In this case, the rounded score is .647, or 64.7 percent. The second step (factoring in the registered voters) produces the predicted residual vote count for auditor.

As easy as it sounds, the second step can be the most difficult in the process. Registration rolls change constantly. Generally speaking, more people are registered in October than in the previous March. Voter registration drives increase the totals. In college towns and areas with seasonal employment, the swings can be substantial. Also, because election registrars sometimes purge outdated registrations—all the better to keep the deceased from voting—researchers try to find out whether they are looking at statistics from before or after a purge, a voter registration drive, or a large-scale population shift.

One way to account for change is to revise strategic estimates as new registration figures become available. The obvious problem with this approach is that it does not allow for much forward planning. Each month would bring a new strategic reality. Another option is to examine past registration trends. For example, assume that the latest available numbers are from March 1, when the registration was 101,409. Assume also that past registration trends for similar election years suggested an average increase of 5 percent between March and November. The next step is to multiply the March registration by 1.05 (the existing registration plus 5 percent), thereby yielding a projected registration of 106,479 on Election Day.

Multiplying this projected registration by the predicted residual vote score, which was .647, one gets a projected electorate of 68,892 for the auditor's race.

To project the number of votes necessary to win, divide the expected number of votes by 2 and then add 1. Again, slightly easier said than done, because two figures have been offered as the expected number of votes: the first projection, from Method 1, averaged the total number of votes from 1994 and 1998; the second, from Method 2, took a big-picture approach by averaging turnout and residual vote over six electoral cycles and then factoring in the projected registration. Which figure should be adopted? Campaign professionals should err on the side of caution and use the higher of the two figures. "Close" will not count on Election Day. In this example, Method 2, which calculated turnout, residual vote, and registration, gave the greater figure at 68,892. Dividing this higher figure by two leaves 34,446 votes. Adding the tiebreaker makes it 34,447.

It is worth noting that this last number is a slightly fictitious estimate. The break point seldom cuts at 50 percent exactly. Some people vote for third-party candidates, while others vote for independent candidates, and a few people write in their own names just to see if they show up in the newspaper. Races can usually be won just under the 50 percent mark, yet, few campaign researchers would average the "other" votes and subtract them from the total. Better safe than sorry.

The calculation for two-candidate races is reasonably straightforward. Multi-candidate elections, however, demand more creative thinking. The formula has to be altered to accommodate the number of candidates in the race; the total number of votes cannot simply be divided in half. If a third-party candidate is at issue in a general election, the best approach is to determine the percentage of votes that similar third-party candidates have received in the past. If no precedent exists, the researcher is left to make an educated guess. In primaries, which routinely have three or four candidates, past elections might show competition between two rival machines, leading to a rough idea of how much of the vote each operation's candidate can expect. Campaigns can sometimes set their sights low. Bill Clinton beat George Bush and Ross Perot with only a 43 percent vote share. In a strong four-way primary the win might be calculated at 33 percent. Although some researchers would prefer a magic formula to project the number of votes needed to win, political judgment must be combined with past electoral data—including imperfect comparisons.

Base Vote and Party Performance

Once the total number of people needed to win the election is determined, distinctions must be made between the portions of the electorate that are in play and those that are not. Professionals talk about "average party performance," "swing vote," "split-ticket factor," "base vote," and so forth. Each measure is designed to carve the electorate into useful categories. Understanding how to calculate these figures is important. Even more useful is an understanding of how they build on each other. Because such formulas must be picked apart, refined, and reassembled to meet the particular needs of individual electoral contests, it is crucial that campaign professionals see how each component operates.

A few thoughts and caveats are in order. First, although these analyses require time, campaign operatives find that the rewards far exceed the cost. The point of electoral statistics is to simplify a complicated data set. The time invested in a few tables pays for itself in ease of management down the road. Second, all campaign statistics must be tailored to the district and race in which they will be used. Statistics like "average party performance" and "swing factor" were developed to handle real-world problems. A campaign professional who remains fastened to prescribed statistical formulas without asking whether they offer the best practical guidance for a given race is courting disaster. At each step, the question should be asked, What is this statistic telling me? and, perhaps more importantly, Is there a better way to approach this strategic problem? Finally, on a technical matter, all decimals in the following discussion (as with the preceding discussion of electoral size) are rounded to the third place (e.g., 0.002). Rounding is done for the sake of simplicity, but simplicity comes at the expense of accuracy. Rounding errors are compounded with each mathematical iteration, so true professionals carry the decimals out as far as their software allows.

Aggregate Base-Partisan Vote. In politics, a "yellow dog Democrat" is someone who would vote Democratic even if the candidate was a yellow dog. Some Republicans are "true-blue" or "rock-ribbed." Although many voters tend to reject party labels, some ostensibly nonpartisan voters consistently vote for candidates of the same party in one election after the next. In this sense, both parties have "base-partisan voters" who, though they might need to be energized now and again, can be counted on in tough times.

Base-partisan voters are critical to campaigns—they are particularly important as volunteers—but to understand a district, it is important to suspend the desire to find them. Aggregate statistics focus on the historic performance of entire precincts, districts, and states. Individuals are all but irrelevant. A precinct where 31 percent of the population is absolutely committed to the party will look no different from one that contains only 11 percent party stalwarts but always seems to gather another 20 percent to vote for the party's candidates. The reason that the calculation is the same is rooted in the overarching purpose of aggregate campaign statistics: charting a winning path regardless of individuals. The aggregate base-partisan vote calculation is simply intended to figure out how many votes can be taken for granted, not who those people are.

The conceptual issue here is critical. When discussing "base-partisan vote," "swing vote," and other such categories, it is important to remember that these terms denote statistical aggregates. They are mere abstractions. They refer not to specific groups of individuals but to recurring electoral phenomena. The distinction is important because the number of true base-partisan voters (i.e., party loyalists who always vote straight-ticket) is probably far smaller than the size of the base-partisan vote (i.e., the number of individuals on whom the party can always count). Even the most die-hard Republican occasionally votes Democratic, and vice versa. Thus, a base-partisan vote of 12,000 does not mean that there are 12,000 base-partisan voters in the district. A district could conceivably be populated with nothing but swing *voters*—everyone splitting his or her vote between the parties, maintaining no loyalty year to year—and still have a strong base-partisan *vote* if the two parties could always count on receiving 30 percent of these fickle voters. In a situation where there is absolutely no partisan loyalty but each of two parties always receives half of the vote, it can be said that the district is entirely made up of swing voters but has no swing vote to speak of! Again, "base-partisan vote" is a mathematical abstraction that can be manipulated to produce useful projections.

"Aggregate base-partisan vote" represents the worst that a party's candidate will do, indicating the number of votes that will go to even a dud candidate wearing the party label. An easy statistic to figure—just find the worst performing candidate—but a researcher still has to be careful. In Smith County, Democrats did worst in the auditor's race of 1996, getting no votes—zero!—but there is a problem with using that election as the starting point for a base-partisan vote statistic. The Democratic Party hit bottom because no Democrat filed for the race. Such elections are not useful; they say little about the district. The next worst election for Democrats was the House race two years earlier, in 1994, when the Democrats had an exceptionally poor showing. On the Republican side, the worst race was for Senate in 1990. Like the 1994 House race, the 1990 Senate race offers a workable benchmark.

Calculating the aggregate base-partisan vote score is a simple matter of finding the share of the electorate that cast their lot with the worst candidate. (See Figure 6.4.) The Democrat in the 1994 House race received 23,582 votes out of 75,452. Divide the first number by the second, and the result is an aggregate base-partisan vote score of .313, or 31.3 percent. For the Republicans, the Senate candidate in 1990 received a mere 18,528 votes out of 75,478, giving the party an aggregate base-partisan vote score of .245, or 24.5 percent. Of the 68,892 voters expected to play a part in the auditor's race, approximately 21,563

Figure 6.4
Calculating Base-Partisan Vote

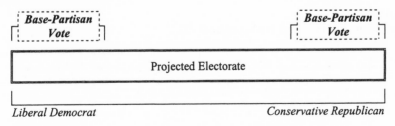

Base-partisan vote = lowest score received by candidate of the party

can be expected to vote for the Democrat, and 16,879 can be expected to vote for the Republican *no matter how bad the candidates might be.* (There is a cruel irony in this: the very loyalty of the base-partisan vote removes it from strategic consideration.)

Average Party Performance. How well can each party expect to do, on average? A party's aggregate base-partisan vote shows the portion of the district vote that the parties can count on through thick and thin. "Average party performance" (APP), on the other hand, reflects the portion of the total vote that candidates of each party generally receive. APP is used to determine the normal percentages of party strength in a precinct (Beaudry and Schaeffer 1986, 30). Functionally speaking, it is the vote that the party can expect to receive when evenly matched candidates go head-to-head.

Average party performance is calculated by first selecting three typical, competitive races in which two quality candidates ran strong campaigns against one another without becoming ensnared in a scandal or falling victim to a disproportionate campaign-spending differential. Presidential races are often used, but the 1992 and 1996 presidential contests included Ross Perot as a third-party candidate, and 2000 saw Green Party candidate Ralph Nader and a pair of Reform Party candidates, making one-to-one comparisons somewhat problematic. Once again, a bit of political judgment is called for. What are the right races to use? Which candidates are quality candidates? Which campaigns were truly strong? Calculating electoral statistics demands that researchers be familiar with the trends of electoral politics and view the district through the lens of history to determine what is meant by "typical." No easy task. It may require extensive discussions with party leaders, a fair amount of time looking at old newspaper clippings, and some educated guesswork. Once the typical races are chosen, the researcher takes the average of the three, finding the vote percentage for each party. (See Figure 6.5.)

In Smith County, an analysis of the past three electoral cycles might show that the best-paired campaigns were the House races in 1996 and 1998 and the gubernatorial race in 1998. For the 1996 House race, the number of votes for the Democrat, which was 42,783, divided by 74,893, the total number of votes cast for auditor, gives the result, 0.571, the score for the race. For the 1998 House and gu-

Figure 6.5
Calculating Average Party Performance (APP)

Average Democratic Performance	*Average Republican Performance*

Liberal Democrat	*Conservative Republican*

APP = ((performance #1) x (performance #2) x (performance #3)) / 3

Figure 6.6
Calculating the Swing Vote

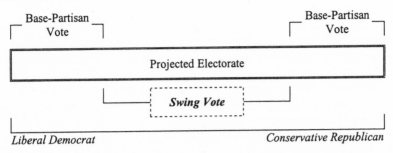

Swing vote = projected electorate – (Democratic base + Republican base)

bernatorial races, the results are 0.590 and 0.556, respectively. Adding these figures together and dividing by 3 yields a Democratic APP score of 0.572. Put differently, 57.2 percent of the electorate generally votes Democratic. The Republican APP score turns out to be 0.424, or 42.4 percent. Note: adding the percentages together often renders a sum that is slightly less than 100 percent. Stray votes for third-party, independent, and write-in candidates cause the discrepancy.

The utility of APP scores quickly becomes obvious. To determine the number of votes that, all else being equal, each party can expect to garner in the Smith County auditor's race, multiply each score by the projected electorate. The Democratic APP is 0.572, and the vote projection is 68,892. Multiply the two figures, and it appears that roughly 39,406 people can be expected to vote for a quality Democratic candidate running a decent campaign. On the Republican side, the APP score is 0.424, which generates an expectation of 29,210 votes for the Republican.

Swing, Soft-Partisan, and Toss-Up

The political contours of the district are coming into view. It is heavily Democratic, with quality Republicans losing to Democrats by wide margins. Almost 56 percent of the vote qualifies as base-partisan—more of it Democratic (31.3 percent) than Republican (24.5 percent). This means, however, that a large portion of the electorate remains in play—the swing vote.

Swing Vote. The measure of persuadable voters—the share outside each party's base—is easy to calculate. The swing vote is the inverse of the combined base-partisan vote (Democrat and Republican). (See Figure 6.6.) Smith County Democrats have a base-partisan vote of 21,563 for the auditor's race, and the Republicans have a base-partisan vote of 16,879. Add the two together, and one finds combined party bases of 38,442. This much of the electorate will not budge. The inverse of the combined base-partisan votes—the 68,892 vote electorate less the

38,442 vote combined bases—is 30,450, or 44.2 percent of the electorate. This swing vote—the portion of the electorate that resides outside the base of the two parties—will decide the election.

There are two variations on this approach, each designed to deal with electoral volatility. The "swing factor" is concerned with the extent to which voters move from one party to the other between two different election years. The first step is to find a party's most successful race in a given year and then find its score, dividing the votes cast for the candidate by the total votes cast for all candidates in the race. Next, one chooses a race during a *different* election year and takes the score of the party's least successful election. The swing factor is simply the difference between these scores, usually expressed as a percentage. The "split-ticket" factor provides information similar to the swing factor, except that it is founded upon intraelection volatility. In other words, it measures the extent to which voters switch from party to party within the same election. To calculate the split-ticket factor, the strategist simply compares a recent race in which a candidate of a party did well to a race in which the party's candidate did poorly in the same election. This score becomes particularly important when there is a strong candidate on the ballot.

Soft-Partisan Vote and the Toss-Up Vote. The generalized definition for "swing vote" might be too broad for a refined analysis. It encompasses all of the electorate except for the portion that the parties hold through thick and thin. Gradations can be parsed within the swing vote, and they should be. The margin between the party bases might be somewhere in the range of 50 to 60 percent. The point of targeting is to economize—to increase the accuracy of the campaign by eliminating wasteful spending of time and resources. A good political strategist refines the swing vote in ways that ensure strategic utility.

Any effort to carve distinctions within the swing vote is bound to be somewhat arbitrary, but reasoned differentiations can be made. Recall that the base-partisan was defined according to the *absolute* worst performance by a party's candidate during a given time period. A "partisan vote" can be defined in accordance with the *average* worst performance in that same time frame. The worst race might keep a quarter of the electorate in a party's fold. An average worst over a five-election period might show a party holding a third of the electorate. There is value in identifying the overlap between the partisan vote and the swing vote. This portion of the electorate votes for less desirable party candidates, even though it might not vote for the worst of the lot. Holding one's own soft-partisan vote is critical; persuading the opposition's soft-partisan vote to defect is difficult but not impossible. Partisans can thus be distinguished between (1) a base-partisan vote, the portion of the electorate that will vote for the absolute worst candidate, and (2) a soft-partisan vote, which can be calculated as the portion of the electorate that will vote for the average worst candidate but not the absolute worst. (See Figure 6.7.) That is, the soft-partisan vote is the total partisan vote minus the base-partisan vote. One additional category, the toss-up vote, would be the remaining portion of the electorate—everyone not in the partisan vote (either base-partisan or soft-partisan).

Figure 6.7
Calculating the Partisan Vote and the Soft-Partisan Vote

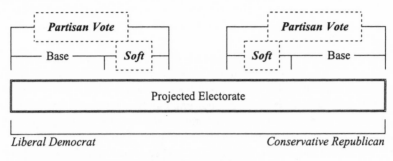

Partisan vote = (vote for average worst candidate)
Soft-partisan vote = (partisan vote) - (base-partisan vote)

The Democratic partisan vote in Smith County is determined by taking the average of the worst Democratic score for each year, 1990–2000. Once again, decisions must be made. In 1992 and 1996 the lowest Democratic score was in the presidential race, both of which had a third-party challenge. The same is true of the GOP in the 1992 auditor's contest. Should races with independent candidates be excluded? It is a judgment call. On one hand, three-way races might depress soft-partisan vote scores, perhaps in ways that distort projections for a two-way race. On the other hand, voters who go for an independent candidate epitomize toss-up voting, so it might be smart to include them in the toss-up category.

For this last reason, three-way presidential races will be used in the analysis of Smith County. For Democrats, take the lowest score for each election, 1990 through 2000. Add the five scores together and then take the average, which is 0.441, or 44.1 percent. Multiplying the score by the number of people expected to vote in the auditor's race finds a Democratic partisan vote 30,381 strong. This vote includes both the soft-partisans and the base-partisans, so the base-partisan vote of 21,563 must be removed from the overall score in order to identify the number of soft-partisans. Subtracting this number from 30,381 leaves a soft-partisan vote of 8,818, which is 12.8 percent of the total projected electorate. The same procedure on the Republican side shows a GOP total partisan vote of 24,043 and a soft-partisan vote of 7,164. The GOP soft-partisan vote is 10.4 percent of the overall electorate.

Finally, the toss-up vote. Four categories have already been calculated—a Republican base-partisan vote and a Democratic base-partisan vote along with a Democratic soft-partisan vote and a Republican soft-partisan vote; combined, these votes represent the partisanship of the district. The toss-up vote is the leftover portion of the electorate. Because the partisan vote is nothing more than the sum of the base-partisan vote and the soft-partisan vote, the toss-up vote is nothing less than the vote that remains after the partisan votes are subtracted from the overall vote total. (See Figure 6.8.) Democrats have 30,381 in the partisan category; Republicans have 24,043. Added together, the partisan vote will come in at 54,424. Subtract the partisan vote from the total electorate, and the toss-up vote is calculated at 14,468, or 21.0 percent.

Target Votes. Just about every candidate will hold the base-partisan vote. The idea is written into the very definition of "base-partisan." If a luckless candidate does worse than all of his or her predecessors, then the base-partisan score is promptly revised downward. It is nearly impossible to lose one's own base, or to reach into the base of one's opponent. Strategic thinking forces the campaign professional to develop a target. In the Smith County auditor's race, a full 34,447 votes are needed to win. A competitive Republican must hold the APP—the first 29,210 votes (42.4 percent) or simply give up the fight. This leaves a vote deficit of 5,237. There are 21,563 votes (31.3 percent) in the Democratic base-partisan vote, and these are, by definition, off-limits. The remaining 18,119 (26.3 percent) is in play. To win, the Republican must garner 5,237 (28.9 percent) of these remaining 18,119 votes—the target. (See Figure 6.9.)

The strategic consequences of this last calculation should not be missed. Looking at the average party performance, the Republican appears to be facing a tough fight. An APP of 42.4 percent means that the GOP candidate needs to get 7.6 percent more of the electorate than average. A formidable task, though it appears doable. But looking at the make-up of the target vote, the job looks nearly impossible. These votes are (1) the portion of the toss-up vote that lies outside the Republican APP, plus (2) the Democratic soft-partisan vote. The Republican, who starts with the low APP, needs to capture a large share of the vote that would ordinarily go Democratic. Classic strategic theorizing would have the Democrat communicating themes that appeal to the natural Democratic constituency. The Republican, by contrast, must pick up a moderate Democratic message in order to capture the middle ground. Complicating matters, this must be done in a way that

Figure 6.8
Calculating the Toss-up Vote

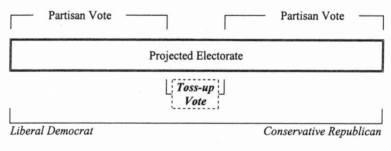

Toss-up vote = proj. electorate − ((Dem. partisan vote) + (GOP partisan vote))

Figure 6.9
Diagramming the Electorate—Smith County, 2002

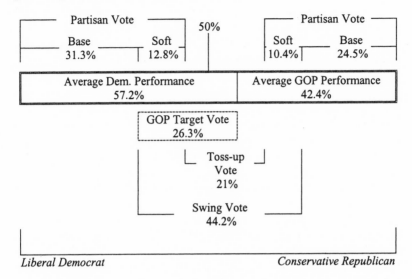

Note: The target vote includes the .4 percent of the projected electorate that is not encompassed by the average performance of either party.

still gives the base Republican vote a reason to go to the polls—letting conservatives feel that there is a difference between the Democrat and the Republican.

A Note on Predictions and Aggregate Statistics. The payoff from these calculations is a clean and simple number. In Smith County it appears that something over 5,000 voters can make a difference. Still, it is important to remember that the quality of the outcome is no better than the quality of the input: "garbage in; garbage out." A great many assumptions were made along the way. It was assumed that past elections are a good guide to future performance, that registration can accurately be projected, that falloff will remain constant, and that the partisan behavior of the electorate will not change dramatically. Human error creeps into these calculations. "Similar" elections were chosen, and "well-matched" candidates were designated. Electoral statistics are not just a product of mathematics; they involve political judgment of the highest order. Without a broad understanding of politics and a deep understanding of the electorate, it is difficult to formulate a strategic awareness of the district.

Judgment is one variable; action is another. Often a campaign team will run the numbers only to find itself on the short end of the stick. The average party performance may be only 43 or 44 percent, suggesting that a candidate of that party will lose. The final picture of Smith County suggests difficult terrain for Republicans. Nevertheless, the difficult numbers accrue from aggregate estimates. They do not reflect all possible outcomes. Another way to examine the partisan disposition is to choose a large number of normal races, perhaps fifteen to twenty over the last ten or so years, and see how often candidates of each party have won. A GOP consultant working in Smith County will take heart in the fact that a Republican won the House in 1994 and that a Republican has held the auditor's seat since that year. There *is* a way to win. Quite frequently, the key to success is parsing the aggregate-level statistics by way of careful targeting.

PRECINCT-LEVEL STRATEGY

Bad odds can be beaten. Consider Democratic contender Bill MaGee's New York Assembly district, which by all accounts was a Republican area. Nearly every local elected official in the district was Republican, and voter enrollment was roughly 2:1 in favor of the Republican Party. Nonetheless, MaGee was able to win the seat. He was elected in 1990, defeating a ten-year Republican incumbent. It was a victory over the fates. MaGee's 1990 campaign team confronted a variety of difficulties, not the least of which was modest funding. MaGee's operation would have to be run with extreme efficiency. A finely tuned targeting plan was devised, combining prior election statistics with polling data.

Rock-ribbed Republican areas were identified. Of the 105 election districts, roughly twenty-five were deemed solidly Republican. The average Republican Party performance in these areas was over 60 percent. Few Democrats had ever won them. Despite criticism from both the news media and local politicos for not working these parts of the district, the campaign directed no energy to the heavily Republican sectors. In addition, the strategy team sought out the few solidly Democratic areas. About twenty election districts were found. Because resources were tight, little effort was made in these areas. If MaGee could not count on solid Democratic voters, he was sunk anyway. Instead of cultivating base precincts, the campaign team was forced to assume that the Democratic voters in these districts were already in the bag and needed only to be reminded to vote on Election Day.

Remaining were the election districts that might, by some optimistic measure, be labeled "swing." Yet the campaign still did not have enough resources to work the voters in all of the remaining sixty election districts. A concerted effort was made to find the districts with the highest propensity toward persuadable voting and to rank order these areas by their relative weight. This information was combined in a series of calculations, using a "votes needed to win" estimate as the guide. For example, considering his base of support, along with that of his opponent, how many swing election districts were needed in a target group if MaGee was able to win them all by 52 percent? By 55 percent? By 57 percent? By 60 percent? In the end, roughly forty election districts formed the principal target group. If MaGee could win more than one-half of these precincts by at least 55 percent and break even in others, he stood a chance.

The campaign proceeded aggressively to court the voters in these precincts, sticking closely to the issues and themes tested in survey research. The most appropriate way to reach these voters, given their dispersion throughout the district, was finely tuned direct-mail, carefully constructed literature drops and canvasses, augmented by an ambitious telemarketing operation. MaGee won the election by less than 500 votes. MaGee's base-partisan vote came through, and, more important, he captured over 55 percent in most of the targeted election districts. The campaign had successfully tackled a serious deficit in resources and voter support and had done so with prior election statistics. The campaign had targeted the right group of voters.

Ranking Precincts

A Republican candidate for auditor in Smith County is in MaGee's starting position. From the Democratic perspective, all is well. True, a Republican has taken and held the seat in the past, but this situation is not unusual. Many Republicans are elected in Democratic districts, and the same goes for Democrats in Republican districts. Some people are good campaigners. With the GOP incumbent gone, the statistics heavily favor a Democrat to win. From the Republican perspective, matters are dire—but not impossible. MaGee offers a model for success. The question is how to tailor an underdog strategy to this particular district.

Once the numbers are drawn for the district as a whole, the research moves to smaller units of analysis. A statewide race might be separated into counties; a county race might be separated into townships; a city race might be separated into wards and precincts. The guiding principle is that election data should be taken down to the smallest manageable unit of analysis. It is a matter of costs and benefits. Keeping the data at a high level of abstraction means cheaper data management but less elegant targeting. As the unit of analysis is refined, the targeting is more exact, but the increased number of electoral units raises the data management costs. The individual segments should be small enough to render precise estimates, but not so small that compilation and analysis become arduous. There may be 250 precincts in a citywide race or 175 in a state Senate district. (Generally speaking, a campaign will find several hundred voters per precinct.) Sorting through the data becomes a chore, particularly if the job is done by hand. The benefits of increased tactical clarity must be weighed against escalating costs of administration.

To allow for the use of smaller units of analysis, new-style campaigns computerize their operations. Small campaigns can probably get by with index cards and spreadsheets. Large operations might want to employ the services of professional data management firms that can maintain, search, merge, and purge enormous data sets. Most of these operations can handle the details of postal regulations, preventing a lot of the headaches that accompany self-service posting. Midlevel campaigns, such as those run in cities and large counties, sometimes invest in middle-range database packages such as Microsoft Access and Lotus Approach. These sorts of relational database applications are principally designed for small business but are readily adapted to political campaigns, able to import a data set, sort it, query it, and with a little work, centralize the task of targeting voters by precinct. Specialized voter contact packages can also help campaign professionals sort and analyze prior election results.

One reason that databasing is becoming a major part of new-style electioneering is the sheer number of calculations necessary for refined targeting. The statistical measures noted earlier are the tip of the iceberg. There are scores of other statistics that one might uncover, conveying new subtleties and findings. Moreover, the calculations are performed not just on the district as a whole but also on each unit of analysis. The size, turnout, falloff, total expected votes, APP, base-partisan vote, soft-partisan vote, and toss-up vote might be calculated for a hundred or more precincts. Each geographic unit must be ranked against the others. After the calculations are completed, precincts are classified by size, performance, and persuadability. Strategists want the ability to call up lists of the precincts, counties, or towns with the greatest number of soft-partisan voters, the ones that candidates from each party can count on, and the ones with voters amenable to the candidate's appeal.

Some operatives establish rank orders according to absolute scores. Precinct 73 might be worth 103.34 points, for example, and precinct 85 might be worth only 24.82 points. Other professionals develop graduated rankings broken into stratified categories such as "high," "moderate," and "low" and then project the rankings on a map of the district.

By calculating the relative priority of each precinct, areas with the most target voters come to light. A precinct with a high APP and low turnout is asking to be courted; a precinct with a low APP, high turnout, and large base-partisan vote in the opposing camp need not consume much of a candidate's time. The "art" of new-style campaigning lies in the creative use of more ambiguous information. Smart consultants know how to read the numbers. There is tremendous leeway in a data set, and consultants are limited by little more than their own ingenuity. Statistics from one source are merged with statistics from other sources, reconfigured, recalculated, and enhanced to produce deeper meaning and improved strategy. Each campaign offers a unique set of constraints and opportunities.

Strategic theorizing can make a grim situation manageable. A consultant in Smith County would probably urge a Republican candidate to concentrate resources on the precincts that hold the greatest percentage of target voters. New problems arise. If it is difficult to guess the number of people who would be registered on Election Day, predicting the share of the target vote that can be persuaded to vote Republican is truly daunting. Political judgment is called upon, past GOP victories are researched, discussions with knowledgeable partisans are held, and ultimately an educated guess must be offered.

A plausible strategy might run as follows. If the entire Republican APP vote sticks with the candidate, the GOP candidate needs another 5,237 votes to win, and these votes must be gathered from the 18,119 votes between the Republican APP and the Democratic base. If 1,540 votes can be produced via district-wide communications (e.g., radio ads and newspaper endorsements), the remaining 3,697 target votes could be picked up through precinct-by-precinct campaign activities. Assume further that precincts targeted for mailings, phone calls, door-to-door visits, and so forth, can yield a full 25 percent of the target vote. For example,

Table 6.2
Ranking Precincts

Targeted Votes Needed to Win				3,697
Rank	Precinct	Target-Zone Votes	Projected Vote Yield	Accumulation
1	56	371	93	93
2	89	359	90	183
3	51	347	87	270
4	81	345	86	356
(Precincts Ranked 5 through 55 Not Shown)				
56	94	267	67	3,569
57	79	260	67	3,636
58	82	255	64	3,700

a precinct with a 200-vote target zone might offer fifty votes beyond the average party performance. Calculating the yield for each of the district's precincts, and then ranking them accordingly, suggests the electoral priority of each precinct. (See Table 6.2.) An analysis of the data might show that most of the precincts at the top of the list come from suburban precincts with high swing factors. Further down the list might be found the solidly Republican rural communities and the equally committed Democratic central city.

Evaluating precincts strictly in terms of available targets is a very crude way of doing business. Additional weights and measures can be added to create the right mix of the base-partisan and swing votes, to adjust for geographic size, or to favor precincts contiguous with other targeted precincts, and then to take account of demographics, polling, volunteer lists, and other such resources. A wise political consultant will work toward the best combination of criteria to develop a general strategy, as will be discussed in Chapter 8. For now, it is important to note the possibility of Republican victory. If the GOP candidate can realistically hope to hold the Republican APP and get a large portion of the target vote in half the district's precincts, the Republican Party can actually capture the auditor's seat. Not easy, but at least it seems possible—and plannable—owing to narrowly focused strategic conceptualization.

CONCLUSION

Strategists pride themselves on the accuracy of their predictions (even if their prophecies might be partly self-fulfilling). Early in the 1996 cycle, the Clinton campaign targeted a list of states designed to give the president his victory. In the Midwest, the campaign focused on Minnesota, Iowa, Missouri, Wisconsin, Illinois,

Michigan, and Ohio. Bill Clinton and Al Gore made frequent trips to the area, ignoring heavily Republican Indiana, Nebraska, North and South Dakota, and Bob Dole's home state of Kansas. The reason for hitting a few states and skipping others should be obvious. Some states *had* to be won; others never could be. (Though there were moments when South Dakota seemed in play.) The result on November 5 was a Clinton victory in all the targeted Midwest states alongside a defeat in all of the midwestern states that were not on the original list, exactly as planned.

The 1996 Clinton campaign benefited from extraordinarily efficient targeting. While presidential campaigns have access to resources that a state or local campaign will never see, the electoral history of a district helps campaign professionals understand the configuration of their districts. History has shown the error of assuming that each geographic area must be approached and solicited on an equal basis. Richard Nixon learned how serious a mistake this was in 1960. No modern consultant would dare suggest such a broad strategy. Prior electoral targeting helps new-style campaigns concentrate their operations on the election's most cost-effective targets.

Chapter Seven

Polling:
The Focus of
Strategic Vision

George W. Bush faced a dilemma in March 2000. He had finally put to rest Arizona senator John McCain's aggressive primary challenge, ending months of speculation that Bush's early lead was soft. The candidate was shifting his sights to Al Gore. The vice president had been second in command during the greatest economic expansion in American history, so the foremost issue in nearly all presidential elections, the state of the economy, seemed an unprofitable line of attack. Crime, a traditional GOP issue, also seemed out of the question, given that Gore favored capital punishment and that crime rates had actually declined during the Clinton-Gore administration. When it came to social issues like protecting Social Security, prescription drug assistance to the elderly, and abortion rights, Gore appeared to be more in tune with middle-of-the-road voters than Bush. Not surprisingly, the Bush plan of attack emerged from a carefully conducted survey of 800 likely voters.

In February the Bush team had run a poll that brought to light Gore's vulnerability on "truthfulness." Early in the questioning, many respondents disagreed with the statement, "Al Gore will say anything to get elected." After hearing a list of charges, stemming from alleged untruthfulness regarding policy issues, personal accomplishments, and campaign finance activities, a lot of the vice president's soft supporters defected. The number of respondents who agreed that Al Gore would "say anything to get elected" rose from 52 to 70 percent. Early on, 42 percent agreed that Gore had "questionable integrity"; following the push this number rose to 69 percent. Twenty-nine percent thought Gore was a "negative campaigner" at first; 59 percent afterward. The Bush campaign had found its message. "This is a man who will say anything to get elected," declared Governor Bush at a news conference on March 12. Bush restated the claim four more times over the next twenty minutes (Yang 2000). It is a sentence that Bush and his allies would repeat again and again, with only slight variation, for many months.

The dramatic jump in Gore's negatives suggested to Bush operatives that many voters were predisposed to like Gore, to trust him, and to believe in his integrity but that this confidence was not deeply rooted. They had found an opening. When Bush began charging that "Gore will say anything to get elected," the two candidates were roughly even in the polls. By late spring, the gap had grown to roughly six points, and by the party conventions of late summer the gap had grown to double digits. There were other forces at work, to be sure, but this tactical approach—garnered from a carefully conducted survey—helped crystallize an attack strategy for the Bush 2000 campaign.

This chapter discusses the most important elements of modern survey research—the need for polling, basic concepts, types of polls, quality control issues, procedural issues, proper sampling, and data analysis. Polling has become the cornerstone of new-style electioneering. Survey research is a critical factor in decisions about the allocation of resources, candidate positioning, and the vulnerabilities of the opponent, as well as the timing of campaign events and paid advertising. Simply put, polling has become the most efficient means by which campaigns come to understand the hearts and minds of voters.

THE NEED FOR POLLING

Polls are costly, leading many to argue that polling data is unnecessary. "I've lived in this district all my life," a candidate might proclaim, "and I know what people are thinking—why should I run an expensive poll to find out what we already know?" A "feel for the district" is basic to old-style party activism. Precinct captains and ward leaders would listen to voters and transmit their interpretations up the chain of command. Additional knowledge was garnered from newspaper reporters and civic leaders. Sometimes political assessments were based upon the size of rallies or number of letters written to officials on a given issue. The quest for public opinion began long before the science of survey research was developed. New-style campaign operatives, however, cannot rely solely on these informal measures—if for no other reason than the breakdown of party hierarchies makes this kind of communication impossible. While much of the electorate distrusts polls (Traugott and Kang 2000, 185), comparisons of polling projections and electoral results show that modern survey techniques render accurate information (Visser et al. 2000, 225). Survey research is often the best way to gain accurate data about the attitudes and perceptions of the electorate. When political operatives want reliable information about voter attitudes, polling is considered a necessity.

POLLING BASICS

Polls are expensive. A "benchmark poll," used at the beginning of a race, might cost some $15,000 to $20,000. When combined with "tracking" and "brushfire" polls, the expense of monitoring public opinion adds up quickly. An outlay of 5 to 10 percent of a campaign's total budget is common. This may not seem exorbitant, but every dollar spent on polling is taken from other campaign activities. For this reason, the price of polling must be recouped via raw utilitarian value.

Survey costs are a function of several factors, mostly questionnaire construction, interview length, and depth of data analysis. A complex questionnaire requires time for development and pretesting. Long interviews and large samples consume interviewer and supervisor time and often long-distance telephone charges. Large samples require the purchase of phone numbers. Given the variety of options, many campaigns request several estimates based on a variety of survey configurations. One consultant suggests that poorly funded campaigns look for an academic to help with the survey (Simpson 1996).

Polling begins with assessments of name recognition and candidate preference. Many who run for public office have been members of civic organizations or have held positions that put them in the public eye. They hope that this visibility will help them in a race for elective office. While community service may aid in fund-raising and campaign organization, it does not necessarily translate into fame. Candidates are frequently humbled by low name recognition in the beginning stages of the race. Candidates who believe that they are known across the district often find one in ten voters recognizing their name. Consider, for example, that in 1994 only 49 percent of voters in Georgia's Tenth Congressional District could identify their five-term incumbent immediately after a hard-fought election. This percentage is perhaps ten points higher than for the average member of the House of Representatives (Shea 1996b, 402). Many are disheartened to find out that they are not well liked.

A second major use of polling is the identification of voter concerns. At the beginning of any campaign, candidates often have a large number of issues that they wish to pursue. The list must be pared. Recalling the way that he helped plan a 1991 Senate victory in Pennsylvania, James Carville wrote, "Harris Wofford believes in a lot of things, but our researchers came up with three key issues that the people of Pennsylvania cared about deeply: a middle-class tax cut, more affordable education, and health care. Wofford did too. That's what we ran on" (Matalin and Carville 1995, 74). Resources are always tight, so campaigns have to focus on topics for which there is a receptive audience. Polling helps a campaign organization find the right issues.

A third broad type of information gathered from polling is the electorate's sense of the candidates. For example, a poll might assess whether the opposition is vulnerable to charges of inappropriate behavior. Just as important, polling data can highlight the vulnerabilities of the candidate contracting the poll. The campaign will want to know what would happen if damaging information were publicized.

Underlying attitudes about various social and political values make up a fourth major area to be investigated. The difference between issue preferences and underlying attitudes is that an issue preference represents a choice among current policy options while underlying attitudes exist even in the absence of specific proposals. A generalized respect for human life, a belief in individual responsibility, and a conviction that the public sector must care for the poor are all examples of underlying attitudes. Campaigns need to understand these beliefs if they are going to frame their policy issues appropriately. A pro-choice policy position might be framed in terms of individual freedom, for example; a flat-tax proposal might go to values like fundamental fairness. Overarching ideology, strength of religiosity, and partisan preference are all clues to the likely behavior of an electorate, and each can be tapped by using surveys.

At their best, polls allow campaign managers to gauge the potential effectiveness of strategies and tactics. With an accurate analysis of the electorate's beliefs, a campaign organization can make informed decisions about message, targeting, and the allocation of campaign resources. As potential donors try to place their best bets and as the news media try to decide which candidates deserve coverage, new-style campaigns gain credibility by showing—scientifically—that they have a shot at winning.

TYPES OF SURVEYS

Political polls can be separated into six major types: "focus group," "benchmark," "follow-up," "tracking," "quick-response" and "push." Generic survey research commissioned by a media outlet is usually intended to sell a story—not to strategize a campaign, so although some information might prove useful, media-backed polls cannot be relied upon when making critical tactical decisions. One reason: campaign operatives do not have access to the raw data. With only the surface numbers, they cannot manipulate the information to discover electorally significant information that might lie inside. Victory is often found in these "internals." When the candidate's future and the consultant's fortunes are on the line, polls conducted by private firms with an experienced understanding of political campaigns are often considered a necessity.

Among the types of research such a firm might offer is the focus group, a type of survey that emerged in the early 1990s. Small groups of respondents "chat" about their opinions, beliefs, and attitudes for up to four hours. A moderator helps "pull" comments from the participants while a survey team records the conversation. Although the sample size is small, the breadth of opinions offered in focus groups often captures the emotions beneath the issues. And although they might appear to be simple affairs, focus groups must be carefully supervised in order to draw out the greatest possible volume of information. Moderators have to encourage shy members to speak and they must prevent outspoken participants from dominating the conversation. Close cousins of the focus group are "dial groups" and "mall intercepts." In a mall intercept, an interviewer approaches a shopper, asks a few questions, and then takes the respondent behind a closed storefront for additional questions. Intercepts are particularly useful for reviewing direct-mail pieces, checking to see how people unfold and skim enclosures. For television spots, a campaign might use a dial group. In a dial group, respondents turn a control knob back and forth, indicating lower or higher satisfaction. This kind of second-by-second analysis can pinpoint strengths and weaknesses within a campaign's message, even capturing problems with wording and sentence structure.

Focus groups are widely used in the beginning of a campaign, setting the stage for a benchmark poll. A benchmark poll is a major survey designed to provide baseline measures on a variety of factors. A large sample is used to assess name recognition, issue preferences, underlying attitudes, as well as prevailing levels of knowledge regarding campaign issues. Measures of partisanship, ideology, religiosity, and standard demographic data are also gathered. This information is used early in the race to design campaign strategy and to choose questions that will be asked in subsequent polls.

A follow-up poll is often conducted around the halfway point of a campaign. The idea is to uncover strategic mistakes and correct them while there is still time. Follow-ups are shorter than benchmarks, and tracking polls are shorter still. They cover a limited range of issues or information, but they are administered on a regular basis—sometimes daily—in order to follow voter trends. Key items are name recognition, candidate support, issue support, and the effectiveness of campaign events and commercials.

A run of surveys makes it possible to observe changes in the overall distribution of preferences in the electorate, but they cannot say much about decisions at the individual level. One way to get at this problem is to gather an initial sample of voters and then reinterview the same panel of respondents throughout a campaign. This approach is informative, but expensive. Moreover, some people quit participating—and indeed repeated interviews may change the attitudes of some respondents. A less burdensome approach is the "quick-response poll," intended to identify the effect of a campaign event immediately after it has occurred. For example, if the opponent launches a series of attack ads, then a quick-response poll determines the effect of the commercials on the candidate's standing.

Some polls attempt to push voters away from the opponent. Usually conducted during the final days of a campaign, "push polls" disguise voter persuasion as survey research. In fact, the term "poll" is inapt, because the calls are not random—usually the caller moves down a list of targeted voters—and the intention is not to collect data but to move support. A question like, Would you still be inclined to vote for Mr. Smith if you knew that he was once arrested for drunk driving? is characteristic of this technique. The practice has caused deep concern among some candidates, consultants, and media commentators, but push polls are done for a reason. As an Illinois pollster recently noted:

> The political process is an advocacy process. For those people in the middle of it, push polls are seen in a very different light than they are by the research professionals. In the real life and death struggle of win or lose, no holds are barred. Everyone thinks that everyone else is doing it. It's on the increase as it goes further down the line to the state representative level. It's a difficult genie to put back in the bottle. (Richard Day, as cited in Bogart 2000, 317)

In a competitive environment, self-regulation is both necessary and impossible.

Allegations of push polling were rampant during Campaign 2000. Prior to dropping out of the race for New York's Senate seat, Rudolph Giuliani accused Hillary Rodham Clinton's campaign staff of using push polls to spread dissatisfaction about his stance on abortion (Bumiller 2000). During the early days of the Republican primary season, presidential hopeful John McCain accused George W. Bush's survey research team of "disillusioning a young boy" with a push poll that portrayed the senator as a "liar and a fraud" (Mitchell and Bruni 2000). The reason that a presumably experienced, professional interviewer would badger a boy too young to vote remained unexplained.

Sometimes the line between legitimate polling and push polling is ambiguous. Did the Bush poll that tested Gore's vulnerabilities on trust issues fit a broad definition of a push poll? Perhaps, but in general terms, the difference is one of intent rather than effect. If the survey is designed to provide feedback from a random sample of voters—that is, if it is intended to gain generalizable information—then it *is not* considered a push. If it is designed to persuade voters, then it *is* considered a push. The American Association of Political Consultants has condemned the practice. Moreover, allegations of push polling make for damaging news. Some state legislators have even proposed legislation to outlaw it. (First Amendment guarantees of free speech would likely preclude any such law.) Consultants are well advised that both the public and the media are poised to condemn the use of push polls, and the repercussions from using them might well outweigh potential gains.

QUALITY CONTROL

To maximize the value of polling, political consultants generally outsource their survey work to professional pollsters. Still, consultants must be, at a minimum, good consumers of survey data, being aware of the many pitfalls of polling. Not every used-car buyer is a mechanic, but an informed shopper can look under the hood for oil leaks and broken hoses, minimizing the chance of being defrauded. The same holds true for consumers of polling services. The better one's understanding of survey techniques and statistical tools, the less likely one is to make a costly mistake.

A "good" poll has minimal error. If 55 percent of the population would vote for a candidate on Election Day, then the poll should represent that fact with little deviation. The difficulty is that a campaign does not know the actual opinions of the population; it just knows the polling data. The only absolute test comes on Election Day itself—too late for corrections. The best that a pollster can do is to make sure that its survey procedures minimize error. Three types of error are particularly salient: "instrument error," "measurement error," and "sampling error." The total error in a survey—the difference between the political reality and the survey results—is the product of these three sorts of inaccuracy.

Instrument Error

Questionnaires are difficult to construct. In a classic piece of research, Howard Schuman and Stanley Presser found that attitudes toward freedom of the press changed significantly as the order of questions was altered (1981). If the survey instrument—in this case, the questionnaire—is poorly constructed, the resulting data will not be a good reflection of public attitudes.

Instrument error is the bias created by the wording of a question or the implementation of the survey. A good deal of instrument error comes from "undecided" voters. The classic example is the question, If you were going to vote today, would you vote for candidate Smith or candidate Jones? With but two choices, many respondents feel the appropriate thing to do is to choose between the two alternatives. Few individuals volunteer, "Look, I haven't made up my mind." Some pollsters *want* to force an answer. After all, Smith and Jones are the only names on the ballot. For top-of-the-ticket races, such as governor or president, most people will make a choice even if they are not very happy about it. But this is not always the case. From the campaign consultant's point of view, undecided voters may be exactly the audience that it wants to identify. Another form of this question is, If the election were held today, would you vote for candidate Smith, candidate Jones, or have you not yet made up your mind? The addition of the phrase "have you not yet made up your mind" enables an undecided respondent to reply comfortably, "No, I haven't thought about it yet."

Measurement Error

Measurement error is the bias created by improper recording of a respondent's answer. It is typified by the mistakes made by interviewers asking questions in the wrong sequence or by data-entry personnel prone to typographical blunders. Even if the question has been properly phrased and duly answered, it is possible for an interviewer to record the answer incorrectly. With pencil-and-paper administration, which must be input for analysis, the data can still be corrupted by data-entry personnel. Large survey houses use computer-assisted telephone interviewing (CATI). Interviewers use a personal computer on which the interview questionnaire is presented one question at a time. As the polling agent records answers from the respondent, each answer is checked to ensure that it is within the range of acceptable responses. The interview is then branched to the next appropriate question. Controls on input validity and branch sequencing increase data quality.

Sampling Error

The third major type of error in a survey is sampling error, the difference between the characteristics of a sample and the overall population it represents. Because only a small portion of the total population is interviewed, from this sample are drawn inferences about the entire population. Unfortunately, each sample will produce a slightly different mix of people. In one sample, there might be a few more wealthy individuals than expected; in another, there might be too many young males; and in yet another, environmentalists might be underrepresented. If the sample is carefully drawn, the extent of these errors can be calculated. In fact, some degree of sampling error must be tolerated. The only way to ensure its elimination is to poll the entire population—an unrealistic approach to public opinion research.

Unbiased samples are difficult to gather. Samples picked out of a phone book, for instance, carry an inherent bias against people without telephones (who may be poorer than average) and people with unlisted phone numbers (who may value privacy more than others). Among those who have a phone, a growing percentage refuse to give their opinion. As campaign operatives, product advertisers, and the media rely increasingly on survey research, polling agents have saturated the public with calls, and the increase in telephone solicitations for sometimes dubious goods and services has been particularly harmful to pollsters. Many people have stopped answering questions. The problem for pollsters is not simply that they have to make more calls to complete their surveys; rather, the type of person who refrains from answering survey questions is not distributed equally among the population. Some demographic groups, such as well-educated men, are less likely to entertain questions than are other groups. Real problems arise. "The key to polling accuracy is the principle of 'equal probability of selection,'" says columnist Arianna Huffington, "[b]ut if larger and larger numbers among those randomly selected refuse to participate, this principle no longer applies" (Daves 2000, 219).

THE INTERVIEW PROCESS

Reliable surveys come from friendly conversations. Interviewers and questionnaires must put the respondent at ease. Useful information must be sought and collected, but the respondent must never feel interrogated. A good interview ends with the respondent feeling grateful for the opportunity to have an interesting dialogue with the polling agent.

The introduction is crucial. The vast majority of refusals come within the first few seconds. A properly constructed introduction should tell the respondent the purpose of the survey and then identify which member of the household should answer the questions. (Many pollsters fear that, say, too many women answer the phone first.) While polls should always disclose the name of the survey firm, the identity of the candidate is often withheld because the very mention of his or her name can skew the results.

Question Design

Pollsters talk about "good" and "bad" questions. A good question will be understood by just about every member of the targeted audience. Clear language and even a bilingual interviewer can aid in the process. The average citizen has little policy expertise, so questions about environmental issues might demand, for example, the use of terms like "the loss of forests" rather than "deforestation." Moreover, the question should not steer respondents toward any particular type of answer, "Do you believe in the constitutional right to keep and bear arms?" predisposes a respondent toward answering "yes." Finally, as noted earlier, a good question offers a range of appropriate responses.

Professional pollsters spend a great deal of time wording their questionnaires properly. Colloquial phrases can skew results. By definition, colloquialisms mean different things to different people. Slang is particularly difficult to use when its interpretation differs by age, class, or ethnicity. Indefinite terms can also become problematic. What does "frequently" mean? What does "several" mean? Even the word "voter" can represent a complex concept. If the interviewer asks a respondent, "Are you a voter?," and the reply is "yes," does this mean a vote in every election, every general election, every presidential election, or a onetime vote ten years ago? Clarity and precision minimize this sort of ambiguity.

Types of Questions

To reduce uncertainty, distinctions are made among "information," "knowledge," "opinion," and "self-perception" questions (Backstrom and Hursh-Cesar 1981). An information question goes to facts relating directly to the respondent, such as standard demographic items (e.g., age, sex, race, and income). A knowledge question goes to the wider domain of facts (e.g., the identity of the respondent's congressional representative). An opinion question asks the respondent for a judgment (e.g., the respondent's attitudes toward an issue or candidate). A self-perception question is an opinion question about one's self (e.g., whether the respondent considers himself or herself a Democrat). By understanding the types of questions being asked, pollsters can gain a better understanding of the types of information they are getting from the public.

Any of these types of questions can be asked in an "open" or "closed" response format. In an open response question, respondents answer questions in their own words. In the closed format, the respondent is asked to choose from a predetermined set of answers. Note that open response formats require interviewers to know a great deal about the topic at hand. Asking, "What do you believe is the most important problem facing America?" might bring a wide array of answers. A part-time interviewer might not understand how to code a complicated answer. Fixed response items are easier to record, but they may force respondents into judgments that they would not otherwise offer.

One important use of closed-format questions is respondent screening. "Filter questions" control the flow of the interview, ensuring the relevance of the questions that follow. For example, it is inappropriate to ask a widow about the effect of the "marriage tax" on her family. Therefore, a marital-status question, "Are you married, widowed, separated, divorced, or never married?" could be used as a filter question. Individuals reporting that they were currently married would receive an appropriate block of marriage-tax queries. Everyone else would branch out to another set. A common filter question asks whether or not respondents intend to vote in the coming election. If they say "no" or "probably not," the survey might end. Why spend money gathering information from a nonvoter? Then again, a campaign might want to know what would make the person into a voter.

Once a respondent gets through the filter, the polling agent might ask a "sleeper" or "probe" question. A "probe" seeks detail about a previous response. For example, if the questioner asked, "In politics, do you normally think of yourself as a Democrat, an Independent, a Republican, or something else?" and the respondent replied "Democrat," a probe might ask, "Do you consider yourself a strong or weak Democrat?" Individuals who call themselves "Independent" would be pressed to see if they lean toward one party or the other. In this case, the probe question seeks intensity. "Sleeper questions" check the veracity of a respondent's answers to other questions. At some point in the questionnaire, the respondent might be asked whether he or she voted in the most recent election; somewhere else in the questionnaire, a sleeper question is asked about the location of the polling place. If the respondent is unable to answer the question about the location, then doubts are raised as to whether the respondent actually voted. Some polling schemes actually check answers against local voting records.

Modes of Administration

Accuracy is paramount, but costly, and each of the four general modes of conducting surveys involve trade-offs. Face-to-face administration has an interviewer go to the home of a selected respondent. A mail survey usually takes the form of a short letter. Internet-based surveys are just now coming of age, whereby surveys may be emailed directly to the respondents, or the subjects are redirected to a Web site where they can complete the poll. The fourth and most frequently used mode of administration in political polling is via telephone.

Each mode of administration has virtues and drawbacks. Face-to-face interviewing usually gives the best results in terms of data quality and respondent cooperation, but the process is expensive and time-consuming. Mail surveys are relatively inexpensive, but they generally offer low response rates—and response time is too slow for campaign work. In addition, since mail surveys depend solely on the respondent's interest in answering, their results tend to be biased. Those who are either very much in favor of or very much opposed to a candidate are more likely to return the survey than those with only marginal interest. The "self-selection problem" should be sufficient to preclude any serious use of a mail poll, but for political campaigns, the difficulty is particularly acute, since unpersuaded voters are usually the campaign's target audience. Telephone interviews dominate political polling by default. They cost about the same as mail polls but they produce much higher response rates and allow for complex question-branching.

In the new millennium, Internet polling is entering the marketplace. Companies such as Creative Research Systems offer complete, Internet-ready software packages. These packages eliminate data entry. Responses are precoded, and upon completion of the survey by the respondent, they are entered immediately and directly into the analysis software. Although rapid turnaround is a great advantage, some concerns about sample bias remain. Internet polling suffers some of the drawbacks of mail surveys. The types of people who go online are disproportionately well educated, young, and affluent—and those willing to respond to an online survey are probably more engaged in politics than the average voter. Perhaps in the years ahead, pollsters will make greater use of Internet polling, but at the outset of the new millennium, its limitations are significant.

Commercial Polling Firms

Campaign polls are usually performed by commercial polling firms, not in-house volunteer operations. The amount of time spent training volunteers is relatively short—usually they want to "get on with the job"—but even the best-motivated volunteers can be unreliable. Attendance is erratic, and the very enthusiasm of campaign volunteers stands in the way of proper survey administration. The collection of data requires a dispassionate approach. Tone of voice, by itself, conveys the desirability of one's candidate. Campaign operatives can try to impress upon volunteers the importance of being neutral, but this is usually an uphill battle. New-style campaigns turn to professionals.

Outsourcing carries its own risks, however. Just as volunteer polling operations suffer from inexperience and overenthusiasm, professional polling firms vary according to the value of their hiring procedures. Recruitment pools, training, and retention rates bear heavily on survey accuracy. While almost anyone can be taught to read a questionnaire out loud, few people are superb conversationalists. Good polling depends, in part, on a firm's ability to recruit good people. Even the method of payment—hourly wage or piecework—affects data quality. An hourly wage reduces an interviewer's incentive to submit a stack of bogus call reports, but because payment will be received regardless of call completion, there is little motivation to get the job done in a timely manner. Piecework payments, by which a caller is paid according to the number of calls completed, rewards persistent employees for recontacting appointments, working numbers at odd hours in order to contact hard-to-reach respondents, and otherwise completing designated calls, but it also rewards the filing of sham call reports. There is no perfect formula. Many survey shops use a combination of an hourly rate and some kind of incentive for completing interviews.

Smart political consultants ask polling firms about their training procedures—manuals, instruction time, and the sorts of behavior expected of employees. The reason: interviewers are themselves a measuring instrument, and a polling-center employee must accurately report all possible information, remaining neutral and unmoved no matter how obnoxious respondents may be.

Many polling firms have their supervisors hook into calls and listen to selected interviews. This type of supervision helps prevent the fabrication of interviews—a form of negligence common among interviewers working from home. A well-run survey firm keeps records of random monitoring sessions. Survey directors adjust pay rates, and manage job assignments accordingly. Interviewers who perform well on these random checks are given difficult, highly paid survey projects. Consultants looking for quality research sometimes verify completed interviews, perhaps by having a supervisor call back random interviewees to confirm that an interview was actually conducted.

SAMPLING

One of the most daunting problems in survey research is determining precisely who should be interviewed. A pollster cannot build a list of possible respondents until the campaign decides which population it wants to analyze. Is it the entire district? Registered voters? Likely voters? Democrats? Registered Democrats who rarely vote? Researchers define "population" as the overall group of people that will be analyzed by the survey. A "sample" is any subset of that population—a microcosm of the whole population. From a scientific standpoint, modern survey research works because pollsters draw their samples from the population at random. Data collected from the sample will be representative of the broader population, and standard statistical equations can then be used for analysis. It is a risky business. In a gubernatorial race, 800 individuals might be drawn from a population of 5 million registered voters. The sample in this case represents only .00016 percent of the registered population. If the sample has been biased in any way, then the data will not be representative, and the survey's conclusions will likely be inaccurate.

One approach to sampling is to use random digit dialing (RDD). RDD is a technique that generates sample telephone numbers based on area codes and local exchanges. A pollster might be tempted to draw a sample from a telephone book, but high rates of unlisted numbers, as much as two-thirds in some areas, would render the sample nonrandom. Random dialing overcomes this bias. The technique is refined by the purchase of RDD lists from specialized sampling firms, which screen out nonworking and business numbers, thereby increasing dialing efficiency. Because an RDD list includes nonvoters, political pollsters often cross-reference them with registered voter lists. The problem with voter lists, however, is that they are frequently out-of-date, and their quality depends on the effort of government agencies to keep the rolls current. Some polling firms rely on "stratification," whereby geographic areas are randomly selected, and then a number of voters within each area are themselves chosen at random.

When deciding on sample size, a consultant must determine how much error can be tolerated. A campaign might be ready to accept a 3 percent margin of error—meaning that a district showing of 46 percent favorability toward a candidate might actually have a population that lies somewhere between 43 and 49 percent favorability. Having decided on the acceptable margin of error, a campaign must decide the level of confidence that it wants to have in the sample. "Confidence" is the probability that the poll actually falls within the margin of error. At 95 percent confidence, there is a 5 percent chance that a perfectly randomized sampling procedure will produce responses that fall outside the margin of error. The reason: random sampling, by its very nature, is a game of chance, and sometimes even randomly selected groups will be highly unrepresentative. Minimizing the odds of a "fluky" poll requires campaign operatives to seek a large sample. A 5 percent margin at 95 percent confidence demands 384 respondents; a 3 percent margin of error at 99 percent confidence demands 1,843 respondents. (See Table 7.1.) Because tighter error boundaries and higher levels of confidence increase sample size exponentially, campaigns must trade money for accuracy—sometimes a tough decision.

If procedures are not random, even a large sample will not solve the problem. Some polls consciously recalculate the value of certain responses in order to ensure balance. Frequently, samples need to be "weighted" to account for problems that arise in the interview methods. For example, 600 interviews might be taken over the course of a single afternoon. At that time of the day, the sample will likely be older and more female than the general population because these groups have a greater tendency to be at home and a greater willingness to field questions. If 250 males are interviewed, but the general demographics of the district show that 312 males would have been needed for the sample to be demographically representative, then greater substance will be given to each response from a male. But even this approach is flawed. The males whom one finds at home might have different party or candidate preferences from those of men at work. They might labor at night jobs or be employed at part-time jobs or simply be unemployed. The same goes for female respondents. Thus, the set of individuals whom a pollster is able to interview in the middle of a workday is not necessarily representative of all the individuals in the district, and even demographic weighting can mislead.

Table 7.1
Margin of Error and Measures of Confidence

Margin of Error	Simple Random Sample Size Confidence	
	95%	99%
+/- 7%	196	339
+/- 6%	267	461
+/- 5%	384	663
+/- 4%	600	1,037
+/- 3%	1,067	1,843
+/- 2%	2,401	4,147
+/- 1%	9,604	16,587

DATA ANALYSIS

Consultants inquire about the procedures used in the construction of a poll, but they are most interested in the results. Tables 7.2 through 7.5 display a set of questions asked in a 1994 poll regarding the Senate race between Ohio Democrat Joel Hyatt, Republican Mike DeWine, and Independent Joe Slovenec.

In the item displayed in Table 7.2, respondents were asked how interested they were in the race. In this case, 452 individuals said that they were very interested in the race, representing 42.6 percent of all the individuals polled. This number is called the "frequency distribution." At the bottom of the panel, there is a value reported as "Don't know." These respondents were unable or unwilling to answer the item. The thirteen individuals coded in that category constituted 1.23 percent of the entire sample. For most purposes, individuals who are unable to answer the question are removed from further analysis. A lot of "Don't know" responses can suggest a badly written question.

The poll shows a clear DeWine lead. Table 7.3 presents reported vote preference, including the breakdown of responses to that item immediately below the question. The results of the question indicate that DeWine was well ahead in the race with about 43.2 percent of the voters who had a preference, as compared to about 33.2 for Hyatt and about 3.8 percent for Slovenec. In Table 7.4 one finds an item that was administered to those individuals who made a choice among the three declared candidates for the race. The computer filled in the question so that the interviewer would have read to Hyatt supporters, "How certain are you to vote for Mr. Hyatt?" A third reported that they were not very sure that they would vote for their current candidate on Election Day.

Table 7.2
Interest Level Question

In the election for the U.S. Senate, the Democrat Joel Hyatt is running against Republican Mike DeWine and the Independent Joe Slovenec. Would you say that you are very, somewhat, just a little, or not at all interested in this race?

(1) Very (2) Somewhat (3) Little (4) Not at all (9) Don't know

Value Labels	Scale Value	Observed Frequency	Percent of Total	Percent of Non-Missing Cases
Very	1	452	42.60	43.13
Somewhat	2	360	33.93	34.35
Little	3	115	10.84	10.97
Not at all	4	121	11.40	11.55
Don't know	9	13	1.23	

Valid Cases: 1,048   Missing Cases: 13

Table 7.3
Candidate Preference Question

If the election were held today would you vote for Mr. Hyatt, Mr. DeWine, Mr. Slovenec, or would you skip the race?

(1) Hyatt (2) DeWine (3) Slovenec (4) Skip (5) Undecided – IF VOLUNTEERED
(9) Don't know

Value Labels	Scale Value	Observed Frequency	Percent of Total	Percent of Non-Missing Cases
Hyatt	1	343	32.33	33.17
DeWine	2	447	42.13	43.23
Slovenec	3	39	3.68	3.77
Skip	4	109	10.27	10.54
Undecided	5	96	9.05	9.28
Don't Know	9	27	2.54	

Valid Cases: 1,034 Missing Cases: 27

Table 7.4
Certainty Probe

How certain are you that you will vote for Mr. _____?

(1) Very certain (2) Somewhat (3) Not at all (9) Don't know

Value Labels	Scale Value	Observed Frequency	Percent of Total	Percent of Non-Missing Cases
	-1	232	21.87	
Very	1	521	49.10	63.30
Somewhat	2	273	25.73	33.17
Not at all	3	29	2.73	3.52
Don't know	9	6	.57	

Valid Cases: 823 Missing Cases: 238

Perhaps the most important category in the constituency is the "undecided" voter. Table 7.5 shows preferences for those individuals who indicated that they had not yet made up their minds or were intending to skip the race. Each was asked which way he or she leaned. The uncommitted are apportioned to the respective candidates. More than 80 percent had some preference in the initial vote-choice question and therefore branched around this item. Those that remained leaned toward Hyatt, but most were truly undecided.

Cross-Tabulations

A "cross tabulation" displays the frequencies of responses to one item within the categories of another item. This type of breakdown helps the campaign visualize the effect of the second variable on the first. Table 7.6 shows candidate preferences cross-tabbed by their interest in the election. The column headed "very" shows the number of individuals who said that they were "very interested" in the race. In that column, DeWine led Hyatt by about 54 to 35 percent. In the second column are individuals who reported that they were "somewhat" interested in the race. Here Hyatt closed the gap to a 41–35 percent spread. Among those individuals who said they are only "a little interested," Hyatt appears to lead by about 39 to 34 percent. A majority of those who said that they are "not at all interested" in the race report that they did not intend to vote.

These numbers would be very heartening to DeWine supporters. Not only does he hold the lead overall, but he is strongly ahead among the people who say they are most likely to vote. And so it went on Election Day. The undecided broke heavily for the Republican. The final tally: DeWine 53 percent; Hyatt 39 percent, Slovenec 7 percent—all within a few points of the poll's prediction for voters who said they were very likely to vote on Election Day.

There are, to be sure, scores of analytic techniques that pollsters can use to coax hidden findings from the data. Some polling firms conduct regression models and probability equations. Others use factor analysis to neatly divide voters into dif-

Table 7.5
Leaning Question

Are you LEANING toward Mr. Hyatt, Mr. DeWine, or Mr. Slovenec?

(1) Hyatt (2) DeWine (3) Slovenec (4) Skip (5) Undecided (9) Don't know

Value Labels	Scale Value	Observed Frequency	Percent of Total	Percent of Non-Missing Cases
	-1	856	80.68	
Hyatt	1	34	3.20	20.36
DeWine	2	27	2.54	16.17
Slovenec	3	4	.38	2.40
Undecided	4	102	9.61	61.08
Don't Know	9	38	3.58	

Valid Cases: 167   Missing Cases: 894

Table 7.6
Cross-Tabulation of Interest Level by Reported Vote Intention

| | *Degree to which the respondent is interested in the campaign* | | | | | |
	Very	Somewhat	Little	Not at all	Margin	Percentage
Hyatt	158	124	43	17	342	33.3%
	35.35%	35.0%	38.7%	14.9%		
DeWine	242	244	38	21	445	43.4%
	54.1%	40.7%	34.2%	18.4%		
Slovenec	18	15	3	3	39	3.8%
	4.0%	4.2%	2.7%	2.6%		
Skip	3	35	11	59	108	10.5%
	.7%	9.9%	9.9%	51.8%		
Undecided	26	36	16	14	92	9.0%
	5.8%	10.2%	14.4%	12.3%		
Margin	447	354	111	114	1026	n/a
Percent	43.6%	34.5%	10.8%	11.1%	n/a	n/a

ferent political groupings. Finally, it is quite common to overlay survey data with stacks of demographic and electoral data. Drawing strategic information from survey results is one of the most important skills in modern electioneering.

CONCLUSION

Consultants must think carefully about their choice of pollster. Trust is paramount. Campaigns expect that pollsters will give accurate answers to pressing questions, even when the news is bad. Done well, survey research affords a campaign one of its best opportunities to understand what the electorate thinks—what the voters care about and who they want to put in office. There are other ways to measure voter opinion, but new-style campaigning is about mathematical precision. Few managers go into the field without survey data.

NOTE

A significant portion of this chapter is adapted from Jesse Marquette, "How to Become a Wise Consumer of Campaign Polling," in Daniel M. Shea, *Campaign Craft: The Strategies, Tactics, and Art of Political Campaign Management* (Westport, CT: Praeger, 1996).

Chapter Eight

General Strategy

In 1984 voters had no doubt where Ronald Reagan stood. He sought renewed economic strength and international security. It was "Morning in America." His campaign theme—romantic in its vision and brilliant in its efficient use of political imagery—has become a legend in the world of American political campaigns. Eight years later, the rationale of Bill Clinton's bid for the presidency was captured on a sign that James Carville posted in the campaign War Room: "Change vs. more of the same; The economy, stupid; Don't forget health care." George Stephanopoulos called it a "campaign haiku" and no matter what the issue was, the campaign wrapped its message around one of these "three commandments." "In our world," Stephanopoulos has written, "the only mortal sin was to be 'off-message' " (1999, 88). A good theme articulates the reason for a campaign's existence quickly and clearly.

In retrospect, the winning campaign themes from 1984 and 1992 seem obvious. When times are good, accentuate the positive. When times are bad, call for a change. But the dilemma facing Bill Clinton in early 1995 was vastly more complex. In late 1994, voters took power away from the Democrats in the House and Senate and gave Congress to the Republicans. "Safe" Democratic candidates went down to defeat. Speaker of the House Tom Foley lost to a lawyer who had never held elective office. It was a dramatic reversal of fortune largely interpreted as a rejection of the Democratic Party in general and the Democratic president in particular. Many thought that Clinton could do little more than bide his time until inevitable defeat in November 1996. Many thought that a challenge would rise from within the Democratic ranks, perhaps defeating the incumbent president in the primaries. It was not clear that any campaign theme could rescue the Clinton White House.

The dire predictions of 1994 never came to pass. Not only did Clinton escape a primary challenge, but he held a consistent double-digit lead over his Republican opponent throughout most of 1996. The press corps even found the race boring, so unflagging was the president's popularity.

Clinton's victory can be attributed partly to the failures of his opposition. The GOP was never able to get into campaign mode, and it often seemed as though the candidate, Senator Bob Dole, was having trouble focusing on a single message— perhaps a natural phenomenon after a heated, multicandidate Republican primary that left almost no time to reorganize GOP support. Success has also been attributed to the Democratic National Committee's spending on anti-Republican ads in 1995, to the support of organized labor, and to the improving American economy. Victory has deep roots. But in many ways, Clinton's 1996 triumph arose from wise strategic positioning.

After 1994 there were two schools of thought as to how the president should proceed. The first was liberal. Several of the losing Democrats were moderate or conservative, and the ones who remained after 1994 were a more partisan lot than their predecessors. The liberal take on 1996 strategy was that the president should concentrate on his core Democratic base of support. The idea made sense. Why should the president move to the right? Why should he cast himself as a Republican in Democratic clothing? After all, it was said, given the choice between a Republican and a Republican, the people will choose a Republican every time! The other school took a moderate approach. The votes that were lost in 1994 fell from the center, not the left. To win in 1996, moderate territory had to be recaptured.

Consultant Dick Morris, who had advised Democrats and Republicans alike, gave the centrist approach his own sly twist: press against the Democratic left and simultaneously against the Republican right, find the center, and then rise above partisan conflict. Morris called the strategy "triangulation." In Morris' words, "The president needed to take a position that not only blended the best of each party's views but also transcended them to constitute a third force in the debate." By taking the prescribed approach, Morris wrote, "either he will be repudiated by the voters and slink back into the orthodox positions or he will attract support and, eventually, bring his party with him" (1999a, 80–81). While the policies engendered by triangulation have been criticized as too moderate or too small, most observers have concluded that the positioning of the Clinton campaign was electorally intelligent. The reasoning behind triangulation becomes clear if one understands the fundamentals of strategic positioning.

This chapter deals with matters of general strategy. Strategic issues have been touched on in previous chapters, and in many ways a discussion of general strategy is the culmination of campaign planning, demographics, candidate and opposition profiles, prior electoral history, and campaign polling. Without a target, a campaign has no direction; without a theme, it has no rationale. General strategy entails the strategic positioning of candidates, mapping the target vote, and developing an effective campaign theme.

STRATEGIC POSITIONING

A wise campaign strategy is selective. The size and disposition of the electorate varies from community to community. A sparsely populated section of a district might supply a rich lode of swing votes, while an urbanized area might offer few.

In some precincts, Democrats never stand a chance, while in others the Republican almost always suffers. From prior electoral targeting, these areas can be labeled "Democrat," "Republican," or "swing." The strategic approach that a campaign takes—whom it will target and what it will do to gain the target votes—stems largely from the known composition of the electorate. A precinct or district with a strong party tradition commands one strategy; an area with a large toss-up vote calls for another. For campaign professionals, there are few immutable rules, but a number of reasoned guidelines are offered.

First, some basics. There are three main goals of campaign strategy: *reinforcement, persuasion,* and *conversion.* To reinforce, a campaign convinces its base voters to stick with the candidate and vote on Election Day; persuasion is the process of bringing swing voters on board; and conversion denotes the act of getting the opposition's voters to switch sides. In campaign parlance, the precise meaning of these terms is somewhat ambiguous—is a Democrat courting nonbase Republicans trying to "persuade" or "convert"?—but in general terms it can be said that a campaign *reinforces its own partisans, persuades the toss-up, and converts the partisans of the opposition.*

It is obviously easier to reinforce or persuade voters than to convert them. In some instances, such as when the candidate is a member of a heavily favored party, the entire focus might be on reinforcement. In this sort of partisan strategy, the objective is to get the party's voters to show up at the polls. In electorally volatile areas, where neither candidate has an edge at the outset, persuasion is usually the central strategy. If most voters are committed to the opponent's party, conversion is called for. In many instances, such as when a challenger takes on a popular incumbent, conversion becomes a necessity.

One way to approach a district is to draw the electorate as a continuum, where the extremes of the line represent the most partisan supporters and the center area denotes swing voters (see Bradshaw 1995, 31–33)—basically the approach taken to Smith County (see Chapter 6). Electoral research, demographics, and early campaign polling can say much about a district, and registration lists can offer some basic facts about individual voters, often including party affiliation. (Party identification is still the best single predictor of voting habits.) Combining this information into a larger portrait should suggest the partisan loyalty of a district. The same calculations can be made for counties, cities, wards, precincts, parishes, or any other unit of analysis that a campaign might employ in its strategic research.

Figure 8.1 illustrates a campaign in which the Democratic candidate is in good shape. Democratic partisans make up about 50 percent of the vote, while Republican partisans are only 30 percent. In fact, the Democratic base is about 50 percent larger than the Republican base. As such, the Democratic goal should be the reinforcement of Democratic voters and the persuasion of a small number of swing voters. Winning does not require a single convert. The task should not be difficult because many of the swing voters would be predisposed to vote Democratic anyway. A Democrat's best strategic position is at the center of the Democratic partisans, or perhaps a bit to their right.

Figure 8.1
Strategizing a Partisan District—The Democratic Favorite

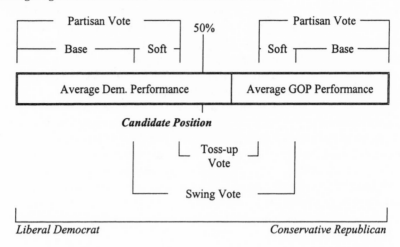

There was little question as to which portion of the electorate Democrat Jesse Jackson Jr. needed to target in his 1995 special election to fill Illinois' Second Congressional District. African Americans make up more than two-thirds of the Second, which extends from Chicago's South Side to the suburbs in the southern part of Cook County (Benenson 1995, 3836). Party enrollment roughly paralleled the demographics, with the inner-city areas overwhelmingly Democratic and the suburbs solidly Republican. The Jackson campaign targeted only the city. On Election Day, Jackson won a whopping 98 percent in the inner-city precincts and 51 percent of the suburban vote. This was enough to give him a 3 to 1 majority overall (D. Johnson 1995, B17).

Some candidates enjoy the benefits of a partisan district; others suffer. Looking at partisan districts from the other direction, one finds the sort of bleak undertaking that faced Republicans in the hypothetical Smith County race (see Chapter 6). In Figure 8.2, a Republican campaign has little choice but to convert a number of Democratic partisans. Because the race is a long shot, it may be necessary to take most of the Republican voters for granted, hoping that they will stick with the GOP candidate. A decision might be made to expend few resources on reinforcement—except, perhaps, for a last-minute, get-out-the-vote drive. Assuming, as one must, that some Republican partisans will be lost and that a fair number of swing voters will go Democratic, a significant number of Democratic soft-partisans must be persuaded. A Republican candidate should take a strategic position at the center of the full electorate, significantly to the left of the GOP base.

This is not to say that Republicans cannot be elected in Democratic districts—it just takes creativity. Republican Bill Redmond was able to prevail in the heavily

Democratic Third District of New Mexico. In 1996 Democrat Bill Richardson beat Redmond with two-thirds of the vote. When Richardson was later tapped to become U.S. ambassador to the United Nations, the seat opened up for a special election in 1997. Like Jackson, Redmond would benefit from low voter turnout, which makes a motivated base vote all the more significant, but Redmond had to do more. In addition to energizing the base, the Redmond campaign moved to break up the Democratic partisans by praising a Green Party candidate who was peeling off left-liberal voters. As the third party increased its share of the electorate, the number of Republican votes needed to beat the Democrat declined accordingly. To rally his own supporters, Redmond charged his opponent with questionable official behavior and made direct appeals to swing voters who usually voted Democratic. According to Redmond's campaign team, the strategy was basic: "By identifying Redmond as a warm, caring person, we were able to blunt . . . textbook Democratic attacks of extremism that hurt so many candidates in 1996" (Wilson and Burita 2000, 98). Having positioned himself as a moderate—not emphasizing his conservative credentials—Redmond won the election with a 43 percent plurality, beating the Democrat by just three points.

Toss-up districts present a different sort of project. Figure 8.3 suggests a district with no clear bias. In one sense the strategy is the same as it would be for an underdog—the candidate should be positioned toward the center of the electorate. Unlike the underdog, who has a broad range of voters to persuade, the Republican in an evenly matched district can focus on a narrower vote range. The strategy for candidates of either party might be to reinforce their own partisans, persuade some swing voters, and perhaps convert a few of the opponent's supporters to guarantee safety.

Figure 8.2
Strategizing a Partisan District—The Republican Underdog

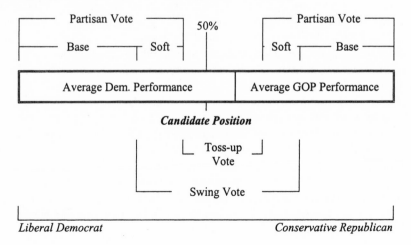

Figure 8.3
Strategizing a Toss-up District

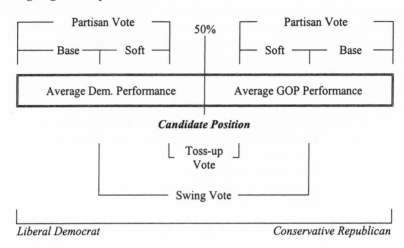

Few races are more evenly matched than the 1998 general election Senate fight between Democratic candidate Scotty Baesler and Republican candidate Jim Bunning. The first was known in Kentucky for his college basketball days; the second, for a career in professional baseball. Each was a sitting congressman in a state that split its votes between Democrats and Republicans. Both were in the conservative wing of their party. Had Baesler run as a moderate and Bunning run as a conservative, it is likely that Baesler could have hung onto his strong early lead. Bunning, however, ran aggressive attack ads after positioning himself as a moderate on the issues. According to a team of political scientists who studied the race, "Bunning . . . lay claim to the traditional Democratic issue of protecting Social Security"; chairmanship of the governing subcommittee "established his sincerity on this commitment" (Gross and Miller 2000, 189). Moderate positioning gave Bunning a strong foundation from which to commence one of the harshest political ad campaigns in recent memory. Bunning narrowly defeated Baesler that November.

Narrow targeting works. Bunning, Redmond, and Jackson ran hard, but they also ran smart. The folly of reaching broadly is twofold. First, campaigns feed off scarce resources. Time and money should be spent only where the expenditures will do the most good. Less obvious is the second problem: campaigning in areas where there is little chance of success can do more harm than good. If voters in precincts predisposed against the candidate start to receive literature, see volunteers on their doorsteps, and hear radio and television advertisements criticizing their party, the opposition interest will be piqued and opponents will be more inclined to vote (the wrong way).

On the other hand, focusing on swing voters carries its own set of problems. In 1998, Ohio Lieutenant Governor Nancy Hollister, a Republican, tried to draw moderate voters from incumbent Democrat Ted Strickland. The Sixth Congressional District had switched back and forth between the parties since 1992, with 2 percent margins each time. By all accounts, Hollister was a quality candidate, but after a bruising primary with conservative GOP rivals, Hollister was caught on the horns of a dilemma. Winning the district meant holding the center, but holding the center meant risking the base. When Hollister's moderate campaign began, the right wing of the GOP had trouble understanding where she stood on key conservative issues like abortion. The more centrist she sounded, the more disenchanted the right-wing base voters became. In the end, Hollister was soundly defeated, losing even her own precinct.

MAPPING THE WIN

Strategic positioning operates in the abstract, and a general strategy is only effective when it synchronizes its component parts. Electoral targeting fleshes out the high-level theory of the race. A campaign must combine polling, electoral research, and demographic analysis, and relate each of these perspectives to individual parts of the district. A difficult chore—but technology is making the job easier.

Computer mapping is the new key. The U.S. Census Bureau's Topologically Integrated Geographic Encoding and Referencing System—"TIGER," as it is usually called—is a street map of the United States. While TIGER does not contain population data per se, it allows researchers to situate data-points in a state, county, town, or even at an individual street address. A political consultant can draw a strategic map that has all the visual impact of a battle plan. "At the onset of any military campaign, decision-makers are constantly reviewing maps to develop strategy, evaluate performance, identify strengths and compensate for weaknesses," writes the president of Spatial Logic, and "[c]ampaigns, polling and political analysis are no different. Maps can be used for any size battle, from a local sheriff's race to the U.S. presidency" (Lindauer 1999, 48).

Many political professionals find the ever-growing volume of useful data overwhelming. A number of businesses sell software to help access and refine data, combining census demographics, business statistics, and lifestyle information. It is possible to merge census data with scores of other government-derived data sets, such as crime reports, health statistics, economic information, and precinct level electoral data. Electoral data is increasingly available online. Two popular computer mapping programs are MapInfo Corporation's *MapInfo* and ESRI's *Arc/Info*. A wide range of Geographic Information Systems (GIS) consultants work with clients to design and support mapping databases, and, in fact, offer a wealth of demographic data ready for importation.

While *MapInfo* and *Arc/Info* are general-purpose GIS packages, data management systems like *GeoVoter*, from Map Applications, Inc., allow campaign operatives to pinpoint voters, donors, and volunteers. These programs let a campaign

Figure 8.4
Mapping Target Votes—Smith City, 2002 (by Voting Ward)

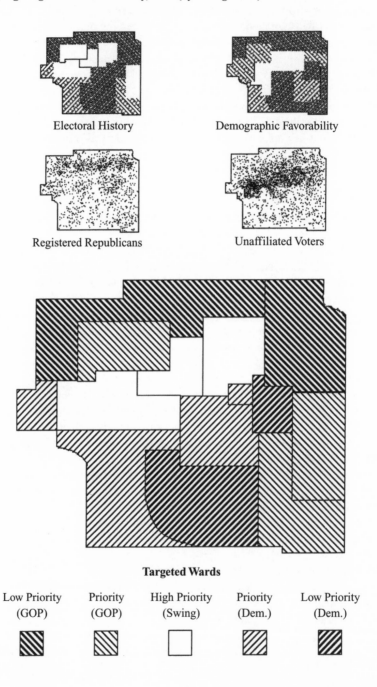

Electoral History

Demographic Favorability

Registered Republicans

Unaffiliated Voters

Targeted Wards

| Low Priority (GOP) | Priority (GOP) | High Priority (Swing) | Priority (Dem.) | Low Priority (Dem.) |

add in-house lists and field reports, further augmenting the value of the database. The capability of these packages is stunning. As long as data sets share a common field of information—voter names, for example, or street addresses—they can become part of the unified database.

By the late 1990s, GIS had become an integral part of the campaign environment. Linking relational databases with visual representations of the district, vote-rich pockets can be rapidly displayed. The idea is not new—crayon-colored maps have long hung on the walls of campaign headquarters—but the advent of GIS has brought nearly instantaneous placement of all sorts of data onto custom maps, with tactics diagrammed street by street, even house by house.

In the hypothetical Smith County race used earlier, Republican strategists might rank precinct targets by prior electoral history alone, or they might take into account the demographic favorability of each voting ward, along with the exact location of registered Republicans and unaffiliated voters. From these data, the campaign might devise a formula to distinguish low priority areas that are solidly partisan (Democrat or Republican) from areas that should be given somewhat higher priority. The highest priority can be given to parts of the city that might go one way or the other. (See Figure 8.4.) GIS software will crunch the numbers and display the result. In one sense, a mapped illustration of the data adds no new information. The numbers have not changed. But the experience of visualizing the numbers, seeing where the average party performance is high and where the swing votes are concentrated, and the ability to manipulate the maps almost at will, gives campaign researchers a unique set of conceptual tools that invite detailed analysis.

CAMPAIGN THEMES

Campaign targets are mapped, in large part, to help a campaign find pockets of support that will be responsive to a campaign theme. A good theme is a carefully crafted merger of what the voters want, what the candidate has to offer, and what the opponent brings to the table. Campaign professionals believe that it is imperative for the voters in the target group to hear the theme repeatedly: "If you stick to it, and say it often enough, you will define the criteria for the voters that they should use to make their choice" (Bradshaw 1995, 44).

Themes can be powerful. Political novice Peter Hoekstra stunned the Washington establishment by knocking off the chair of the National Republican Congressional Committee, Michigan Republican Guy Vander Jagt, in a 1992 primary contest. On a shoestring budget, Hoekstra pounded home the idea that Vander Jagt was a career politician, more interested in national affairs than in the voters back home. The message was echoed when Hoekstra appeared in a parade: he rode in a 1966 Nash Rambler, made the year Vander Jagt was first elected. The sign on the car read, "Isn't it time for a change?" (Morris and Gamache 1994, 116). Jesse Jackson Jr. turned his youth—he was just thirty years old—into a powerful message.

Throughout the campaign, he argued that he was "young enough to stay long enough" in Congress to reap the fruits of Washington seniority for his constituents (D. Johnson 1995).

The goal of a campaign theme is to find and push the right button for the right voter. Demographic research and polling data told the Redmond campaign that "a plurality of [toss-up] voters said 'restoring honesty and integrity to government' was most important to them in deciding their vote" (Wilson and Burita 2000, 94). The campaign worked hard to focus the voters' attention on government ethics. Treating all voters as a homogeneous unit is a grave mistake.

Targeted themes are vital to contemporary campaigns. As partisanship became a less meaningful voting cue (see Wattenberg 1998), voters had to find other ways to distinguish among candidates. Scholars who study campaign politics have suggested that incumbency filled the vacuum (Mayhew 1974b; Ferejohn 1977; Cover 1977). Though it is difficult to test empirically, David Mayhew writes, "A logic suggests itself. Voters dissatisfied with party cues could be reaching for any other cues that are available . . . incumbency is readily at hand" (1974b, 313). Conceivably, the shift from partisanship to incumbency helps explain high reelection rates.

This line of reasoning has its limits. First, the theory implies that voters pay virtually no attention to a candidate's qualifications, the issues, the national trends, or a host of other forces that may pull them toward a challenger. This perspective demands, as noted by Linda Fowler, "a level of pessimism about democracy that is difficult to accept" (1993, 79). The incumbency theory minimizes the importance of retrospective evaluations of incumbent performances and presupposes that weak party identifiers and independents are more inclined to support incumbents than are strong partisans, which does not appear to be the case (Krehbiel and Wright 1983). An alternative explanation is that voters seek concise messages to explain what the candidate stands for and then relate this information to their own ends. For some voters, party-based appeals might still work; for others, incumbency could be the cue; for still others, a host of messages might combine into an effective set of decision forces.

If voters care about factors beyond just party and incumbency, campaign themes become critical. It is the easy way for voters to make an informed choice. As Joel Bradshaw notes:

> It is the single, central idea that the campaign communicates to voters to sum up the candidate's connection with the voters and their concerns and the contrast between your candidate and the opponent. It answers the question: Why should your candidate be elected? (1995, 42)

If the candidate is a member of the majority party in a heavily partisan area, party-based appeals might be the key. If the candidate is the incumbent and voters are found to prefer experience, then knowledge of the people and a record of accomplishment could provide the theme. The important point is that voters rarely have time to assess candidate appeals on each and every issue. A carefully constructed theme links the voters' concerns with the candidate's approach.

While thematic simplicity is important, some candidates fail to see the need for it. They believe voters will make sense of disparate policy stands. Few voters have the time or energy to do this—and the ones who do, tend to confirm the choice that they have already made. Campaigns must offer voters a coherent rationale. Indeed, from the perspective of a campaign team, a central theme guides the message, ensuring that statements do not crisscross and contradict one another, leaving the voters even more confused.

Selecting and Implementing a Campaign Theme

There is a certain redundancy to campaign themes. Catherine Shaw, an Oregon mayor who also works as a campaign consultant, has compiled a list of campaign slogans drawn from political brochures: among them, "We all win with [name]," "A leader for [name of the place]," and "A concerned candidate for all of [place]" (2000, 28). It seems as though campaign themes are interchangeable. But Shaw is quick to point out that the choice of an appropriate campaign theme is contingent upon the campaign context. Which is better, "A New Voice! New Energy!" or "Leadership in Action: [name]"? The words often sound simplistic; in actuality, the construction and implementation of a theme can be a complicated venture. Development of an appropriate theme is an artful combination of what the voters want and what the candidate has to offer, never forgetting what the opponent might say. (See Bradshaw 1995, 43; Salmore and Salmore 1989, 126–135).

Finding "what the voters want" is an uncertain proposition. A benchmark poll may indicate a number of salient issues—perhaps none being mentioned by more than a small number of respondents. When asked to name "the most important problem facing this country today," those who answered a March 2000 Gallup Poll said "education" more often than any other answer. It got a 16 percent score. The AIDS epidemic did not even register, getting less than 0.5 percent. Perhaps the numbers would have been higher if the pollsters had prompted the respondents— "Is AIDS an important issue?"—but a campaign professional would then wonder if the poll measured what was really on people's minds.

Although data are always subject to interpretation, theme development must find a message that summarizes voter concerns. Generally speaking, themes are intended to be *inclusive*. They try to encompass a diverse set of issues or a broad range of qualifications. In most instances, it is a mistake to bill a candidate simply as an "environmental leader," even though concerns about pollution might be apparent and the candidate might be well suited to deal with them. Environmentalism might alienate some target voters. Some campaigns find that a more general theme, something like "a candidate concerned about the future" works best for them. A variety of issues can be fitted into this overarching message. Likewise, instead of being the "tough-on-crime-candidate," a better tactic might be to say that the candidate favors "a safer community." The fear of crime suggests, at its core, that one is not safe in the community. To make an area secure, many changes could be sought—more cops on the beat and tougher sentences for criminals, surely, but also a better educational system, promotion of family values, investing in housing and infrastructure, and so on. Broad themes can incorporate several related ideas, thereby appealing to more voters.

Some observers talk about a difference between "positional" issues and "valence" issues (Salmore and Salmore 1989, 112–13). Positional issues are those that have well-defined sides. People have to take a position. Abortion and gun control are divisive issues and this sort. Valence issues, on the other hand, are concerns about which everyone can agree, such as a strong national defense, decreased crime, the elimination of pollution, and the creation of jobs. For the most part, campaign themes center on valence issues. There is an exception, however. A "wedge" strategy—the name comes from a chess tactic whereby an opponent is forced to sacrifice a piece—highlights issues that divide the opposition. A liberal constituency that holds both environmentalists and organized labor gives a Republican the chance to pit a "jobs" message against environmental activists in an effort to bring middle-class workers on board.

Sometimes candidates are not given an opportunity to choose between positional and valence issues, as when a single issue engulfs the concerns of nearly all of the voters. Such issues are labeled "referenda" issues (Salmore and Salmore 1989, 113). In many cities, voters are asked to support a professional sports team, footing the bill for a new stadium. Even though successful teams can mean big money for a city, supporting one can mean less revenue for existing roads, bridges, and schools. Issues of this type can divide a city, forcing candidates to run on one side or the other.

The office sought may also constrain the choice of theme. Voters may well expect different ideas from candidates for different offices. Candidates for executive posts—such as governors, county executives, or mayors—might wish to focus on leadership and competence. Rather than merely responding to the needs of particular interests, they are expected to lead. Candidates for legislative posts, on the other hand, might make more hay out of their ability to deliver pork-barrel projects along with their routine constituent services.

The candidate's status also matters, and incumbents face special restrictions. Judith Trent and Robert Friedenberg suggest that candidate status is a key element in communications strategy (2000, 76–78). Incumbents cannot stress messages strictly related to "change" without asking to be removed from their jobs. Incumbent campaign themes highlight the need to "stay the course." Unlike challengers, incumbents can use the symbolic trappings of the office—strength, integrity, competence, and legitimacy—but they also have a record from which they cannot hide. Most incumbents do their best to find positive aspects of their record, a "record of accomplishment."

Challengers enjoy more latitude in their choice of theme—they do not have a record that limits its selection—but the need for a powerful theme is heightened. Challengers must convince voters to change their past voting behavior. It is nearly always necessary to attack the incumbent (Trent and Friedenberg 2000, 91–101). As scholars Barbara Salmore and Stephen Salmore note, "Most challengers must simultaneously erode the favorable reputation of the incumbent and build a positive case for themselves" (1989, 128). Without a cutting edge, voters have little reason to seek change. Thus, in a 1992 U.S. Senate race, the late Paul Coverdell successfully portrayed himself as an average Georgian, while painting his opponent as an extremist. In one powerful television spot, an elderly woman tells voters that Coverdell is "like us," while opponent Wyche Fowler "is just like Ted Kennedy." Georgians are proud of their state; Massachusetts liberalism is not for them.

Whether designed for a challenger or an incumbent, the theme must be easy to understand. Once again, voters are much more likely to grasp simplicity than complexity. Simple messages like integrity, experience, concern, change, hard work, family values, and other valence issues are easily understood and have almost universal appeal. In his successful 1990 challenge for the Minnesota U.S. Senate seat, Paul Wellstone developed a straightforward theme, "A man of ordinary means," a not-so-subtle contrast to his opponent, who was exceedingly wealthy and ready to spend $6 million on the race. Eight years later, Minnesota voters made former professional wrestler Jesse Ventura their governor, based largely on his defiance of traditional authority. The campaign theme became a no-message message. One political analyst has said, "Unlike the practiced politicians he was up against, he never stayed on message, deflecting the tough questions. That really set him apart." This is not to say, however, that there was no theme: an Independence Day T-shirt screamed, "Retaliate in '98" (Beiler 2000, 128.)

CONCLUSION

"Theme is not a word that should have an 's' on the end" (Bradshaw 1995, 42). The theme provides voters with a cognitive shortcut, and if there are many paths from which to choose, voters will simply choose none. Ventura's reformist theme gave his campaign a hard cutting edge that fit his strategic goals. If a campaign fails to generate an overall strategy—if it does not think about its strategic position, its target vote—and perhaps most importantly, a reason for persuadable voters to cast their ballots, success is not likely in the offing. Then again, it is not enough to know where the votes are and what theme will bring them into the fold; a campaign must undertake a concerted effort to reach its potential supporters. Voter contact is the subject of Part 3 of this book.

Part Three

VOTER CONTACT
TECHNIQUES

Chapter Nine

Fund-raising Strategy and Tactics

Campaigns need money. Volunteers, issues, good looks, and a winning personality can take a candidate only so far. Poorly funded candidates occasionally win, but the shortage of exceptions tends to prove the rule. Campaign expenditures remain a strong predictor of electoral success. Even social activist Ralph Nader, who ran for president in 1996 under the Green Party label, spending almost nothing and consequently receiving very few votes, chose to run a serious effort in Campaign 2000, complete with earnest fund-raising—this despite the candidate's protest that the existing campaign finance system corrupts American politics. Senator John McCain, who made campaign finance reform his flagship issue, was forced to raise millions of dollars to be competitive with George W. Bush. The new political environment requires candidates to raise money—and lots of it.

Money is valuable, in part, because it allows a campaign to acquire political resources on short notice. Old-style campaigns relied on endorsements and volunteers. But volunteers take time to organize, and they can sometimes be an unreliable source of labor in an enterprise that demands efficiency. The endorsement of a key political figure is helpful on its own—few would deny that the publicity does a campaign some good—but an endorsement carries far more weight if it means a powerful name on a fund-raising letter, access to donor lists, and money calls made on the candidate's behalf. Bankable support has become a necessary precondition of successful electioneering.

This chapter is designed to acquaint the reader with campaign fund-raising. It provides a brief look at the history of campaign finance, the reasons that people and groups give to campaigns, and some of the strategies and tactics involved in fund-raising operations.

A BRIEF LOOK AT MONEY IN CAMPAIGNS

Campaigns have never been cheap. In colonial times, candidates were expected to treat the voters with food and drink. George Washington's campaign gave away 160 gallons of alcoholic beverages, about a quart and a half per voter, in his first bid for the Virginia House of Burgesses (Dinkin 1989, 3). During most of the nineteenth century, campaigns were conducted in the partisan press and through party organizations. Rallies and events were held, party workers "hit the streets," and handbills were printed and distributed. Parties, rather than candidates, raised the necessary campaign funds. In turn, candidates were expected to contribute to the party—frequently, it was a necessary requirement for receiving the party's nomination. Urban Democratic machines were funded by a system that George Washington Plunkitt called "honest graft" (Riordon 1995, 3). When Mark Hanna used millions of dollars, donated in large gifts by wealthy industrialists, to fund the "Front Porch" campaign of William McKinley, the Republican Party all but purchased the White House. The politics of old were thoroughly scandalous by today's standards.

Although the parties would lose ground in the twentieth century, they continued to play an important role in campaign finance. In most areas the party leadership still controlled a number of party workers, and it was able to manage the nomination process. Perhaps most importantly, parties were still able to amass huge war chests. The money came from a generalized entanglement of cash and clout. To influence government decisions, one would contribute to the party. If money did go directly to the candidate, the candidate was expected to replenish party funds, since the candidate was just a creature of the larger organization. The result was massive party funding by business, labor unions, and wealthy individuals. In 1928, for example, roughly 70 percent of the funds raised by the two national parties came in contributions of $1,000 or greater—enough to buy a couple of Model T automobiles (Sorauf 1988, 3).

In the 1960s and 1970s, the political landscape began to shift. Corruption was still rampant—Vice President Spiro Agnew was forced to resign in 1974 after Justice Department officials happened across kickbacks that he was still receiving from his days in Baltimore—but the parties were no longer running the show. Before and after Watergate, Congress passed a series of campaign finance reforms that put much of the burden for fundraising in the hands of the individual candidates. While the courts have watered down campaign finance rules, leading to a rise in the use of soft money—party spending that helps candidates—individual contenders still have to raise a great deal of money on their own. In fact, candidates without money are rarely taken seriously by their parties.

Fundraising has become a full-time job. A large number of U.S. senators retired in 1996, and nearly all suggested that the pressure of raising massive sums for reelection played a role in their decisions. Senator Paul Simon, who had to raise $8.4 million in his last reelection campaign—"and that's not easy with my voting record" (1999, 306)—told *60 Minutes*, "When I first came here—man, when there was a Democratic fund-raising dinner, I was so eager to go. Now I drag myself. And it's probably a pretty good indication that this is a good time to step aside" (Simon 1995). The price of a Senate seat used to be obeisance to party leaders—in an era of new-style politics it became their dedication to endless campaign fund-raising.

Simon can be forgiven for thinking that costs are spiraling out of control. There are more people to reach—the baby boomers of the 1940s and 1950s, the Voting Rights Act of 1965, and the Twenty-Sixth Amendment (which gave eighteen-year-olds the right to vote) all expanded the size of the electorate (Adamany and Agree 1975, 21). In an effort to reach the voters, competitive campaigns avail themselves of new technologies. Sophisticated survey research, direct mail, telemarketing, computerized targeting, not to mention radio and video production, have driven up the cost of getting elected. Campaign consulting has added new burdens. A good consultant will charge hundreds of dollars per hour, and the introduction of Web-based communications has added a whole new category of consultancy. For the 1997–1998 campaign cycle, the Federal Election Commission reports that House and Senate candidates spent more than $740 million—and only a fraction of those candidates won office.

One might ask whether all this spending is really necessary. Could candidates spend less and still win? Perhaps the cost of campaigning has increased because candidates mistakenly believe that victory requires spending as much as possible on television, radio, and direct mail. Perhaps incumbents and other experienced officeholders were going to win anyway—so contributors are merely giving to the eventual winner. Is there a relationship between money and the likelihood of success? While the precise cost per vote might not be calculable, most agree that money does make a difference in American political campaigns. In the 1990 state legislative races in California, for example, 96 percent of the candidates who had the most money won. The same is true for federal offices. Successful candidates in open-seat elections outspent their rivals by 48 percent in 1998, according to Paul Herrnson, "lend[ing] credence to the point that money matters" (2000, 243–44). Campaign riches might not determine victory, but they seem to improve the odds. More importantly, few candidates or consultants are ready to gamble on the idea that money is meaningless.

Money and the Incumbency Advantage

Are campaign finances at the root of high reelection rates? Do incumbents win because it is easier for them to raise money? Or is it the other way around? The answer is difficult to find because the questions are hard to parse. Herrnson's careful study of electoral success shows that challengers are more likely to win when incumbents spend a lot of money on campaign communications (2000, 232). Presumably, a safe incumbent does not need to spend money, whereas an endangered incumbent has to start buying media. One of the first to explore this interesting paradox was Gary Jacobson. When a challenger poses a serious danger, the incumbent can raise the money needed to counter the threat. Jacobson has said that "the incumbency advantage depends not so much on what incumbents do, but on what potential opponents do" (1997, 37). So, is campaign spending a cause or an effect of electoral competition? The record is not entirely clear. Most likely, incumbency and campaign finance share a mutually reinforcing relationship.

Whatever the answer may be, PACs give disproportionately to incumbents. Herrnson reports that sitting members of the U.S. House raised an average of $320,574 from PAC contributions in 1998, whereas challengers received just $37,660 (2000, 155, 165). A strong incumbent advantage exists at other levels of government as well. Organizations wishing to promote their interests give to projected winners, since there is no payoff in losing candidates. As noted by a former director of the Democratic Senatorial Campaign Committee, "Washington money is, by and large, smart money. Most PACs are not a bit interested in supporting people they don't think will win" (Luntz 1988, 178). Because incumbents usually prevail, they can therefore expect to receive a large share of contributions—and they do.

Other factors may also be in play. Incumbents often have cash left over from their last campaign, making their next effort seem credible from the start, attracting a good deal of "early money" from PACs and individuals. Early money further discourages quality challengers—the ones who can spot the danger signs—from jumping into the race, leaving the field to less qualified contenders (Maisel 1990, 125). Finally, incumbents have fund-raising experience. After all, if they did not know how to raise money, they probably would not have been elected in the first place! Once in office, they maintain a reliable list of contributors, spend time learning from other candidates, and continually refine their fund-raising operations.

Campaign Finance Law

Federal candidates are subject to strict fund-raising rules. The regulations are extremely detailed, and for this reason wise campaigns keep attorneys and accountants on board to sort through the regulatory maze. That said, the Federal Election Commission (FEC) has made a strong effort to distribute its rules and regulations in easy-to-digest formats. Virtually all current documents are available on the Web, including a detailed "Campaign Guide for Congressional Candidates and Committees," frequent news releases, a series of brochures, and a monthly newsletter called "The Record," which provides campaign professionals with up-to-date information on campaign finance and reporting requirements. In keeping with the needs of campaigns in the Digital Age, campaigns may now file mandated reports online.

These reports are intended to keep campaigns within the letter of campaign finance laws, which were passed in the 1970s. The Federal Elections Campaign Act (FECA) and a series of amendments set a $1,000 limit on individual contributions at each stage of the election—primary, runoff (if applicable), and general. National parties were given a $5,000 cap, but they could also provide assistance through "coordinated expenditures"—usually in the form of voter registration efforts, shared polling, and get-out-the-vote drives. Coordinated expenditures were capped by a formula based on population and inflation. For the 2000 cycle, House candidates in states with more than one congressional district were allowed $33,780 in both state and national coordinated spending. Depending on the size of the state, Senate candidates were allowed up to $1,636,438. At the time of publication, the constitutionality of the cap on coordinated expenditure funding was being challenged in the courts and comprehensive campaign finance reform legislation was being debated in Congress.

As the new millennium began, labor unions, corporations, and incorporated trade and membership organizations were prohibited from making direct contributions to candidates, but were allowed to participate financially through segregated and highly regulated accounts. They could establish political action committees (PACs), which could give $5,000 in direct contributions to a candidate at each stage of the election process. During the 1997–1998 cycle, the FEC reported donations of just under $.5 billion from 4,699 PACs. In a way, PACs are simply responding to candidate needs. Candidates want more money to run their races, and PACs fill this demand. When one candidate accepts PAC funds, other candidates must usually respond accordingly.

Similar rules apply in state and local campaigns, where the growth of special interests roughly parallels the national trend. Insofar as state and local government has become much more involved in regulatory matters, business, labor, and consumer groups have made the decision to get more deeply engaged in the campaign process at this level. In states like Michigan, roughly three-quarters of candidate war chests come from interest groups and political parties, while in others, such as North Carolina, about two-thirds have come from individuals (R. Jones 1991, 52–53). Financial regulations at the state and local level vary. The FEC tracks state regulations and publishes a comprehensive list every two years, but candidates must consult their state's regulatory body for specific information.

Recent years brought widespread calls for campaign finance reform legislation that seemed poised for passage as the new millennium commenced. Much of the focus has been on "soft money"—the money a party legally raises or spends outside the bounds of FECA. The term generally refers to money used on nonfederal campaigns and on "issue advocacy ads" sponsored by a political party. The latter are more controversial than the former. In 1996, for example, the Democratic National Committee ran a series of issue advocacy spots that steered clear of expressly advocating Bill Clinton's reelection. They showed a hard-working Clinton laboring in the serenity of the Oval Office, but they never said, "Vote for Clinton." As such, the ads did not qualify as "express advocacy" for Clinton's reelection, and hence they did not fall under the FECA rules. In 2000, soft-money spending shattered all records. Leaders in both parties called for reform, and in 2001, legislation sponsored in the Senate by John McCain and Russ Feingold, which would, among other things, impose heavy restrictions on national party spending, passed the Senate by a wide margin. In previous years, a similar bill had passed the House after an extraordinary parliamentary coup was instigated by reformers (Dwyer and Farrar-Myers 2000). At publication time, no major campaign finance reform had been signed into law.

In the middle of Campaign 2000, however, Congress questioned the propriety of "section 527" money. The reference is to groups organized under section 527 of the Internal Revenue Code, which allowed for unlimited and undisclosed raising of money used at election time to run "issue ads." McCain castigated his GOP presidential primary rival, George W. Bush, for declining to forbid Republicans for Clean Air, a group formed by financial supporters of Bush, from running ads touting Bush's record on environmental issues. Defenders of 527 money said that it was protected by the First Amendment, which gives wide birth to political speech. There is, they argued, no reason that a person should be exposed to retribution just for making a political point. In July 2000, new legislation was signed into law, requiring the organizations to disclose their leadership and funding sources.

The free speech argument arises from a Supreme Court case, *Buckley v. Valeo* (1976), which arose from a constitutional challenge to FECA. The Court held that restrictions on campaign contributions were generally constitutional, but that some sections of FECA violated constitutionally protected rights by attempting to place overall caps on campaign spending. To maintain the constitutionality of FECA's independent expenditure provisions, *Buckley* redefined the legal definition to include only "expenditures for communications that in express terms advocate the election or defeat of a clearly identified candidate for Federal office." While the precise contours of this definition are vague, "express advocacy" has come to mean a narrow range of statements such as "Smith for Congress" or "vote against Old Hickory." Without these "magic words" or some other statement that leaves no doubt about the electoral nature of the advocacy, the communication is not an independent expenditure under FECA and therefore is not federally regulated.

REASONS FOR INDIVIDUAL AND GROUP DONATIONS

Whatever one might think of the existing campaign finance system, candidates are forced to live under its rules. They have to raise money if they want to win, and in order to raise money, they must understand why individuals and groups give to campaigns. "The process is bilateral," writes Sorauf; "both contributors and candidates pursue political goals" (1995, 78). In the days when Spiro Agnew charged a percentage on government contracts, campaign donations were easily understood. Campaign finance in the new millennium, however, is more complex. Most constituents would be amazed at the spectacle of a "photo line," in which individuals pay $1,000 or more to stand in line for a quick "grip and grin" snapshot with a Senate candidate. No policy issues are discussed, and those who try to take a moment of the candidate's time for a discussion of a pet project are hurried off by staff. Some aspects of modern campaigning are almost imponderable.

Individual Donors

Of the roughly $750 million raised and spent in congressional elections during the 1998 campaign cycle, almost a third was given by individuals. For the 2000 elections, FEC reports showed that individuals had given more than $120 million before the calendar year had even begun. These figures tell only part of the story. State and local campaigns are not included in this sum, nor are presidential campaigns. Suffice it to say that individual donors are putting a lot of money into the system.

Many people give to campaigns because they are asked. The act of solicitation greatly increases the chances that an individual donor will produce a check. Without the request, even the most supportive citizen might not think to offer financial support. Perhaps the campaign already has enough money—after all, no one came looking for it. Among those who intend to give, many simply like to hear the request. The solicitation makes donors feel that they are needed and appreciated. Possibly, as Sorauf suggests, "the request for money activates some generalized, even vague, feeling of loyalty or sympathy, whether for the cause or the solicitor" (1988, 49). The loyalty thesis is strengthened by a common practice in state legislative politics whereby party leaders request that members with safe elections contribute to colleagues who do not have that luxury (Shea 1995a).

Many individuals are interested in government, and by helping a favored candidate win office, they can change the course of political events. Sometimes the contribution is related to a single issue, such as the candidate's stand on abortion, gun control, or economic deregulation. Sometimes the contribution is meant to further a larger set of beliefs, such as a party platform or political ideology. Party activists and those keenly interested in the outcome of government are more likely to give, obviously, but loyalty to nonpolitical organizations may also impel them to send a check. If, for example, a professional association has long opposed an incumbent's political agenda, the association's membership may believe that their best interests lie with donations to the challenger.

Retrospection is a powerful force. A candidate who voted for lower property taxes might benefit from contributors who simply want to demonstrate appreciation for these efforts. Retrospective donations can also work in favor of the challenger. One prominent GOP leader has advised GOP fund-raisers, "Ask yourself, who hates the incumbent, who wants to beat him as bad as I do. This starts the donor list process" (Shea and Brooks 1995, 25). Once on the list, some people fall into the habit of giving (Yeutter et al. 1992). Indeed, about 10 percent of Americans contribute to one or more political candidates in any given election cycle (Sorauf 1988, 47).

Habit, retrospection, policy preference, and loyalty to the solicitor are powerful forces—but so is celebrity. It is an interesting paradox: as a class, politicians are disdained, while as individuals, many public officials are held in high esteem. Officialdom has its own magnetism. Some people want to be seen at a fund-raiser with successful candidates, particularly those who regularly appear on television. Often the contact takes the form of a personal telephone call or an autographed picture. The celebrity factor in politics explains the success of fund-raisers that include popular figures from the worlds of entertainment, sports, and politics. Perhaps for the same reason that some people give to the arts—the chance to participate in the glamour and excitement of a well-known event—many choose to share in the experience of politics by writing a check to a political candidate.

Interest Groups

The incentives for individual campaign contributions apply to interest group contributions as well. The main difference is that groups are more likely to base their donations on policy grounds. Fund-raiser Carl Silverberg lists four reasons that a PAC might give money to a candidate: "[T]he legislator voted with them on their issues. . . . The legislator sits on a committee that has jurisdiction over the majority of the legislation the PAC has set out as its priorities for the year. . . . There is a good following in the district. . . . The corporation represented by the PAC has a good number of employees in the district" (2000, 62). PACs want to elect officials sympathetic to their concerns—to have access to officeholders who handle their issues. This is precisely why incumbents receive the vast majority of group contributions: there is no advantage in funding losers. Hence it is common to see interest groups giving money to both major political parties to make sure their voices will be heard.

While the donations may be offered out of a concern for policy, there is little reason to believe that interest groups are "buying" candidates when they provide funds. Rather, groups probably contribute heavily out of a desire for access—the hope that they will be allowed to present their position to the elected official. Groups seek "a chance to persuade, an opportunity to make a case or argue a point" (Sorauf 1988, 314). Paul Simon has put the matter bluntly: "I have never promised anyone a thing for a campaign contribution. But when I was in the Senate and got to my hotel room at midnight, there might be twenty phone calls waiting for me, nineteen from people whose names I did not recognize, the twentieth from someone who gave me a $1,000 contribution or raised money for me. . . . Which [call] do you think I will make?" (1999, 306).

The Decision *Not* to Give

As a final note, it is important to understand why people and groups might *not* contribute to a given campaign (Yeutter et al. 1992). First, many would-be contributors are not asked. Few people know intuitively that they are supposed to give money to a campaign. Second, sometimes no amount has been specified in the appeal. Without knowing how much is needed, a potential contributor may simply pass up the opportunity. Third, the potential contributor might not have provided a clear way of giving. A fund-raising letter that does not include a return envelope has wasted a lot of money. Simple issues can have a profound impact on fund-raising efforts, as can more substantive difficulties. If a candidate uses a racial appeal, many prospective donors may be offended and then choose not to give. Sometimes solicitation leaves the supporter feeling used, belittled, or underappreciated. Along similar lines, the appeal may be unconvincing on its face. Potential contributors need to believe that their money will make a difference. If prospects sense that their money is unneeded or will be wasted—or if they do not trust the solicitor's judgment—they have no compelling reason to send a check.

FUND-RAISING STRATEGY AND TACTICS

According to fund-raising expert Mary Sabin, there are three keys to successful fund-raising, "and they are work, work, work. If you are not feeling anxiety and stress, you're not doing your job. . . . This isn't rocket science or brain surgery. What it is is working hard, staying at it, and concentrating on raising the money while feeling completely obsessed about it" (Shea and Brooks 1995, 25). Part of the work is careful attention to planned objectives. Robert Kaplan is adamant on this point: "[O]nce you've bought into the plan, it's your job as a candidate or campaign manager, to work full force to implement it, notwithstanding any mid-course corrections" (2000, 64).

There are four principal elements to a strategic fund-raising plan: quantity, timing, sources, and tactics. Some campaigns mistakenly base their plans on an assessment of the amount of money that can be raised (Himes 1995, 63). The correct approach is to figure out how much money will be needed to implement the overall campaign plan. By setting specific goals, the fund-raising team has a clear motivation. Targets and deadlines are strong motivators. If, for example, the campaign strategy calls for a massive television buy in early spring, fund-raising efforts begin well in advance. Traditional sources of money (party funds, local contributors, and the PACs that contributed to other members of the candidate's party) may suffice, but if they do not, the candidate must think about alternatives (regional contributors, PACs that have not contributed to the party, etc.).

Wealthy candidates have an edge because they can give money early in the cycle, signaling a concrete commitment. One of the greatest financial obstacles that a campaign faces is "seed money." This is the funding needed before the campaign can move into full gear, including consultant fees, benchmark poll costs, and money for electoral targeting data. Pro-choice Democratic women often look to EMILY's List. The "EMILY" in EMILY's List stands for "Early Money Is Like Yeast—It makes the 'dough rise.' " Without early money, a campaign finds would-be contributors hesitant to give. EMILY's List scouts candidates, trains them, and provides campaign funding, thereby helping selected women get past the first major obstacle to campaigning.

For all candidates, potential sources include family, friends, colleagues, and associates; partisans; political action committees; habitual givers; adversaries of the opponent; and political parties at all levels. Many candidates group potential givers, or "prospects," into three general categories: small, medium, and large. Precisely how these categories are defined depends on the specifics of each race. A large contributor in a city council campaign might be considered a small donor in a congressional race. In fact, most candidates prefer that the general public not believe that they are relying on "fat cat" donors. Former Republican senator Rudy Boschwitz, in his 1996 rematch against Paul Wellstone, went out of his way to let Minnesota voters know that he was drawing large portions of his campaign money from "skinny cats" who gave less than $100.

Because fund-raising tactics vary depending on the prospect, broad-based plans work best (Beaudry and Schaeffer 1986, 164). No technique is sure to work in every race, and often the proper mix depends on the candidate and the consultant. Some candidates, for example, are more comfortable asking for money, just as some consultants are more skilled in direct mail than in PAC solicitation. Some prospects consider direct mail abhorrent, preferring that someone verbally request the money, while others think that mail is convenient and that phone calls are intrusive. Not all tactics work equally well in every district. Nevertheless, campaign operatives should be familiar with each of the most commonly used fund-raising techniques.

Personal Solicitation

When GOP representative Rod Chandler of Washington decided to leave Congress in 1992, fellow Republican Jennifer Dunn saw her chance. What she lacked in campaign experience she made up for in fund-raising savvy. Having run the Washington state Republican Party for eleven years, Dunn understood that the best way to raise money is to ask for it personally. "With help from friends and volunteers, Dunn worked her way through the 5,000 names in her personal files, raising $492,442 from individuals and $168,373 from PACs" (Morris and Gamache 1994, 152). She outraised her opponent by a two-to-one margin the "old-fashioned way"—she asked for it!

"Dialing for dollars" is an unpleasant way to spend an afternoon, but personal solicitation has proven to be extremely productive, particularly for up-front money from large donors in a short period of time. In general, a master list of prospects is drawn to include wealthy individuals in tune with candidates' views (Allen 1990a, 49). Personal solicitation can work with small-scale donors, but it takes the same amount of time to ask for $10 as it does for $1,000—with about the same rate of return. New-style campaigns use the candidate for big donors, in part, because personal requests are often the only way to get fat cats to give.

Success often lies in the personal and professional interests of the prospect. Solicitors must be ready to detail precisely where the campaign is going and why the money is needed, offering polling information, campaign brochures, a summary of the candidate's policy stands, and a list of expenses the money would cover. In some instances, it is worthwhile to provide a shortened version of the campaign plan. The goal is to make prospects feel as though they are being asked to join a tightly run, highly organized campaign team.

One of the hardest things that a professional fund-raiser confronts is a candidate reluctant to ask for money. Kaplan calls this phenomenon "fund-raising fear" (2000, 64). When making the "ask," Kaplan advises, "Choose a number that is 10 to 25 percent in excess of what your research shows contributors should donate" (1991, 54). Some consultants look at the situation from the potential contributor's point of view: Why donate money to the campaign? Consultants often recommend that separate fund-raising accounts be established for each aspect of campaign operations. A donation to underwrite an ad buy shows a specific return for the campaign dollar. A telephone script for a typical request might read: "We're trying to raise $12,000 for some TV spots that have to be bought now for the November election. Would you be willing to make a pledge or send a gift to support our efforts?" (Shaw 2000, 79).

A number of campaigns have profited from the development of "pledge systems," where the contributor is asked to donate at periodic intervals. This approach can often increase the overall contribution (Beaudry and Schaeffer 1986, 168). The more common technique is contacting those who have given once to give again. Both approaches are risky: it is almost always better to get as much as possible all at once, since future donations may taper off. Large-scale fund-raising operations use fund-raising hierarchies. A wealthy donor might promise to sell a table of seats at a high-dollar fund-raising dinner. An individual donor is worth some money, but someone who can get others to contribute is worth even more.

PAC and Interest Group Solicitation

As noted earlier, national and state political action committees have become first-string players in new-style campaign finance. The average congressional incumbent received over $320,000 in PAC funds in 1998 (Herrnson 2000, 155), and yet, campaigns cannot presume that these organizations will flood a race with donations simply because the candidate holds the right policy stand. Challengers are in a particularly tough spot, as they receive little more than a tenth of the PAC money that incumbents get.

To find PAC money, careful strategizing is in order, beginning with a long list of potential donors. At the federal level, PACs are registered with the FEC, and at the state and local level most are required to register with the elections commission or the secretary of state. If a candidate is on the wrong side of the policy fence, a donation is probably not forthcoming. PACs that consistently give to the opponent and the opponent's party are poor prospects as well. Once the list is trimmed, a campaign might look for "hooks"—bits of information that could draw a PAC into the race. An association might count the candidate as a member, an ideological PAC might take note of issues raised in the district, or a business group may be against the opponent's record, as shown in bill sponsorships and floor votes (Yeutter et al. 1992). Developing a PAC list is a time-consuming chore, but the more detailed the database, the better.

From this list, the campaign can develop specific arguments for each PAC, often assembling "PAC kits." A typical kit might place a cover letter on top of biographies, district profiles, prominent consultants, leadership endorsements, and issue papers, along with campaign materials, poll results, and favorable press clippings (see Yeutter et al. 1992, 24–26; Himes 1995, 66; Herrnson 2000, 160). PAC kits are generally mailed, but a follow-up telephone call by either the candidate or campaign official is made after an appropriate interval (see Silverberg 2000). For "hot prospects," it is often deemed wise to have the candidate hand-deliver the packet.

Sending or delivering PAC kits is by no means the only way to get special-interest money. Incumbents host periodic receptions on their own behalf, often with the help of colleagues. PAC officials are invited to meet the candidate in a social setting. Receptions in Washington and some state capitals commonly cost $1,000 or $2,500 per person. The more prestigious the incumbent, the higher the price tag.

The process is more difficult for challengers and open-seat candidates than it is for incumbents, but party campaign committees can be tremendously helpful. The campaign committees can provide strategic advice about PACs and the right way to approach them. Most PACs send questionnaires wherein even the slightest mistake can prevent a candidate from receiving funds, so parties tutor candidates on proper completion of these forms. Furthermore, while "it is illegal for the parties to 'earmark' checks they receive from individuals or PACs for specific candidates," Herrnson notes, "committee members and staff can 'suggest' to contributors that they give to one of the candidates on the committee's watch-list" (2000, 107). Party organizations also hold "meet and greet" receptions, where PAC decision makers and selected candidates are invited to the same gathering, allowing candidates direct access to donors—often a difficult hurdle in the PAC fund-raising process. Like a dating service, the party's goal is to bring the candidate and the PAC together. (See Hernson 2000, 106–7.) Party leaders can also prod the news media to see certain races as competitive—leading perhaps to more PAC money. Overall, party committees can be a great help with PAC fund-raising, but to get this assistance, the committee must believe that the candidate stands a good chance of victory.

Direct Mail

Direct-mail solicitation can be a powerful fund-raising tool. The modern approach was developed by Richard Viguerie, who, as a fund-raiser in the early 1960s, preferred mailing fund-raising letters to making personal solicitations (Blumenthal 1980, 224). In 1965 "Viguerie hired two employees and the three of them copied [by hand] the names and addresses of the 12,500 major donors to the Goldwater campaign" (Friedenberg 1997, 104). The successful use of direct mail by George McGovern's campaign in 1972 was followed by the rapid growth of Republican National Committee fund-raising efforts in the late 1970s. The 1980s and 1990s saw an explosion in the number of mail-service professionals. Dwight Morris and Murielle E. Gamache report that in the early 1990s several dozen direct-mail firms were making huge amounts of money from House campaigns. They note that in 1992, for example, several made over $400,000 and some over $1 million (1994, 221). Mail houses flourish because the process can be complex and confusing, far beyond the familiar task of writing a letter and sending it off. In many ways, direct mail epitomizes new-style campaigning.

Direct mail is a step-by-step process in which previous losses are absorbed in expectation of future gains. The operation begins with a "prospect list," a collection "based on some characteristics or qualities thought likely to make them susceptible to a candidate's appeal for funds" (Sabato 1989, 88). Often, lists may be available through a government agency (such as the board of elections), the state or local party organization, or prior candidates of the same party (and even for the same office), or they can be pulled together from a variety of nonpolitical lists. List vendors offer the use of magazine subscribers, mail-order purchasers, boat owners, and professional accountants, attorneys, and medical doctors. Everyone is on a list of some sort. Law restricts the use of some lists, so caution is in order.

The trick to profitable direct mail is the acceptance of early losses (see Sabato 1989). Assume that the prospecting list contains 40,000 names. Production costs and postage for this large group might run approximately $.50 per letter, for a total of $20,000. It is customary to receive roughly a 2 or 3 percent response rate from a prospecting list, meaning that a great letter will bring about 1,000 respondents. The average contribution from the group as a whole will generally be rather small, maybe $19. The gross income from this mailing would therefore be $19,000, in which case the campaign has incurred a $1,000 loss. Or has it? There is another way to look at the mailing: a list of 1,000 proven donors was purchased for just $1 each. Once this "house list" has been established, the cost of a new mailing is much smaller (the list is only a fraction of its original size), and the rate of return is much higher. The second appeal will be more refined, with the campaign spending, say, $.65 per letter on production and postage. It is mailed to contributors only, requiring just a $650 outlay. The response rate might be as high as 20 percent, with an average contribution of $18. The $650 investment would therefore gross $3,600—a $2,950 net return.

Mailings to the house list can be repeated several times. The rate of return will probably become smaller with each mailing as people grow tired of sending more money. Each mailing will bring a slightly different set of contributors. Checkboxes on the donor card set the lowest suggested amount at the donor's highest previous contribution, perhaps pressing a steady donation increase. Fund-raising consultant Neesa Hart suggests that a campaign can send the house list a new mailing every week (1992). A direct-mail consultant who worked with Congressman Mark Neumann has noted that his 1998 Senate campaign "grossed over $1.1 million in the mail, and grew challenger Neumann's housefile from 7,000 names in June 1997 to over 36,000 names . . . in-state!" (Thibodeaux 1999, 61, ellipses in original). To increase the campaign's fortunes, "We mailed 28 different prospecting packages, to 756,948 names and grossed over $510,000. And an amazing 70% of the prospecting packages netted money!" (61).

One way to enhance a direct-mail program for lower-level races is to begin with a "suspect list" rather than a "prospect list." Instead of sending letters to a large group, the campaign looks for specific individuals who are likely to give.

For example, it may use a list of habitual party donors or the candidate's business contacts. A candidate for county commissioner may draw up a list of her personal friends. A statewide Democratic candidate might solicit all the Democrats in his hometown. The idea behind the suspect list is to improve the rate of return—to perhaps as high as 15 or 20 percent. Hart suggests a number of other refinements (e.g., weeding out unlikely donors and combining households into one mailing) to improve efficiency (1992). Small lists can be created, personalized, and mailed in-house, perhaps saving production costs.

Whether the campaign proceeds from a big or a small list, several elements of a direct-mail appeal must be kept in mind. The letter must convey an urgent message to the reader. "Dull is dull," writes Ron Kanfer, so "the most successful direct-mail programs are built around [a] compelling story" (1991, 22). Appeals must be personal, or they have to discuss a hot issue. Readers are given the impression that the campaign is behind in the polls, but within striking distance. (Nothing kills a small-donor program faster than the perception that the race is in the bag.) Finally, a successful letter will provide a response card and a self-addressed envelope.

As to style, many argue that longer letters, with handwritten notes in the margin, work better than short notes. It seems that, in order for people to send their hard-earned money, the case must be laid out in detail—even if most people do not read beyond the first page. Large donations are often followed up with a personal thank-you note from the candidate—partly out of gratitude but also because the heart of direct mail is the notion that people will give more than once, and one never knows when the candidate will seek higher office. Details matter.

Direct-mail programs are complex and risky. Many candidates and consultants outsource the task to mail houses. These firms are often one-stop units that provide copy, layout, printing, list rental, and postage know-how. Billing is generally handled in two ways: a retainer or a fee per piece mailed (Kanfer 1991). But any investment can go bad. A mailing that costs more than it returns produces out-of-pocket costs that some campaigns cannot absorb. Good targeting and production are critical. A dozen years ago, Larry Sabato wrote, "Many direct mailers foresee a time when they will commission extensive psychological testing of word patterns, colors, and approaches, and use focus groups and much more sophisticated list selection techniques" (1989, 99). In the new millennium, variations on these functions are routine in high-level campaigns.

Events: Big and Small

When the president, the vice president, governors, and members of the congressional leadership travel around the United States, they often stop in at candidate fund-raising events. So do Hollywood stars. At these affairs, the honored guest shakes hands with high-dollar donors, perhaps having a picture taken with the celebrity and the candidate, and then everyone joins the low-dollar crowd for dinner and a few words about the future. Fund-raising events can be large-scale affairs, such as dinners, cocktail parties, concerts, or boat tours, or they can be small events, such as coffees, ice-cream socials, and chicken barbecues. Done well, these activities can produce large sums of money, demonstrate to the media and the general public that the campaign has momentum, reward past donors, and build a list of contributors (Yeutter et al. 1992). They can also serve an important social function. Many voters and contributors are drawn to candidates for the excitement, as massive rallies for Ralph Nader showed in Campaign 2000. Campaigns must know how to build a good event.

Like direct mail, large-scale fund-raisers are a gamble. The logistics of an event, particularly a large one, can be overwhelming and can tie up the campaign team for weeks. Ticket sales may falter, and uncontrollable circumstances can court disaster. An event that flops causes financial problems and, more important, suggests to the media, voters, and potential contributors that the campaign is struggling.

Small-scale events do not court disaster in the same way that large-scale events might, but they do risk tedium. Small-group chitchat can be painfully dull. A smart campaign uses some imagination, perhaps holding auctions, wine and cheese receptions, folk dances, and so on. Location is important. Successful event planners go out of their way to find interesting locations, but whether the event is on the waterfront or in a neighbor's backyard, most consultants insist that the setting should have an air of success. Campaigns are cautioned, "Perception is reality—especially in the event business. If you're having a small reception with 20 people, don't book a room that can hold 100" (Meredith 2000, 62). In fact, a good event staff ensures that a room can be "cut" with draperies, movable walls, or greenery, just in case the expected number of tickets is not sold.

Telemarketing

One of the newer techniques in campaign finance is telemarketing. The process is similar to direct mail, but suspect donors are given a pitch over the telephone. Also, like mail, telemarketing as an investment is only as good as the list with which it starts. Kaplan suggests that the basic telemarketing approach can be improved with a "peer-to-peer" program. Instead of having anonymous callers phone people whom they have never met, peer-to-peer telemarketing encourages business, industry, and professional organization leaders to call others in their field. Providing volunteers with an assistant to help with the dialing enhances efficiency. Kaplan suggests that this method doubles calling volume while increasing the dollar return per call (1993, 41–42). Working in conjunction with direct mail, telemarketing operations can reactivate donors who have not contributed in some time, prompting lost contributors to give again (Himes 1995, 76). Two or three days after the prospect receives a fund-raising letter, a campaign telemarketer calls "just to make sure the note from the candidate arrived." Response rates for direct mail can rise significantly, possibly because telephone solicitation gives form letters a more personal appeal.

Recent Innovations

Lately, a number of fund-raising innovations have been collecting money in ways never before envisioned. For example, some campaigns bridge the gap between personal contact and blind prospecting with a paid canvass. Workers are assigned to potentially productive districts and asked to walk door-to-door in search of funds. As compensation for their efforts, the canvassers receive a percentage of the collection. This process is used by environmental and Public Interest Research Groups across the nation. It can serve several goals simultaneously: raising money, building a house list, and distributing campaign literature. A drawback to the paid canvass is that many workers are motivated by money, not by the campaign or the candidate. Managers might sometimes wonder if the message is getting out as well as the money is coming in. More importantly, the use of this technique might signal desperation. The thought of mercenaries scouring the district in search of funds may be too much for some candidates to bear.

An alternative is offered by campaign consultant Bill Wachob, who suggests that one-page flyers asking for donations of five dollars to twenty-five dollars be distributed at every campaign event (along with a return envelope). The idea is to hook people with small donations and put them on a monthly newsletter list. These reports, filled with "confidential campaign information," are designed to bring the donor into the race emotionally and to prepare the donor for future fund-raising solicitations. Wachob suggests that small-scale, volunteer-driven strategies like this can yield big bucks (1991, 51–52). In 1992 presidential candidate Jerry Brown asked his supporters to call a 900 number, and each time they did, ten dollars would be added to his treasury—and to the caller's telephone bill. This mass-based approach was particularly appealing to Brown, as his campaign theme was "an insurgent campaign against an entrenched leadership." Over 280,000 callers made the effort (R. Hart 1994, 1).

The new-millennium version of the 1990s-era 900-number is Web and email fund-raising. While still an unproven vehicle—one that costs a great deal of money to establish and maintain—there are signs that Internet solicitation is more than just a gimmick. The McCain campaign claimed to have raised millions on the Web in just a few days. Whether this was new money or just the cash that would otherwise have been given through traditional means remains to be seen, but McCain, along with fellow presidential candidates George W. Bush and Al Gore, created sophisticated Web sites with user-friendly donation systems. Privacy, security, and legal information were offered, and mailing addresses along with toll-free telephone numbers were listed for those unwilling to send credit card numbers over the Internet (Jalonick 2000a, 48). Furthermore, an increasing number of candidates are sending their pitch via email. Combining the new technology with the old idea of letting people know what their money is going to be used for, Republican congressional candidate Charlie Gerow gave "donors a tangible goal by listing some campaign expenses (100 Gerow yard signs cost $241, a one month supply of Gerow bumper stickers costs $391, etc.)" (48).

CONCLUSION

The precise manner in which campaigns should go about raising money is a topic of much speculation—perhaps more than any other area of new-style campaigning. There is, however, agreement on a few fundamentals. As Kaplan puts it, fund-raising "is about asking—and knowing that one dollar early is better than one hundred dollars late" (2000, 64). Still, while consultants are paid well to give new and improved advice, each has a slightly different spin. One of the most successful conservative fund-raisers, Bradley S. O'Leary, made his name with large events, including a million-dollar affair in an airline hangar. O'Leary says, "[F]or a big fund-raiser, I want the biggest place I can find" (Hallow 1997b, 22). At the same time, another consultant confides, "I know a campaign is in trouble when they tell me they are large event driven" (McDevitt 1996, 50). What is the right mix? Few can say for sure. The winning combination can be determined only in light of the campaign's specific time, place, and strategic context.

Chapter Ten

Strategic Communications

At the Republican Convention of 1996, Senator Bob Dole accepted his party's nomination for the presidency with a moving speech. Dole, a war hero who had served in public office for decades, articulated a heartfelt vision of conservative America. Noting that "age has its advantages," Dole offered,

> Let me be the bridge to an America that only the unknowing call myth. Let me be the bridge to a time of tranquility, faith, and confidence in action. And to those who say it was never so, that America has not been better, I say, you're wrong, and I know, because I was there. And I have seen it. And I remember. (*New York Times* 1996a)

The penultimate paragraph captured the essence of the oration: "Tonight, I stand before you, tested by adversity, made sensitive by hardship, a fighter by principle and the most optimistic man in America. My life is proof that America is a land without limits" (*New York Times* 1996a).

To those who watched from the floor of the convention hall, it was a great moment. Even those in Bill Clinton's White House gave the speech its due. But the Clinton campaign saw opportunity in Dole's words. The Republican candidate had submitted himself as a bridge to the past. Clinton, however, would talk about the future. When the president gave his own acceptance speech, he listed his past accomplishments, along with some unfinished business, and then intoned:

> I love and revere the rich and proud history of America, and I am determined to take our best traditions into the future. But with all respect, we do not need to build a bridge to the past. We need to build a bridge to the future, and that is what I commit to you to do. So tonight let us resolve to build that bridge to the twenty-first century, to meet our challenges, and protect our values. (*New York Times* 1996b)

The Clinton campaign thus crystallized its central theme, variations of which would be pressed through campaign ads, media interviews, stump speeches, news releases, and the campaign Web site. The tightly coordinated, forward-looking message soon overwhelmed the GOP's vision of the past. After the election, Dole's communications director said that his candidate's "instinct . . . from the very beginning . . . was that the one thing critically missing from [his speech] was there was not enough about the future" (Institute of Politics 1997, 127).

The battle of the Republican's past versus the Democrat's future was a head-to-head contest of campaign communications. Throughout 1996, the Dole camp struggled to synchronize a disparate collection of messages. They never seemed to come together. Before the convention, Senator Dole, a longtime deficit hawk, chose as his running mate former congressman Jack Kemp, a strong advocate of business tax breaks. The days leading up to their formal nomination were therefore filled with questions as to how the two men would work together. After the convention, Dole–Kemp campaign events looked amateurish. Colors clashed, backdrops failed to convey the appropriate message, and Dole operatives always seemed to be putting too many white male elected officials in the picture. Some White House staffers thought, only half in jest, that it made the whole business of campaign communications look bad.

The haphazard nature of Dole–Kemp message coordination is particularly interesting when one considers that Republicans invented new-style communications strategy. Dwight D. Eisenhower had aired the first television commercial used in a presidential election. While Richard Nixon did not pay close attention to television in 1960—John F. Kennedy's win is often attributed to his performance in the televised debates—the 1968 Nixon team made the first comprehensive use of television marketing professionals. The defining presidency was Ronald Reagan's. One of Reagan's advisers, Michael Deaver, figured out that the medium truly does define the message—and even more importantly, "the message" is conveyed by "the picture." Deaver implemented a communications strategy that made imagery the primary focus of event planning. Deaver understood that "unless you can find a visual that explains your message you can't make it stick" (1987, 141). Because Reagan "knew exactly what he was and where he was going," Deaver has said, the image-maker's task was merely to "draw the image around that, so that the public could see it clearly" (Hines 1992).

The idea goes to the heart of campaign communications. While scholars may disparage George Bush Sr.'s decision to hold a campaign event at a New Jersey flag factory, thinking the message shallow politics, the event was reported faithfully by the news media. It was a powerful image: the vice president draped in patriotic symbolism. Furthermore, the imagery was not necessarily misleading. By appearing at a flag factory, Bush aligned himself with traditional patriotism, setting himself apart from the more civil libertarian views of his opponent, Massachusetts governor Michael Dukakis. The imagery even had power in the policy arena. When the Supreme Court handed down a decision allowing protesters to burn the American flag, President Bush had no wiggle room. Having used the flag so prominently in his campaign, he could not have backed away from its protection even if he had wanted to do so. The dangers of such symbolism can be seen in Bush's appearance at Boston Harbor, a polluted body of water that mocked Dukakis' environmental record. The assault on Dukakis was helpful in 1988—Bush became "the Environmental Candidate"—but four years later, with a meager record on environmental issues, the message came back to haunt the president. In 1992 the only people who called Bush "the Environmental President" were derisive Democrats.

Political communication is a complex endeavor. Armchair analysts sometimes think that it is all about money and message—and it *is* about these things—but it is about much else. Communications directors must know the fine points of television (broadcast and cable), radio, print, and new media (primarily the Internet). They need to appreciate the tactical differences between paid media (advertising) and earned media (news coverage)—how to buy one and how to attract the other. They must also be able to orchestrate all these media into a coherent, strategic unit. This chapter discusses some of the general strategies that campaigns use to maximize the power of their message, the fundamentals of media strategy, the differences among the various types of paid media, and the resources that campaigns use to find the media appropriate to their constituencies. News coverage, which often runs counter to a campaign's strategy, is examined more fully in Chapter 11.

MEDIA STRATEGY

Renowned scholar Marshall McLuhan popularized the idea that "the medium is the message" (1964). McLuhan intended this maxim as a critique of a culture that venerates televisions and computers. The written word and its culture would soon give way to more compressed informational structures and these structures were creating a new culture. Whether the shift is good or bad, it is deeply felt. Print journalists say television offers less information, while television reporters note that a picture is worth a 1,000 words. At any rate, research shows that people are more likely to believe what they see on television than what they read in the papers—and in a surprising twist, they are even more likely to believe a news outlet's Web site than the broadcast version of the same information (Pew Research Center 2000). If the choice of medium in any way circumscribes the message that it will convey, then political professionals working in an intensely competitive environment must pay heed to the nuances of the various media. Professionals must, in short, know how each medium works and how these media can be made to work together.

Coordination is crucial. The overall image of the candidate is created largely by the general strategy of campaign media. If the media do not mesh, then voters will not know where the candidate stands on the issues. Will the electorate see this as a reflection on its own inability to understand public affairs? More likely, the conclusion will be that the candidate does not really stand for anything. To build a coherent image, a campaign must commit itself to consistency, efficiency, proper timing, effective packaging, and a well-played expectations game.

Consistency. Media consultants seek "message discipline"—trying to stay "on message" and never getting "off message." During Campaign 2000, George W. Bush kept the focus on "leadership." Whether the specific issue was foreign policy, the domestic economy, or the need to change the education system, leadership always held center stage. Likewise, Bush's main rival in the primaries, Senator John McCain, also held a singular theme. For him it was good government. The failings of the political system—high taxes, irrational policy, and so forth—could all be tied back to special interests that had an unduly large role in funding American elections. Proof of McCain's determination could be found in his dogged fight on behalf of the McCain–Feingold campaign finance reform bill. While pundits often criticized Bush for his relative lack of leadership experience and McCain for accepting funds that would not be allowed under his legislation, both campaigns hammered home the central message of their respective campaigns over and over again.

Consistency is demanding. A campaign's theme must be communicated up and down the chain of command. Typically, only designated staffers speak for the campaign—the candidate, the campaign manager, and the press secretary or communications director. In the ordinary course of business, consultants are expected to stay out of sight. The campaign theme must also be consistent with the candidate's past record. One function of opposition research is to locate discrepancies between a candidate's actions on the job and words on the campaign trail. A candidate who says one thing and does another courts misfortune—even if the statement fits with the campaign theme. Finally, the theme must be reasonably consistent with the views and actions of a candidate's supporters. Staffers and contributors who may have once worked against the candidate's current policy proposals can become an unwanted part of a news story. Ironically, however, if the staff and contributors are *too* consistent with the candidate's beliefs—if, for example, the candidate's platform is friendly to major donors—then conflicts of interest may be charged. Once again, politics is not an easy game.

Simple consistency is not a sufficient strategy in itself. Two of the most unswerving presidential candidates in recent years have suffered the consequences of unshakable regularity—Senator Tom Harkin of Iowa and publisher Steve Forbes, son of the founder of *Forbes* magazine. Forbes made his name in politics by pushing for a flat tax in 1996 and 2000, making the case time and again that his proposal would be equitable for the taxpayers and profitable to the economy. The problem was that Forbes could not talk about much else, and using the same phrases over and over, he was criticized as a "one-note-Johnny" (Tuttle 1996, 3). Much the same problem bedeviled Tom Harkin in 1992. Harkin conveyed a progressive message aimed at unions and other traditional Democratic base groups. He got strong support from these sectors but could not make his case elsewhere. When, in the face of pending defeat, he stuck to his original campaign themes, one political reporter said that Harkin's "solution to the problem [was] to turn up the volume rather than change the tape" (David Yepsen in Kurtz 1992).

Efficiency. Despite complaints that consultants drive up the cost of campaigns, new-style political operatives are known for their efficient use of resources in difficult media environments. They want to eliminate "waste." Consider the problem of a congressional candidate running in Chicago. Credibility demands that the candidate use television advertising—for some people, a campaign is not real until they see it on television—but Chicago stations reach a dozen or more congressional districts, many of them in Indiana and Wisconsin. The viewers who cannot vote in the candidate's congressional district represent wasted media. The job of the campaign professional is to maximize the number of times that persuadable voters can be reached with a campaign pitch, either through paid advertising or through news coverage.

For electronic media, communications specialists think in terms of "reach" and "frequency." Reach is the portion of the viewership that actually receives a given message. The concept is typically bounded by some time frame. For example, a campaign might reach 30 percent of the market in a given week. Frequency, on the other hand, is the number of times that a person is reached. The principal measurement, however, is neither reach nor frequency but a combination of the two, expressed as "gross rating points" (GRPs). GRP is nothing more than reach times frequency. A message that plays three times on a show having an 11.2 percent reach adds up to 33.6 GRPs. These notions offer communications personnel a powerful means of analyzing media efficiency.

Demographics matter. *NYPD Blue* may offer the largest viewership, but it is not necessarily the best audience for every candidate. The show's reach skews toward a cosmopolitan audience aged eighteen to forty-nine. Would *NYPD Blue* be the right show for a campaign that wants to reach older, more socially conservative voters? The better approach might be to place ads on reruns of *Matlock*—a much smaller audience but a much more efficient media buy. Moreover, the demographic of *NYPD Blue* tends to represent good consumers. The classic young, upwardly-mobile professional likes the show, spends a great deal of money on high-priced consumer goods, and is therefore popular with product advertisers. The cost of advertising on a show like *NYPD Blue* rises and falls according to the spending habits of its viewers and the efficiency of its targeting. This audience is expensive to reach. For the same reason, some programs with a small audience can be worth the money. MTV's audience is not large, but it is valuable to some advertisers because it skews toward a narrow, youth-based demographic. If people of all ages watched MTV, its audience would be valued less—even if it attracted more people—because fewer advertisers would be interested in a scattershot viewership.

As a rule of thumb, a political campaign thinks not in terms of simple GRPs but in terms of the cost-per-point (CPP) of persuadable voters. Everything outside the district is waste. Everything outside the targeted demographics is inefficiency. The more precisely that a campaign can aim its message at targeted voters, and the more options that it has for reaching them cost-effectively, the more efficiently the campaign can spend its money.

Note that these considerations are relevant for news coverage as well as paid advertising and for print as well as electronic media. Ads consume campaign cash whereas news coverage consumes the precious time of the candidate, staff, and consultants. A congressional candidate in Chicago has to work hard to win a profile piece in the *Chicago Tribune*, and if this widely circulated paper eventually decides to run the story, many of the candidate's new admirers will be Wisconsin voters. Additionally, the demographics may be all wrong. For some campaigns, an interview with a reporter from *Crain's Chicago Business* would be a far more efficient use of a candidate's time. More likely, however, the best investment would be a neighborhood weekly, which might reach targeted voters more efficiently.

Dealing with the press is a profession of its own. Likewise, the purchasing of media time and space is so complicated that most midlevel and some lower-level campaigns delegate media strategy to outside consultants. Where advertising is concerned, many of these consultants subcontract the purchasing of ads to professional ad buyers who take a negotiable commission of about 15 percent on every dollar spent. The cost of expertise is presumably recouped in the efficiency gains of carefully targeted ad purchases.

Timing. Part of the efficiency equation is the timing of the message. A standard sequence for a challenger campaign might be to establish the candidate in the public mind by doing a series of press interviews combined with "establishment" ads—those designed to let viewers know who the candidate is in the broadest terms. Once a positive impression of the candidate is created, the campaign might build credibility with a series of "issue" ads, laying out the high points of a candidate's agenda. If the incumbent starts to respond, the challenger might return fire with "attack" ads. At the end of the campaign, it is the responsibility of the campaign strategists to decide whether the challenger should go negative, go positive, or stay the course. Incumbents might follow roughly the same pattern, but they start off with better name identification, so they may not have to get into the business of establishment ads. Incumbents must, however, decide whether they want to strike back at a challenger who attacks their record.

Timing is important to message development for another reason. Ad buys and news coverage require advance planning. Reporters do not sit down with a candidate at a moment's notice—relationships take time to build. Moreover, an opponent who enjoys a long-standing association with a reporter might have been subtly dropping insinuations about the candidate since the beginning of the campaign year. If the challenger waits too long, there may be no way to erase the bad impression that has been built over time. With paid electronic media, the problem is far more acute. Buying ad space in a newspaper is a simple matter of phoning the advertising department and requesting display space. Electronic media, on the other hand, is a scarce resource. Only a fixed number of radio and television spots are available during the course of a race. Timing becomes critical. A campaign must make early determinations about how much money it will be able to raise and when it will be able to get the cash in hand. A campaign's income and outflow must match an odd quirk in the tactics of ad buying: the last days have to be purchased first. Because every campaign wants to grab the last few days before the election, a campaign that waits until a month before Election Day to buy the final slots will likely walk away empty-handed—another reason for raising early money!

Packaging and Effectiveness. A voter who always votes Republican need only be informed that the candidate is a member of the GOP. Signs, radio ads, endorsements, and television spots might make the candidate's party affiliation explicit: "Senator Jones: Republican for U.S. Senate." Sometimes, however, the cues must be more subtle. As partisanship fades and complex policy issues take hold in American elections, the skillful use of metaphor can help a campaign make its case.

In the 1980s, there were few issues facing national politics more difficult than the nuclear standoff between the United States and the Soviet Union. Between Democrats and Republicans, the question was whether the appropriate strategy was a buildup, a freeze, or a drawdown. President Reagan stood firmly with those who sought to increase U.S. nuclear superiority. The 1984 Reagan team needed a way to make its case in simple terms. The campaign used a well-constructed metaphor. A Native American faced a "bear in the woods." Noting that there was disagreement as to whether the bear is dangerous, the well-armed hunter forced the bear to literally back away. The message was clear: "[T]he best way to avoid a military confrontation with the Soviets was for America to be stronger than [its] Cold War rival" (Weaver 1996, 204).

Campaign ads fall into three general categories: positive, comparative, and negative. Advertising designed to establish a candidate's credentials and to lay out a policy agenda are usually positive in nature. The Reagan ad is a good example, but there are others. In a 1998 Georgia race Republican Dylan Glenn was trying to become the first black Republican congressman from the South since Reconstruction. To introduce himself, he ran a biographical sketch—"From Georgia; for Georgia." Comparative ads lay out differences between the candidates. In the 1998 Ohio race between Congressman Ted Strickland and Lieutenant Governor Nancy Hollister, one thirty-second ad was literally split in half. It began with a harsh attack on Hollister's record ("41% Income Tax Increase"), complete with black-and-white imagery and a discordant musical score, and then in midcommercial, the music lifted, the colors flowed, and the ad turned decidedly positive ("Ted Strickland is working to cut taxes"). Across the Ohio River in Kentucky, the 1998 Senate campaign of Republican congressman Jim Bunning included a fiercely negative ad against his opponent, Scotty Baesler. Baesler was shown shouting into the microphone at a campaign rally, to which was added Richard Wagner's "The Ride of the Valkyries," a score often associated with Nazism. According to scholars who followed the election, this ad and related attacks "would help propel the race into one of the nastiest in the nation" (Gross and Miller 2000, 190).

Skeptics would be forgiven for believing that the increasing use of media in American campaigns stems, in part, from the fact that ad buyers and consultants receive a percentage of the ad buys. George Stephanopoulos, discussing the huge sums that Dick Morris made from the 1995–1996 campaign cycle, said, "It's inarguable that there's a conflict of interest. . . . That doesn't mean it was bad advice, but it certainly wasn't disinterested advice" (Harris 1998). Some consultants advise that campaign polling be kept institutionally separate from the purchasing of campaign ads. At least one pollster believes that those in his profession can serve as "independent auditors," making sure that the candidate knows how well the media efforts are working (Friedenberg 1997, 56).

Expectations. An important element of communications strategy is something that political professionals call the "expectations game." "News" is that which is new, and if a front-running candidate wins, then there is not much new news. If, however, a dark-horse candidate comes in a close second, then there *is* real news—though not the type that the actual victor desired.

George W. Bush suffered from inflated expectations in early Campaign 2000. Through most of 1999, Bush was the presumptive winner of the next year's primaries. As such, he had nowhere to go but down. When Steve Forbes ran just eleven points behind Bush in Iowa, and John McCain won New Hampshire by 19 percent, virtually all attention shifted to Forbes and McCain. The question was whether the front-runner had hit a roadblock. More realistic observers saw that neither Forbes nor McCain had sufficient money and organization to win. Forbes had no genuine organization outside of Iowa. McCain had some people beyond New Hampshire but nothing to rival Bush's national web of establishment Republicans and certainly nothing to compare with Bush's ability to raise money. Yet, operatives for Bush's nationwide campaign—ahead in virtually all of the post-New Hampshire states—were forced to call supporters with reassurances that Bush still had good prospects.

The expectations game demonstrates the relative nature of news. The question is not, Did Bush win Iowa? but rather, Did Bush win Iowa by the number of votes anticipated? Critics say that the outcome is all that counts, but it is not clear that the failure to meet expectations does not signify underlying truths. Even though Forbes had little hope of eventual victory, his strength in Iowa exposed weakness in the Bush camp. His advocacy of the flat tax had forced Bush to respond with his own tax cut plan. Forbes' effort *was* news. But the deeper meaning of the story is that political campaigns must work in an environment where success is a comparative quantity. Perception becomes reality. Campaigns must therefore do their best to control expectations.

There is a fairly routine cycle to the effort. At the beginning of a campaign, a challenger wants to give the impression that victory is possible, hoping to get at least minimal coverage. An incumbent, on the other hand, wants to show that victory is inevitable, hoping to scare off challengers. Once a competitive election begins, both sides want to show that the race is close. To make sure that voters go out to the polls, front-running candidates highlight the possibility of a loss so that their supporters do not just sit out the election. Even an incumbent with a commanding lead tells supporters on Election Eve that the race is not yet won, that there is still plenty of work to do. It is a message that wise campaigns press through news coverage and paid campaign advertising.

PAID MEDIA

The unique value of paid media is that it gives campaigns the ability to control their message. Unlike news coverage, which puts a reporter between the campaign and the public, paid media allows campaign operatives to script the message, target the audience, and, for the most part, to select the timing that best suits the needs of the campaign. The downside is that paid media costs money (by definition). Television ads can run tens of thousands of dollars. Even a small display ad in a college newspaper can cost hundreds. The costs of paid media can be staggering. According to congressional scholar Paul Herrnson, "Hopeful challengers committed an average of $410,000 to campaign communications" (2000, 230). Campaigns must be efficient in their targeting, and they must choose the right medium for their message.

Communications consultant Craig Shirley says, "When I first began doing public relations in Washington back in the '70s, media options were the large city daily newspapers, the secondary city newspapers, the wires, the three networks, some radio . . . and the local affiliates" (1997, 22). Campaigns in the new millennium have a wider variety of options, from new broadcast channels, to cable systems, to Internet media. Each has its own advantages. Cable allows for narrow targeting. Broadcast television and radio have wide reach and are required to sell ad time to candidates at bargain prices. Newspapers, while losing market share, are doing their best to remain competitive by offering deep discounts. Campaign Web sites, unknown before 1996, are becoming a critical means of voter outreach.

Television

Television is a powerful medium. Combining audio with visual imagery, it absorbs its viewers in ways that radio and print cannot. Joe McGinniss wrote more than three decades ago that television was "[s]omething new, murky, undefined," that "[t]he mystique which should fade grows stronger. We make celebrities not only of the men who cause events but of the men who read reports of them out loud" (1969, 28). Why? Because television makes its images more "real" than do any of its competitors. Thus, "The medium is the massage and the masseur gets the votes" (29). Most political consultants would agree.

Production costs are high, to be sure. Assembling a television spot requires the assistance of a producer, photographer, assorted gaffers, and a postproduction house to edit the raw footage. An independent filmmaker forewarns campaign consultants, "In the quick turnaround, high-pressure world of media production, there are few situations where margins of error are smaller, time crunches more acute and smooth sailing more essential than in the production of political ads" (Arnold 1999, 62). The process is complicated, taking time that campaigns cannot spare. Campaigns that shoot on film, which is strongly preferred over video, need to factor in the hours, or even days, required to develop film stock. The competitive nature of politics puts a premium on speed, and television is the slowest and most expensive of the media to produce. It is cumbersome and resistant to real-time changes, but no campaign turns down the opportunity to use television ads if it has the money to do so.

Communications scholar Robert Friedenberg notes that consultants see 300 to 500 GRPs as the minimum threshold for going on television (1997, 174). Because each GRP represents a percentage of potential audience tuned in at any given time, 300 gross rating points means that, theoretically, everyone saw the campaign ad three times. With GRPs priced into the thousands of dollars, the costs add up quickly, and consultants are upping the ante. After the 1996 elections, when the television marketplace was crowded with political ads, recommendations started to exceed the 1,000-point boundary (1997, 175). One consultant whom Friedenberg interviewed said that "he would like to see every voter exposed to his ads 10–14 times or more, to help account for the problems inherent in the new media environment of the 1990s" (175). This kind of advice might well be contributing to the upward spiral in the cost of campaigns.

Broadcast Television. The most familiar means of receiving television is via broadcast. In the mid-1970s, it was practically the only way to see a television program, but with the rise of cable in the 1980s and 1990s, broadcast lost a significant share of the video audience. Videocassette recorders, digital video players, and video game systems reduced the broadcast television audience further still. Furthermore, the increasing number of channels available to the viewer—especially those who watch network broadcast television on cable television systems—means that there is a greater tendency for people to "zap" commercials, including political spots. Nonetheless, broadcast television continues to be the mainstay of larger, new-style campaigns.

The reason is reach. A campaign can send a powerful message to wide swaths of the electorate with a single ad buy. While broadcast has lost audience to the cable companies, it remains the dominant video medium. Many homes are not wired for cable. This fact causes a problem for consultants who think about skipping broadcast television. As noted by one media specialist, "To be successful, we must obtain a market share of 50 percent plus one of the potential pool of political customers. This fact requires us to be mass marketers. We want market share, not unit sales" (Hutchens 1996, 42). Especially for candidates who must reach lower-income voters, broadcast remains a powerful medium.

There is another advantage to broadcast television. Because it is regulated by the Federal Communications Commission as a public resource and because the FCC's mission is to render broadcasting friendly to political discourse, federal candidates have a legal right to buy ad time at discount rates. Prior to 1992, there was some question as to whether nonfederal candidates were entitled to the low rate, but the FCC determined that they were not. Even for federal candidates, there is a catch. Low-cost purchases provide no guarantee of placement. If a candidate buys a spot at a certain time using anything less than the higher "non-preemptable rate," another of the broadcaster's clients can pay top dollar to bump the candidate's ad from its time slot. To use low rates well, ad buyers must pay attention to day-to-day fluctuations in the broadcast marketplace.

Close monitoring is possible because candidate ad-buy records are public by law. Everyone has a right to view up-to-the-minute reports and to make copies for a reasonable fee. Researchers who look at the files find everything from purchase orders and canceled checks to scribbled notes of phone conversations. If a campaign is making a heavy ad buy on daytime soaps early in the electoral cycle, all the paperwork related to the acquisition, right down to the specific time slot sought, is supposed to show up in the file. What the researcher does not find, however, is documentation as to whether the buy went through. Was the requested spot actually run at the date and time ordered? Or was it bumped by a higher-paying customer? The answer might be inferred by totaling up invoices, but inferential measurements in lieu of after-the-fact affidavits are mere approximations. In addition, the station rep and the ad buyer might rearrange time slots over the phone, leaving no paper trail. Furthermore, not all stations fully understand or comply with the rules. It is not uncommon to find that a media outlet has not kept its records current. The researcher may end up waiting at the reception desk while the designated file keeper assembles the data as best as possible on short notice. Finally, there are varying interpretations of the law. Some stations classify issue advocacy ads by outside groups as being subject to disclosure, while others do not, and short of a legal battle it is not always clear that the matter can be resolved.

In the Digital Age, some campaigns might wish to avoid manual records searches. Fee-based ad detection systems claim to track television spots by their audio signature (Friedenberg 1997, 180–83), but even if the system works well, its use is expensive and alerts the campaign only after the opposition's ads were run. It is important to trace the station's sales ahead of time. Despite the incompleteness of public records, weekly or daily trips to broadcast stations can serve as a distant early warning system. A campaign that buys early has tipped its hand. Its strategy is out in the open. An additional reason to watch the opposition's ad buys in advance is to monitor broadcasters' compliance with the Equal Time Rule. Broadcasters are not required to sell time to candidates, but if they choose to sell to one candidate, they must offer time to everyone in the race. Keeping a close eye on public records can let a campaign know when it should jump into the market.

The trend that grew in the 1990s was early ad play. Congresswoman Nancy Johnson, a Connecticut Republican who nearly lost her seat in 1996, made a strong comeback in 1998 by running spots that might be termed "reestablishment ads." Her media consultants describe the overall strategy as follows: "[I]t was decided that she needed to 'reconnect' with voters, and make them remember what they liked about her in the first place" (Weitzner and Geller 1999, 56). Instead of waiting until the fall of the election, Johnson ran her spots early, before the rates went up, so that by Labor Day she had already done the heavy lifting. She targeted voters concerned with "health care, education and taxes," talking about the issues in terms of policy, not partisanship. "When Johnson's opponent tried to run negative ads against her, the attacks weren't credible—voters were familiar with her record" (56). By seeking out her best demographics, maximizing efficiency, and playing her cards strategically, Johnson was able to stay in the game.

Cable Television. Broadcast television reaches the largest audience, while cable television targets the most specific selection of voters. At the turn of the twenty-first century, 80 percent of homes in the United States were wired for cable, providing ad buyers with a whole new category of paid media. On one hand, there is no difference between broadcast and cable advertising. Viewers watching a major-network television show transmitted via cable might be unable to distinguish between ads run by the network and those inserted by the local cable company. On the other hand, the ability to run ads in a single cable market fundamentally changes the tactics of video ad placement. Cable offers narrowly defined markets. Local cable companies have fixed borders—towns, cities, counties, and other municipal entities—and these boundaries are contiguous with many electoral districts. Waste is minimized. Moreover, because cable offers dozens of channels, cable channels and networks are forced to "narrowcast" their programming. That is, the History Channel, A&E, BET, and MTV each seeks its own slice of the pie. Candidates have started to work their way into Spanish-language networks like Telemundo. As if to emphasize the tremendous ability of cable to segment a political marketplace, some campaigns have even found it profitable to run different ads in different locales within a single electoral district.

The benefits of cable are not without cost. First, the cable audience tends to be highly desirable to product marketers. Cable is a fee-based system, so the demographics of the cable viewership skew up the economic scale. While it has been reported that cable customers vote more regularly than broadcast viewers (Friedenberg 1997, 184–85), campaigns that wish to target these voters are competing with powerful economic interests. Hence, to those who think cable is less expensive than broadcast, media consultant Jon Hutchens replies, "Not on a cost-per-voter-impression basis, not by a long shot" (1996, 42). Second, the cable marketplace is decentralized. Because there are more than 10,000 cable companies across the country, buying cable ads can be a tough job. Media buyers often feel compelled to use the services of "spot reps" to facilitate the acquisition of ad time in more than one market. Finally, as noted earlier, there is some question as to whether an all-cable strategy is politically wise. Cable penetration is deep, but it is not total. Says Hutchens, "Excluding any significant-sized audience from receiving your communications only invites peril" (42). Broadcast and cable are each important in their own way.

The distinctive value of cable is revealed by Hutchens' own experience. In 1992 Hutchens was working for Democratic congressman Jim Bacchus, whose redrawn district made for a precarious reelection cycle. To lift its prospects, Bacchus' people targeted a small area of his Florida district, Indian River County, that had not been with the congressman in the past but that seemed to offer a fair amount of opportunity. Writes Hutchens, "[I]n addition to direct mail, we bought heavily on Indian River cable (25 spots per day on all available networks) and supplemented our reach with local, non-metro radio" (1996, 43). On Election Day, "The additional vote out of Indian River County made the difference in what turned out to be a very close race" (43).

Changes in the cable industry are helping to make it more competitive with broadcast. Two of the most important trends are that (1) cable penetration has continued to increase, while network market share has decreased, and (2) cable company mergers and the rise of cable "interconnects" have eased the problems of purchasing cable in several markets at once. As local cable companies are absorbed into larger systems, billing and invoicing are centralized. Where the companies remain separate, some cable systems share digital interconnects that allow ad buyers to run a spot on several systems at once. The advantage to a campaign is paperwork efficiency: a single phone call can request ad time on several cable systems, and at the end of the process the campaign receives just one bill. For a political campaign, which must operate on speed while ensuring compliance with campaign finance laws, any decrease in complexity is appreciated.

Radio

Radio obviously lacks the visual element of television, but in some ways it offers the best of broadcast combined with the best of cable. Like broadcast, it has a powerful reach, and it follows the same discount rules as broadcast television. Like cable, it can be used for precision targeting and constant repetition. For example, talk radio attracts a decidedly more conservative audience than pop stations. A radio-based strategy is therefore low-cost, allowing a campaign to buy a great deal of time. Moreover, fast production means that radio is suitable for rapid response. Campaigns can react to events in a matter of hours. In an interesting tactical twist, a radio-based strategy helps a campaign "fly under the radar," escaping the sorts of "ad watch" scrutiny that sometimes makes negative advertising difficult. As Friedenberg points out, "Generally, radio ads are not taped, nor are the transcripts of them closely analyzed by the press" (1997, 143).

An interesting aspect of radio is that consultants tend to talk about its "intimacy." It is not the words alone that make radio intimate; "[Radio's] impact is significant because the images it conveys exist in the listener's minds" (Sweitzer and Heller 1996, 40). Radio imagery can be seen in a pair of radio ads that the Senate campaign of John Warner produced for the 1996 elections. The *Washington Post* described the predicament that Warner faced in the GOP primary: "[H]e must drive up turnout dramatically. He hopes to do that with an aggressive media blitz aimed at mobilizing women, moderates, and especially Northern Virginians, while giving reason to doubt his rival's credentials as a true believer" (Baker 1996). Evidently in an effort to tweak the demographics, "Warner aired a radio commercial featuring a male voice assailing his Republican primary opponent for masquerading as a conservative. It ran just once before being taken off the air. A few days later, it resurfaced—but this time with a woman's voice" (1996). The Warner campaign, it seems, wanted to paint a more feminine picture in the mind of the radio audience.

Newspapers

Newspapers, once the primary means for propagating partisan ideas, have lost a great deal of market share. Fewer people are reading newspapers, and less money is spent advertising in them. There are, however, a few reasons that newspaper ads remain part of new-style campaigns. First, ad space is always available. Whereas television and radio are scarce commodities, newspapers can always find space for display ads—even if they have to add a few pages to accommodate an end-of-the-campaign advertising blitz. Second, newspapers are responding to market pressures by segmenting their markets. High-tech printing operations allow for geographic variations in advertising content, whereby each suburb in a metropolitan area might receive its own set of display ads. Finally, there is a fear factor at play. Many political operatives believe that failure to buy newspaper ad space can lose a campaign its rightful endorsement and might even creep into decisions about news reporting. It is an economic pressure that is presumed to work both ways. One former elected official recommends the following to candidates in local races: if a paper never runs with a campaign's news release, "threaten to cancel [campaign] ads and ask for your money back. The editors will hate me for telling you this, but for a small paper on a tight budget, this is an effective technique for your campaign" (Grey 1999, 182).

New Media

Newspapers are old media; campaign Web sites are new media. In the mid-1980s such resources did not exist, but now a presence on the World Wide Web is considered essential to campaigns at almost all levels. A candidate without a Web site seems to lack seriousness. A candidate with a disheveled site gives the impression of having a disorganized campaign. A visually attractive, user-friendly Web site that offers an abundance of informational content—one study showed that visitors spend the most time with "issue sections, candidate biographies and comparative sections" (Hockaday and Edlund 1999, 14)—can help deepen voters' impression of the candidate. During Campaign 2000, it became common for campaign Web sites to post news releases, calendars of upcoming events, and even streaming video and audio, showcasing the ads being run through more traditional media. Until the next advance in communications technology takes hold, well-built Web sites will be an integral part of campaign advertising.

Most Web sites offered during Campaign 2000 had a professional look and feel. They offered policy records and comparisons with the opposition and made personal appeals—and they did so with much stronger graphics than in years past. During the 1996 cycle, the reason to have a campaign Web site might have been to avoid newspaper stories about the lack of a Web presence. In the new millennium, when far more people have access to the Internet and when campaign Web sites offer a wealth of information about candidates, the new wisdom is that the Web can offer a strong foundation for campaign communications.

The difficulty with campaign Web sites is that people must make a conscious effort to travel to the site. Radio and television reach all the listeners and viewers who do not zap the ad. They are "opt-out" media. The Web, however, is an "opt-in" medium, meaning that some sort of off-site market is necessary to bring a substantial surfer-base or user-base to a Web site. Media consultant Mike Connell points out that the Web can serve as an extension to broadcast media. Campaigns try to purchase "30-second spots in which the candidate must explain to all the electorate who they are, what they have done, their vision for the future and why they are the best candidate. But put the campaign's Web site address on the advertisement and suddenly you've given the electorate access to complete, in-depth information on the candidate" (Connell 2000, 58). Donald Dunn, running for Congress in 2000, "ran a list of [Utahns] who are owed money from their 1998 tax returns on his Web site." It proved to be a smart strategy: "The Dunn campaign then held a press conference announcing that they would be posting the names, after which the Web site had nearly 20,000 hits" (Jalonick 2000b, 62).

Another strategy is the political use of "banner ads." The digital version of newspaper display ads, these banners are the small advertisements that most Web surfers know from the top of major search engines and online directories such as Yahoo! and Lycos. In 1998, New York City Council speaker Peter Vallone used banner ads in his bid for the New York governorship. Banners are similar to traditional voter contact media in that they build name identification, but "[w]hen a user clicks on your banner ad (called a 'click through'), they immediately leave the site they were on and move to your site" (Hockaday and Edlund 1999, 14). Furthermore, "[c]lick-through rates on banner ads are comparable to direct mail prospecting rates, and there is strong evidence that voters who visit campaign Web sites make good use of the resources available" (14). One consultant notes the specificity with which banner ads can be placed: "Current local ad-targeting capabilities by national newspapers such as *The New York Times* and *USA Today* mean they can now be included in your media plan. Each site has different targeting abilities. Some target by market, others by state, ZIP code or phone number prefix. National TV and cable sites (such as MSNBC.com and CNN.com) can, in most cases, be bought by state or market" (Mentzer 2000, 69). By reaching out to other sites and even other media—both paid and earned—a campaign can increase traffic and broaden the reach of its strategic communications.

FINDING THE MEDIA

Finding media outlets requires careful research. Take, for example, the search for print media. While just about everyone knows the major papers in a big city, a number of smaller publications might go unnoticed. With geographically large districts, such as rural congressional districts, just getting a handle on the television stations that serve the electorate can become a chore. Media advisers must inventory the outlets that serve a district—not just those that are published in the district but all those that reach the district's voters. The principal resources are Editor and Publisher's *International Year Book, The Gale Directory of Publications and Broadcast Media, SRDS TV & Cable Source, Broadcasting & Cable Yearbook,* and *SRDS Radio Advertising Source.*

The *International Year Book* lists publications from major daily papers down to shopping guides. A researcher studying the Miami Beach market will find a handful of major newspapers serving the metropolitan area, including the *Miami Herald* (in the "Dailies" volume) and the Spanish-language *el Nuevo Herald* (listed in the "Hispanic Newspapers" section). For each paper, the *Year Book* lists circulation, advertising rates, special editions, special weekly sections, and the newspaper's magazine. In addition, technical specifications—ranging from the width of a paper's columns to the types of software and printers in use—help a media consultant plan the details of an ad buy. To find smaller papers, the researcher looks to the "U.S. Shoppers" section of the *Year Book*, or to the *Gale Directory*. There one finds that Miami Beach has the *SunPost,* affiliated with the Post Newspaper Group. Contacts and ad rates are supplied. Even with all these resources, a prudent operative will actually travel the district to see what publications are sold at the newsstands and offered at the local libraries. Looking at the news boxes on the sidewalks makes clear that the *Miami New Times* and *Street,* both of which focus heavily on Miami's nightclub scene, are widely read in the South Beach area.

Also in the *Gale Directory* are broadcast media. Returning to the Miami Beach example, one finds that there is a 1,000-watt gospel radio station, WMBM. Of course, those who live in Miami Beach are likely to be listening to stations aired from the city of Miami, a few miles away. A researcher should therefore look at the whole media market. These stations can be found in the *Gale Directory, Broadcasting & Cable Yearbook,* or the *SRDS Radio Advertising Source. SRDS* divides the state of Florida into markets. Miami Beach lies in the "Miami–Fort Lauderdale–Hollywood" market. In the section devoted to this region, the researcher learns about a variety of radio stations, including WLYF, a 100,000 watt "adult contemporary" station licensed out of Miami. It has women aged thirty-five to forty-four years as its primary audience and men and women aged twenty-four to fifty-four as its secondary audience. The *SRDS TV & CABLE SOURCE* shows WAMI-TV in the Miami–Fort Lauderdale market. In fact, the station is located in the heart of Miami Beach's historic Art Deco district. Through careful investigation, political researchers can efficiently pinpoint media outlets appropriate to campaign marketing.

Television resource information is structured in much the same way. Using the *SRDS TV & Cable Source*, to look at Miami Beach once again, it appears that the Miami–Fort Lauderdale market is served by a number of broadcast stations, WFOR among them. This station is shown to be a CBS affiliate out of Miami. In addition, one finds that cable spots in Miami Beach zip codes are handled by TCI Cable Advertising of Miami. With a little investigation, the astute researcher can map out a rigorous media strategy.

CONCLUSION

The point of such research is purely strategic. Media buying has as its primary goal the purchasing of spots and ad space that will most likely move the candidate closer to electoral victory. The business of paid advertising—the most controllable form of voter contact—becomes unpredictable as soon as the opposition candidate enters the fray. Charges are followed by countercharges as each campaign seeks to push the other side off-message. To reinforce its own themes, a campaign must use all available means of reaching the voters, including news coverage, in the quest for an integrated series of campaign messages.

Chapter Eleven

News Coverage

A sizable war chest, a strong message, and a smart strategy each help a campaign present its candidate in a positive light. Paid media offers nearly complete control over the timing, audience, and message, but few campaigns have unlimited funds, and while news coverage is not truly free, it can be significantly less expensive than paid advertisements. The most important benefit of news coverage, however, is its credibility (Salmore and Salmore 1989; Herrnson 2000). The message is coming from a seemingly neutral observer. It also comes within a context—on the television news, in the newspaper, or during a radio news segment—where people are thinking about politics. In other words, the news media reach people when they are in the market for political information. Getting into the news is a wise use of a campaign's time. Indeed, a campaign that fails to court reporters may leave the impression that it has something to hide. News coverage is fundamental to campaign strategy.

Political consultants talk about "earned media." The term refers to coverage on television, radio, and in the newspapers. Consultants call it "earned media" rather than "free media" in order to emphasize the hard work that goes into the quest for coverage. Perhaps the only office for which candidates are guaranteed regular news coverage is the presidency—and even then, front-running candidates complain that they are not getting enough attention or that the coverage they are getting is not entirely fair. For years, reporters have objected that politicians try to "manage" the news, even as candidates feel put upon by an unwieldy press. Moreover, while pundits grumble that candidates offer nothing more than "sound bites," the news media continue to run them as real news.

Positive coverage is never assured. When Democrat Bob Graham of Florida decided to run for the U.S. Senate, he planned a large press event to kick off the race— a multicity, satellite-driven extravaganza that unfortunately coincided with the explosion of the *Challenger* space shuttle. During Campaign 2000, George W. Bush was taken aback when an on-air radio personality asked him to name the leaders of various foreign nations, and the candidate's inability to do so raised questions about his knowledge of foreign affairs. Whether the line of questioning was fair or not, the damage was done. As noted by one observer, "If you are brilliant, the media will make you appear even better. If you are foolish, incompetent, indecisive, or wimpy, the media can cripple you" (Phillips 1984, 77).

To understand how campaigns operate, it is important to understand how candidates, consultants, and campaign staff view the media. The press is a blessing and a curse, an opportunity and a danger—a necessary part of the campaign process but one that always looms as a threat. Among political operatives, there is little confidence that the press is "objective" in the sense that it merely reports the facts. Rather, a campaign understands that the news media are forced to pick and choose which facts are going to be reported. To say that a paper contains "All the News That's Fit to Print" merely begs the question, What counts as "news"? Likewise, it is too easy to assert that reporters are generally liberal while editors and publishers are conservative, or that news organizations are just profit-seeking enterprises, or that reporters always base their stories on personal opinion. Political reporting is complicated. This chapter tries to understand news-based campaign strategies by discussing the history of news reporting, with an eye to "newsworthiness," and the tactics that campaigns bring into play.

A SHORT HISTORY OF NEWS REPORTING

A *Gazette* or *Intelligencer* of early America looked nothing like today's *New York Times*. Without a drive for objective, dispassionate reporting, the "news" was unabashedly partisan (Dinkin 1989, 7–9). Newspapers, such as they were, aligned themselves with one side of a debate or the other, and they did so according to the whims of the parties that funded them. In the first half of the 1800s, however, publishers began to understand that people who wanted to read the news might be willing to pay for it. The "penny press" was born. For one cent, readers could get the news of the day along with feature stories to keep things interesting. More readers meant more profit, so there was little reason to restrict a paper's viewpoint to that of one particular party. Thereafter, publishers came to understand that even more money could be made if space was sold for advertising. With the rise of profit-driven "yellow journalism" in the late 1800s—which gave front-page coverage to crime, scandal, and tragedy—newspapers became big business.

The profit motive was not the only force in journalism. In much the same way that broader sales freed newspapers from their partisan roots, the Associated Press (AP), a national wire service, started to release the press from its local, parochial points of view. The AP was formed in 1848 as a cooperative that pooled the resources of New York newspapers. Instead of sending ten reporters to get the news from Europe, the AP could send one. As the AP co-op spread across the United States, reporting on the Civil War and other domestic news, the regional interests of AP reporters gave way to a more national perspective. At the end of the nineteenth century, a backlash against yellow journalism reinforced the idea that "objectivity" should be the guiding principle of journalism. Progressives in the early 1900s hailed the arrival of "muckraking" journalism, which sought corruption in government and greed in the private sector. Advocating a form of reporting that focused on journalistic responsibility, the muckrakers paved the way for the new professional standards—a form of journalism that distinguished "facts" from "analysis" and "editorializing" that is now taught in schools of journalism around the country. A strong ethical framework that would have seemed foreign to the early partisan press had taken hold in American journalism.

The difficulty with the concept of journalistic objectivity is that the meaning of reportable news has fluctuated considerably in the past 100 years. In the first part of the century, politicians were treated with kid gloves. Journalists accepted what they were told and rarely scrutinized the private lives of candidates—leading to a period Larry Sabato aptly labels "lapdog" journalism (Sabato 1991, 25). During the 1960s and 1970s the news industry entered a period of "investigative journalism." Shocked by revelations of governmental misinformation, reporters who covered the Vietnam War and the Nixon administration no longer took for granted the sincerity of politicians. They scrutinized the words and behavior of candidates. Reporters dug to find the dirt, leading some to call this period one of "watchdog journalism" or even "attack dog" journalism. There was a growing interest in the horse race—who is ahead and who is behind—and even the internal workings of campaign operations. In a sense, "the mechanics of campaigning have become a better story than the campaign itself" (Luntz 1988, 33).

Most criticism of the media is reserved for television news. In the early 1900s radio started broadcasting news events, but unlike print outlets, which cover news in depth, radio reporting was exceedingly condensed and required all the day's news to be delivered in a few moments. Radio was criticized for its superficiality. Nevertheless, the medium was given credibility by serious journalists like Edward R. Murrow, whose voice gave urgent, passionate reports from Europe at the outset of World War II. After the war, a number of radio reporters, including Murrow, moved to television news. Television suffered the same time constraints as radio. Indeed, the cost of television production and transmission meant that viewers had limited options: three broadcast networks decided what constituted "the news." Lacking depth, the medium was open to attack by the likes of Marshall McLuhan, Joe McGinniss, and before them, Daniel Boorstin. Boorstin wrote, "Our national politics has become a competition for images or between images, rather than between ideals. The domination of campaigning simply dramatizes this fact" (1964, 249). The news media, Boorstin thought, were full participants in the problem, having allowed themselves to become mesmerized by "pseudoevents" (7–44).

Boorstin's critique can be directed at all news media. Journalists chafe at the idea that their profession is anything less than objective, but objectivity is an elusive ideal. The fact remains: media outlets that go out of business are not able to inform the public, so news content must be able to hold the interest of consumers. Some stories are more interesting in one medium than another. When Republican candidates in 1994 walked in front of the U.S. Capitol to sign the

GOP Contract with America, almost every detail was staged for the television cameras (Tron 1996). Although the story was fed to other media, the event was designed for video. At the same time, complicated stories that involve detailed information work better in print. In the middle of Campaign 2000, the *New York Times* ran an extensive biographical profile on U.S. Senate candidate Rick Lazio, analyzing the congressman's policies, his personality, and his approach to politics. It is difficult to imagine that a drawn-out life history of any non-presidential candidate could have attracted a sufficient television audience to warrant a producer's approval.

Even if publishers did not have to worry about the bottom line, the problem of preconceptions would linger. Reporters cannot help but bring their outlook on the world to bear on their coverage of the news. Reporters work hard to separate political partisanship from news coverage, and they are perhaps more aware of the distinctions between facts and analysis than most. Still, they are forced to make decisions on the credibility of sources and the importance of events. Are politicians, as a class, believable sources of policy information? In the early 1960s the answer was yes, but no longer. Does money corrupt politics? Perhaps. Furthermore, the history of the journalistic profession requires journalists to write stories that are both fair and newsworthy. But what happens when fairness is not newsworthy? Some would argue that, when the news media reported Dan Quayle's mistaken spelling of "potato," they should have made clear that the vice president had been reading from a cue card given to him by a schoolteacher. The event was newsworthy, but was it fair? To the vice president's office, the episode reconfirmed its fear of the "liberal" press. But it is likely that the press thought the vice president's mistake was indicative of larger issues.

COMMUNICATIONS TACTICS

The history of earned media bears directly on communications tactics. For a campaign to bring in media attention, it must understand the needs of the press. Stories must be newsworthy. A campaign-related item must be fresh and it must usually relate to public affairs in a way that is likely to affect the lives of readers, but two caveats are in order. The first is strictly economic. The media marketplace is extremely competitive, with an array of vehicles ranging from newspapers to cable opinion shows to Web sites offering up-to-the-minute news reporting. Without good stories, readers and viewers will not consume the information and advertising dollars will dwindle. Dull pieces are a hard sell to reporters, producers, and editors. Similarly, because every news organization operates on a budget, stories that are expensive to cover will not get much play. A story that would require a television crew to lug its equipment over a mountain pass is far less likely to get covered than one conveniently situated near the television station. The second caveat goes to journalism as a profession. Reporters are trained to uphold standards acquired over a century and a half of professional development, complete with heroes like Bob Woodward and Carl Bernstein, who literally changed history with their reporting of the Watergate break-in and the subsequent cover-up. To be true to their profession, journalists must adopt much of their colleagues' view of newsworthiness, appropriate press scrutiny, and the relative importance of stories. Campaigns that fail to recognize the dual standards of American journalism are unlikely to get the attention of journalists.

The News Release

With a general understanding of journalistic principles, a new-style campaign understands that stories can be marketed to the news media. The campaign operation puts its best foot forward, even if it can never really manage the news. The most important tool for selling a candidate is the news release. Releases are used to issue statements, announce upcoming events, spin breaking news, highlight endorsements, respond to attacks, and provide background facts that help reporters make sense of the race. This form of communication, inexpensive in both production and distribution, plays a central role in any campaign's earned media strategy.

The difficulty is that media outlets receive countless news releases from businesses, organizations, and individuals, not to mention other campaigns. Some are selected, but the vast majority are not. The cardinal rule in release-writing is that one should make the text newsworthy to the editor and informative to the reporter. Few editors wish to have boring, unimportant articles in their papers or on their radio or television news broadcast. Still, puffery is the single most common flaw in news releases (Randolph 1989). Facts are best. To make life easy for reporters, campaigns provide everything that they need to write a positive story. Many find that the best approach is to write the release exactly the way the campaign would wish the news to appear in the paper. Press secretaries are advised to employ the same notation that reporters use, adding, for example, a "###" or a "-30-" to indicate the end of the release (Hewitt 1999, 57).

The reason that campaigns imitate the journalistic style is twofold: (1) it helps to fit the story into the mind-set of a reporter, editor, or broadcast producer, and (2) some smaller newspapers will run the story word for word. Thinking like a reporter, press secretaries will include at least one quote from the candidate or some other pertinent figure (clearly identifying name and title). Usually, the quote will be in the form of a "zinger"—a pithy remark with a powerful message. News releases stand a better chance of unedited publication if they contain a headline, a strong lead sentence, and relevant photographs, particularly when they are written in the journalist's inverted pyramid format—with the most important information at the top and the less important information further down. Many consultants suggest brevity. The shorter the releases are, the more likely that the outlet will find room. Of course, it is also possible that long news releases are more helpful to reporters.

In format, campaign news releases hew to a fixed standard. They are written in the third person, using action verbs as much as possible, relying on facts instead of opinionated generalities. To the greatest extent possible, they are written in simple language. The style of good releases tends to match that of the targeted outlets.

Radio, newspaper editorial pages, and Sunday morning magazines each has its own manner of speaking. Furthermore, candidates must establish credibility with the media so that reporters feel comfortable using their releases. If a campaign maintains accuracy, it will not lose the trust of news organizations. Also, the name and telephone number of a campaign "contact person" are usually noted at the top of each release, as well as the recommended timing of the story. Some stories are "embargoed" for later release. "For immediate release" indicates that the story can be run whenever the editor sees fit.

As to how many releases should be sent, the profession seems divided. Some believe "the more the better," arguing that the campaign can never tell when an outlet will have a slow news day. Every press secretary can point to favorable news stories that followed releases they never expected to see picked up. Frequent releases also keep the election at the forefront of an editor's mind and lets reporters know what is going on in the race. More likely, however, daily releases lead to summary dismissal. Reporters and editors who receive bundles of releases from the same campaign quickly tire of them and assume, perhaps rightly, that the releases contain fluff. The most important releases end up being rejected along with all the rest. Media consultant Steve Snider recalls a time when an opponent was overzealous with his releases, leading a columnist to write about the waste: The releases were used as a scratch pad for the columnist's three-year-old (Snider 1990).

Actualities and Feeds

While radio and television stations also receive news releases, the odds of the message being run are increased dramatically if the candidate goes directly to the station. Many radio news editors appreciate the fact that a candidate went to them, and as a consequence they sometimes feel obliged to provide some airtime. At the very least, the candidate will generally be allowed to give a quick statement to be used at the station's convenience.

This type of contact requires a fair amount of time and trouble. There are easier ways—rather than walk into a studio, a campaign can send clips. To get radio air, a campaign distributes news advisories in advance, allowing for any necessary planning and preparation on the station's part. The press secretary then calls and asks if the campaign can send an "actuality" (also called a "beeper" or an "interface") over the telephone. The actuality will be a short statement from the candidate (just a few seconds, definitely not more than twenty or thirty). The press secretary also provides the reporter with a written account of the information so that the news director has something from which to write the story. Many radio stations use the process heavily because it gives the listener the impression that reporters went into the field to get the story, when in reality the campaign came to them.

There are several ways to provide radio stations with actualities. The simplest is the spoken word. The candidate phones in a quick statement, which is recorded on tape at the station. Although effective, this approach generally yields metallic-sounding audio. Worse, calling all the stations ties up the candidate's schedule. To save time, a candidate might tape a statement, which the press secretary would then use with each radio station, holding the recorder to the telephone so that the station can capture it. But this approach worsens the quality of the transmission. To overcome problems of sound quality, campaigns use "electronic couplers." The candidate's statement is recorded on tape, and the statement is transmitted over telephone lines wired directly to a playback unit. Candidates sound as though they are sitting in the studio. To broadcast a single statement to a large number of radio stations at once, campaigns rely on "actuality machines," which employ digital technology and yield a recording of even greater quality.

For television, the process is much the same, but the technicalities are far more complex, and the costs of satellite time are much higher than telephone charges. To do satellite feeds, studio production must be moved to an uplink station—all of which requires professional assistance. For this reason, many campaigns still rely on "sneaker" connections, running a tape to the station and handing it off.

A masterful use of actualities and video feeds was the distribution of the Contract with America signing. According to Barrie Tron, who built the event, "[W]e produced a multicamera live broadcast" that was distributed to news departments around the country (1996, 51). Writes Tron, the "signal was distributed live, via satellite . . . to every television station around the country. The feed was free and produced as if we were feeding our own network" (51). The whole event, from start to finish, was offered to the media because "[n]ews directors want the most options—especially in the midst of a campaign" (51). For radio, "an audio bridge fed the audio portion of the program, [accessible] via telephone and made available free of charge to radio stations" (52). As a result, the hard work that went into setting up a massive, tightly choreographed event on the Capitol steps paid off with a day's worth of heavy, nationwide coverage. "Demand was so high" for the audio feed, Tron says, "we even scheduled a highlights replay for additional stations" (52).

Mass distribution feeds have become commonplace, and, as such, news directors are beginning to ignore them. As the Internet opens new channels for the distribution of audio and video—both to stations and to the public at large—campaigns must find new ways to distinguish themselves. One strategy is virtual personalization, by which the candidate goes to each station electronically. "Satellite media tours" allow the candidate to reach a large number of stations in a short period of time with each appearance tailored to the individual station. From a single studio, a candidate can be interviewed by one television reporter after another. A media specialist notes that "in one hour you can talk to ten stations, each getting an exclusive interview," and "radio is done in much the same way, only you can be anywhere there is a phone" (Ouzounian 1997, 51).

News Conferences

If the news release is the earned media workhorse, the news conference is the showhorse. News conferences bring reporters into a controlled environment so that the candidate can talk about a significant campaign development. They allow for personal explanations of complex issues or dramatic new developments, as well as an opportunity for the press to ask questions about the matter. Although the odds of coverage are not great for routine political items, many candidates use news conferences to announce their candidacies. News conferences are also used to level attacks against the opponent, defend against charges made against the candidate, introduce new rounds of campaign commercials, announce important endorsements, highlight fund-raising activities, introduce celebrities, and so on.

Deciding whether to cover a conference, assignment editors undertake a cost-benefit calculation. They weigh the merits of getting the story firsthand with the price of sending a reporter into the field to get it. To the campaign press team, this balancing act suggests that the issue to be discussed must be exceptionally important and that it must be easy for the press to cover. When these two conditions are met, most candidates for lower-level offices still have a hard time getting coverage, but without them it is nearly impossible. If reporters do choose to cover a candidate's news conference, chances are better than not that they will run a story—though not always the message that a campaign has in mind.

A waste-of-time news conference is scorned by the media and will, in all probability, be the last one that reporters cover. Campaigns are warned, "If you call a press conference and it ain't news, they might not cover you again" (Shirley 1997, 23). The campaign may even be written off or, worse yet, be ridiculed in the public eye. After all, the campaign wasted precious time; someone has to pay. Before a conference is called, the campaign communications team must be certain that the topic will be found newsworthy. If so, it chooses to proceed, a notice is sent to each outlet, outlining the importance of the issue, where and when the conference will be held, and the name and telephone number of the contact person. Campaigns follow up with a telephone call or even a visit to the assignment editor or reporter. Occasionally, this sort of prodding tips the scales in a campaign's favor. Pushing too hard, however, can have the opposite effect.

The days of the informally prepared news conference are long gone. In new-style campaigns, close attention is paid to the backdrop behind the candidate. Good visuals are a boon to both the candidate and the media—a powerful shot helps the candidate convey the right message while giving an incentive for the media to run the story. Well-prepared campaigns help the shoot go as smoothly as possible. A "mult box" is provided so that several television and radio stations can plug directly into the candidate's microphone. Good angles are established in consultation with camera operators, and the distance between the press stand and satellite trucks will be paced off before the conference so that there are no surprises. A wise press secretary keeps an eye on deadlines. If, for instance, the campaign wishes to make the local 6:00 P.M. news, the event might be held before 3:00 P.M., giving the stations plenty of time for editing. The same logic applies to newspaper deadlines. It is a matter of convenience. Asking reporters to drive an hour out of town is a sure way to minimize press participation. Finally, coverage is assumed to be affected by limited parking and insufficient electrical power, insufficient seating, and the failure to provide room for tape recorders, lights, and cameras.

Media Events

The struggle for media attention has led candidates to walk across states, work blue-collar jobs, sleep among the homeless, serve food at soup kitchens, clean up neighborhoods, visit toxic waste sites, meet with senior citizens, greet workers at a factory gate, and climb into hot air balloons. Creativity is vital. On one occasion, a candidate who was attacked for putting campaign posters on public utility poles called upon the local Boy Scouts and Girl Scouts to help him take them down, offering $1 for every poster—a novel idea. Nearly all the district's media outlets covered the clean-up day. There was little doubt that the few hundred dollars paid to the Scouts was well worth the coverage. Not all press events go as planned. During his 1994 gubernatorial race, George W. Bush participated in an annual ritual, the opening day of dove-hunting season. He invited the press along to take a few pictures. One of the birds that he felled, however, was not a dove, but a protected songbird. Bush received a $130 fine.

What distinguishes a media event from a simple news conference is that the focus of the news conference is the spoken word, whereas the focus of the media event is the action and context. The signing ceremony for the Contract with America was among the best media events of the 1990s. In the 1980s the best events were scripted by White House aide Michael Deaver, who has defined the essence of a quality event by example:

> [W]e were searching for any development that we could showcase to reflect a good trend. A staffer walked into my office one day and said housing starts were up for the first time in five years and we ought to get the president down to the press room to make an announcement.
>
> At such moments, you go with your instinct. This was mine: "No, find me a city with the most dramatic increase in housing starts in America. And get it back to me fast."
>
> The city turned out to be Fort Worth, Texas. I had the president fly to Fort Worth, and he made the announcement at a housing development there, surrounded by a bunch of construction workers in hard hats. (1987, 140–41)

Deaver adds, "My standing joke with Bill Hinkle, the head of the advance team, was: If you can't give me a good visual, give me a big sign" (141).

There is an art to the construction of media events. All the rules for advancing news conferences apply—there must be enough chairs to seat the attendees but not so many that the event looks poorly attended, and the lighting must be sufficient to allow for video but not so bright that the candidate starts to sweat. But, unlike a standard news conference, the idea behind a news event is that the action itself is the message. If things go right—as when, during Campaign 2000, George W. Bush went to the nation's most prosperous border town, San Diego, to say that he would reduce immigration waiting times—the result is positive press. When things go wrong, the message can be disastrous. During the 1996 presidential campaign, Bob Dole leaned forward to shake supporters' hands. Unfortunately, the railing he pressed against gave way, and Senator Dole fell into the crowd. The accident was portrayed as a metaphor: Dole's campaign had lost its balance. Good advance staffers check every detail of event staging. It is not beneath them to jump up and down on a riser to check for squeaky joints or weak spots.

As Michael Deaver's work taught, the image must convey the message before a single word is spoken. "I am sure the purists, who want their news unfiltered and their heroes unrehearsed, gag on the word *visuals,*" he wrote, "but in the Television Age, [an event] hasn't happened, or at least it hasn't registered, if people can't see what you see" (1987, 141). Matthew Bennett, former trip director for Al Gore, says that the reason that visuals are so important is that "we can't control the decisions made by the writer or editor about what will be covered" (Bennett 2000). But, he adds, if the media wanted to run a "horse race story" and Al Gore wanted to talk about policy, the advance team can at least convey the intended message visually.

Debates

For many local candidates, debates are the only opportunity to get free press. Reporters cover most of these events, perhaps from a desire to "inform voters," and they might feel obliged to print a few lines about each candidate. Coverage is generally balanced, meaning that each candidate gets about the same amount of ink. Unlike higher-profile presidential or gubernatorial debates, there are few clear "winners" or "losers" at the local level. Not enough people see them to make a difference. If, however, the coverage complements themes articulated in paid media, the one-two punch can prove effective. Debates can help poorly funded candidates get their names out—precisely why candidates ahead in the polls are often reluctant to debate. Why give the challenger this kind of exposure?

Candidates who want to maximize press coverage gear most of their remarks to the press, not the audience at home. A vast majority of those who attend debates personally or watch them on public television have already made up their minds and merely wish to see their candidate win. Very few uncommitted voters watch debates, but reporters and editorial boards pay close attention. Candidates strive to make clear, brief, novel, and sometimes confrontational statements. It is important to reinforce the campaign theme, but simple repetition can be interpreted as "old news" (Hershey 1984, 23). New wrinkles and off-the-cuff deviations can draw media attention. Reporters realize that nothing is more boring than a photo of two candidates standing stiffly on stage, so anything out of the ordinary catches their eye. A candidate who knows this tactic might hold up a piece of the opponent's campaign literature to highlight a contradiction—but if a candidate uses this tactic too aggressively, as when Rick Lazio walked right up to Hillary Rodham Clinton's lectern, media backlash may be the result.

Candidates generally want to be well prepared for debates because the media will be ready to seize upon gaffes. Candidates who deviate from prepared material place themselves at risk. When Ronald Reagan suggested in a debate that trees were the major cause of air pollution, the press pounced (Hershey 1984, 23). Opponents join in the attack, and the result can be disastrous. There are few things in politics more fearsome than a media attack on live television. It has become commonplace for campaigns to prepare briefing books on the issues and to work with the candidate on sharp replies, cutting attacks, and strong defensive maneuvers.

Interviews, the Editorial Page, and Nonattributed Information

News conferences and media events are open invitations for candidate interviews. Other earned media possibilities include radio and television talk shows and community service programs. When Democratic senator Dianne Feinstein of California struggled to hold her U.S. Senate seat in 1994, she faced an increasingly conservative electorate and a multimillionaire opponent. When her lead began to slip, the Feinstein team went on the offensive. Feinstein's opponent, Michael Huffington, had fully endorsed Proposition 187, designed to limit the flood of illegal immigrants into the state. It was discovered, however, that he had employed for some time an illegal immigrant as a houseworker. The hypocrisy was sure to drain support from Huffington, but getting out the word quickly and inexpensively was problematic. Feinstein decided to lead the attack on CNN's *Larry King Live,* and the charge was then picked up by more traditional media. Huffington's negatives skyrocketed; Feinstein was returned to the Senate.

Candidates for local office are rarely invited to appear on national television talk shows, but there are opportunities on local radio and television programs. That same year, Ohio gubernatorial candidate Robert Burch found it difficult to garner newspaper coverage, but he was able to appear on talk-radio programs throughout the state, including several in large media markets. Burch did not win, but he showed the viability of talk-radio outreach, a form of communication that serves much the same function as newspaper "op-eds"—opinion pieces that run on the editorial pages. The prevailing wisdom is that "placing an op-ed is one of the most difficult things to do in public relations. Especially if your client or candidate is not a well-known figure" (Shirley 1997, 23). But the reason that editorial pages are so difficult to break into is that they are so influential: everyone wants to get his or her opinion in the paper, so editors have a large number of op-eds from which to choose. An alternative route is a letter to the editor. Campaigns coordinate letters to all the newspapers in the district. In addition to being a means of easy access, letters to the editor are one of the most heavily read parts of the newspaper (Beaudry and Schaeffer 1986, 138).

A campaign that does not have to fight for coverage can get its message out with nonattributable backgrounders. The messages might be called "leaks," except that the term sounds devious and underhanded—perhaps even unauthorized. The fact of the matter is that a large portion of news provided to the public as independent research is actually given to reporters by authorized parties who strike a deal to remain anonymous. Campaigns that have gained the trust of a reporter can disseminate their ideas "on background."

While the boundaries are hazy, there are four general levels of reporter–source communication. First, "on the record" conversations can be printed with direct attribution to the source. All conversations with a reporter are assumed to be on the record unless another agreement has been made ahead of time. Second, "background" conversations are those that can be attributed to a nonspecific source. The campaign staffer might, for example, negotiate for references to "a campaign official." Third, "deep background" exchanges cannot be attributed at all, but they can be used to guide a reporter's research. The most famous example is "Deep Throat," the hidden voice behind the *Washington Post*'s coverage of Watergate. Finally, "off-the-record" conversations cannot be used in any way. For the most part, the only remarks that are kept off the record are discussions about family and other personal matters—friendships between reporters and political professionals are included here—and in any case, conversations off the record often turn up in the paper anyway.

Nonattributed conversations—talking to reporters "on background"—can be used to help reporters write their stories. One consultant says, "On background is useful to outline a complex plan yet to be announced or to explain something not generally understood by the media in which the speaker is not the primary source" (Scudder 1997, 25). Research on nonattributed sourcing will always be sketchy, but the anatomy of "backgrounders" can be seen in the White House's handling of the fund-raising controversies that followed the 1996 elections. White House special counsel Lanny Davis was charged with handling press inquiries. His job was not to deflect reporters' questions but rather to answer them as fully as possible. The idea was to establish a "baseline." "Help the reporter write the first story, make sure it's complete, with everything in it," Davis says, and "[f]rom that point on, other reporters will find it when they search the LEXIS-NEXIS database of published newspaper stories, and so it will become the starting point for all future reporting" (1999, 43). Many of the campaign finance stories that appeared to have been leaked by Republican investigators actually got their start at the White House.

As Election Day nears, most daily and weekly newspapers note their preferred candidates in editorial endorsements. New-style consultants are mindful of the fact that reporters play only a supporting role in the endorsement process. Although the exact steps involved in the endorsement decision vary from paper to paper, most often the decisions are made by the editors and, occasionally, by the publishers. Reporters are sometimes asked for their opinions, but the final determination is not theirs to make. Special efforts are made to win the favor of decision makers. Periodic visits help, as do personal notes from the candidate thanking the editor for a "fair and accurate" story, and certainly the candidate will attend any meeting requested by the editorial board. Campaigns that get the nod will reprint the endorsement for last-minute literature drops. Democratic state Senate candidate Gordon MacInnes was given an immense boost when the leading paper in the district called his opponent, among other things, "a walking argument for term limits." The piece was reprinted and dropped to swing areas throughout the district (Beiler 1994c). Of course, there is always a possibility that an editorial decision will go the wrong way. In this case, media consultant Robert Shrum recommends a paid media counteroffensive, saying, "500 gross rating points of media can answer a lot of largely unread editorials" (1997, 24).

CONCLUSION

James Carville calls news media "the Beast"—if the campaign does not feed it, it feeds on the campaign. Whether or not this assessment is accurate, the media play a critically important role in new-style campaigns. As CNN has erased the old deadlines in favor of a twenty-four-hour national news cycle, with regional and statewide news networks doing the same transformation to statewide and congressional races, the political world is truly changing. Earned media is difficult, and paid media is expensive. *SRDS* lists the average cost-per-point for prime-time Miami television airtime at $707—a great deal of money for any campaign. A campaign that effectively gains news coverage can begin to shape the electoral debate with minimal cost.

Chapter Twelve

Returning to the Grassroots

A dominant theme of this book is that new-style electioneering is expensive. Chapter 9 underscored the importance of fund-raising, Chapter 10 discussed communication strategy, and Chapter 11 looked at news coverage. These forms of campaigning take place in a world where party politics has become professionalized. Whereas in the past candidates might expect legions of party activists to help carry the banner, today money and professional campaign services are funneled in from Washington and the state capital. Local party volunteers are not the force they once were.

But has volunteer-based, grassroots campaigning become obsolete? Consider two brief anecdotes. First, Democratic U.S. representative Frank Pallone Jr. was in the fight of his political life in 1998. The attack, however, did not come directly from his opponent or from the GOP. Rather, it came in the form of a heavily financed, independent expenditure campaign. A group calling itself Americans for Job Security (AJS), a conservative, pro-business organization, had set its sights on Pallone and by the end of October was pumping millions of dollars into a television assault. A Pallone operative commented, "Every time you turned on the television there would be, like, 'Frank Pallone baby killer, child molester.' It got to the point that you did not want to turn on the TV" (Duncan 1999, 425). Most of these spots were aired from the highly expensive New York City media market and were even run during prime-time programs. For example, AJS ran hardhitting anti-Pallone commercials during *60 Minutes* and the World Series. In all, they spent some $2 million on the assault. Early in the race Pallone was considered safe, but with the pounding that he was receiving at the end of October the outcome seemed less certain.

Pallone's response to the assault was multifaceted and included some radio and television—but not too much, given their cost. Direct mail was heavily used. The Pallone team also cultivated the sympathy of the local media. One drawback of most independent expenditure campaigns is the wrath of reporters. (There is a strong sense of localism in American politics, and "outsider" groups are often assailed.) Another critical piece of the counterattack came from a carefully orchestrated grassroots effort. During the final weeks of the race an army of volunteers set about calling voters, dropping literature, and canvassing face-to-face. According to commentator Philip Duncan, "New Jersey's Democratic Party has a number of strong and sometimes competing factions, but the AJS campaign provoked a 'circle the wagons' response. . . . Marshaling a force that included students and union members, Pallone deployed yard signs, doorknob hangers and other old-fashioned campaign tools to supplement his phone bank operation" (Duncan 1999, 425). In the end, Pallone netted 58 percent of the vote.

Second, consider the upset defeat of Democratic Congressman Michael Synar. In 1994 Synar was considered a powerful force in Congress. He had served only eight years, first coming to Congress when he was twenty-seven years old, but he was a rising star and was seen by his colleagues as "one of the most popular and respected middle American liberals" (Reeves, 1994). His Oklahoma district was more conservative than he was, but Synar's post seemed secure.

Synar's opponent in the Democratic primary was Virgil Cooper, who had no previous political experience and was a seventy-one-year-old retired school principal. During the race, Cooper bought no television time: instead, he barnstormed the district himself, putting up homemade posters and handing out small leaflets. Because he was retired, Cooper was free to spend six days a week pounding the pavement. He was able to cultivate a pool of dedicated activists to work on his behalf. It is hard to know whether these volunteers were energized by their devotion to Cooper or disdain for Synar, but either way their efforts were significant. Cooper defeated Synar in what was termed "one of the biggest political upsets in Oklahoma history" (Martindale, 1994). While Synar spent nearly $600,000, Cooper won the election with just over $16,000, most of it his own money.

Every election season produces examples of grassroots campaigns that prevail on Election Day. Personal contact remains the single best means to win votes, and grassroots efforts are important in any new-style campaign. A team of dedicated volunteers can help compensate for weak finances and, at times, help push a well-financed race over the top. This does not mean that grassroots campaigning is simple and unsophisticated. To the contrary, in order to optimize the help of volunteers, careful attention must be paid to planning, targeting, and resource allocation. All of the basic principles of new-style campaigning apply to the grassroots operation. Because the "soldiers" in the grassroots effort are generally untrained, they often need supervision. Without order and direction, well-intentioned volunteers can become detrimental to the campaign.

This chapter discusses reasons why direct voter contact works, describes various types of grassroots activities, and outlines some ways to optimize the aid of volunteers and other direct-contact activities, often termed "fieldwork." Candidates like Pallone and Cooper were successful with volunteers who rely upon sheer grit and determination. Still, poorly planned grassroots efforts can prove disappointing. Cooper shocked the political community by knocking off a rising star in the Democratic primary, but his approach proved unsuccessful in the general election. The old-fashioned way of getting votes remains one of the best, but only if it is combined with new-style strategies.

THE POWER OF DIRECT VOTER CONTACT

Direct voter contact works for a number of reasons. First, it brings the voter to a different cognitive level from that of other campaign communications. There is a qualitative difference between a volunteer's talking with the voter on the front porch and a piece of campaign literature in a mailbox. The voter becomes more engaged and is more attentive for a longer period of time. Second, direct contact allows two-way communication. Voters are given a chance to share their own views. When voters have the opportunity to meet the candidate, they become more invested in the campaign (Trent and Friedenberg 2000, 300–302). Additional benefits of direct contact are physical cues, not otherwise afforded by indirect means. For example, a voter may be persuaded by the physical appearance or body language of the candidate or volunteer. Facial expressions, hand movements, and voice inflections can mean a great deal in interpersonal communication. Some of this might be captured by radio or television spots, yet voters are not as engaged by this media.

Grassroots campaigning also humanizes the candidate. Put differently, campaigns conducted over the airwaves can seem distant and impersonal. When a candidate or volunteer makes direct contact with the voter, a better connection is made. In the new millennium, voters need to be reminded that candidates are people, not products. Along similar lines, fieldwork can give the impression that there is a groundswell of support for the candidate. Voters like being on the winning side. An enthusiastic volunteer effort leads them to believe that others in the community are supporting the candidate. This can bring in still more volunteers as well as support on Election Day. There are few better ways of getting the bandwagon rolling than with a visible outpouring of help by members of the community.

Fieldwork costs money, but the use of volunteers can keep expenses low. If the campaign is out of funds and receives a last-minute endorsement, for instance, a massive volunteer literature operation can spread the message quickly. Grassroots campaigning offers one of the most targeted voter contact activities available. With careful planning it can bring the right message to the right voters, without the waste that normally accompanies broadcast media.

Finally, fieldwork can lead to greater enthusiasm in the race, leading to more media attention and easier fund-raising. Campaigns engulfed by hordes of volunteers are conspicuous—they stand out and send a positive message. This leads potential contributors to take notice and catches the eye of news editors and reporters. An air of grassroots popularity can be a self-fulfilling prophecy.

The advantages of direct voter contact are numerous. But is grassroots organizing easier said than done? How does a campaign recruit the number of volunteers necessary for a strong campaign? The first place to start is always the candidate. It is difficult to ask others to lend a hand if the candidate is unwilling to do so. Again, the most persuasive message is the one delivered by the candidate, and the candidate's family and network of friends are the next logical resource. Often this effort takes some prodding—those close to the candidate presume that their efforts should be geared only to "strategy," as opposed to implementation. Successful campaigns revise this notion early in the race.

Some local parties are as robust as they have been at any time in the past thirty or forty years. Local party operations can offer a deep reservoir of potential volunteers. Many party workers have campaign experience. Grassroots campaigning is not difficult, but there are some "tricks of the trade." Local organizations and interest groups can provide volunteers as well. Many Democrats are assisted by labor unions and many Republicans get a boost from business organizations. If the candidate is a member of such a group, certainly fellow members can be approached. Yet another source is the pool of student organizations at the local college or university, and at the other end of the spectrum, senior citizen groups. Older Americans are politically active and often have a good deal of spare time.

TYPES OF GRASSROOTS ACTIVITIES

Contemporary fieldwork is systematically targeted. While direct voter contact is often the *best* means to win votes, it is also the *slowest* means to win votes—and time is a precious campaign resource. In addition to standard measures of persuadability, grassroots organizers look to reachability. For example, geography is an important factor in door-to-door campaigning. Suburban areas are more amenable to a precinct walk than rural areas, where the number of households approached might be only four or five an hour. The benefit of a well-targeted grassroots effort is that it can be aimed very narrowly. A media-based campaign that relies on radio might reach listeners across an entire county, including many of the opposition's base voters. A carefully planned door-to-door effort might have the candidate walking right past the homes of opposition loyalists.

The Candidate Walk Plan

In congressional campaigns and races further down the ballot, candidates themselves often canvass the prime target areas—the most important marginal neighborhoods in the district. This effort entails more than just sending the candidate out to meet voters with a handful of literature. It is meticulously planned, down to the finest detail. A good candidate walk plan consists of several elements.

Walk Sheets. The first step is to acquire walk sheets. These lists contain the names (and in some states the party affiliations and limited biographical data, such as date of birth and occupation) of voters at each house on each street in the area.

They exclude those not registered and list the households along each side of the street, rather than in numeric order. For example:

1. Alma Jones (R), Morris Jones (R); 1 Maple Street
2. Bert Smith (D), Carol Smith (R), April Smith (D); 3 Maple Street
3. Andrew Johnson (I); 7 Maple Street
4. Betty Hill (D), Stephen Fisher (D); 9 Maple Street.

This format allows the candidate to skip households without registered voters and to work each side of the street at a time. Voters enrolled with the opposing party are skipped. Walk sheets can usually be purchased from the board of elections, the office of the secretary of state, or a commercial list vendor.

A Local Volunteer. The candidate rarely goes into the field unaccompanied. A volunteer, preferably one from the area where the candidate is assigned to walk, can serve many roles. Volunteers can introduce the candidate to the resident, provide some background information on each voter ("Mrs. Smith is a retired teacher who loves to bird-watch"), or give a quick rundown of the neighborhood ("We used to have a toy factory here"). The volunteer can carry the walk sheet, allowing the candidate to shake hands with the voters. He or she can keep the candidate on task, provide directions, and most importantly, serve as the "bad cop" if needed. If the voter is eager to have the candidate in for coffee, the candidate might appear accommodating, but the volunteer will suggest that they need to be moving along. In all likelihood, the voter will blame the staff for the misfortune.

Pre-walk Cards. Approximately two weeks prior to the candidate's walk in an area, pre-walk cards are mailed to each household (or, if the campaign is short on funds, the materials are hand-delivered). These cards might contain a picture of the candidate and a small note, something like:

> I'll be stopping by in the next few days to visit. I hope we get a chance to chat about your concerns and what I might do in the state legislature to help.

These cards serve several purposes. They get the candidate's name and message out, prime the voter for the visit, and maybe provide a picture of the candidate so the voter knows who is at the door. Even if the voter will not be home on the day of the visit, the cards suggest that the candidate is willing to "listen to average folks." Once the cards are sent, the candidate is obligated to walk in the area. Accordingly, the pre-walk can also serve as a strong motivator for the candidate.

The Drop-off Pamphlet. After shaking hands at the door, the candidate often provides an informational pamphlet in the hope that after the candidate has departed, the voter will return to the couch and read the material. This one-two punch of meeting the candidate at the door and then scanning the pamphlet provides powerful repetition—the heart of voter contact.

Careful Notes. Immediately after the candidate departs from each voter's doorstep, the volunteer takes notes about the conversation: the name of the person contacted, the voter's concerns, the voter's comments about the candidate, and so forth.

The Follow-up Card. If the voter is not at home, the candidate leaves a *handwritten* note on the back of the literature:

> Sorry I missed you. I stopped by to say hello and chat about your concerns, but you were out. Perhaps we can get a chance to talk another time. Please feel free to call.

The cards are written in advance so that the candidate and the volunteer can move along on the night of the canvass. To those voters who were home, a follow-up mailing is sent about a week after the visit. It thanks the voter for his or her time and highlights the candidate's commitment to voter input. Additional content parallels the notes taken during the conversation (see Careful Notes). If, for instance, the voter was concerned about environmental issues, the follow-up might outline the candidate's environmental priorities.

Additional Follow-ups. As a final step, any requested information or material is mailed, delivered, or telephoned to the voter immediately. This chore can be done by a volunteer.

A multistep program of this sort is time- and resource-intensive. But if it is done in the prime target areas of the district, the costs are justified. Repetition and careful attention to message distinguish this type of walk plan from traditional canvasses, in which the candidate simply knocks on doors.

The Canvass

In many ways the canvass mirrors the candidate walk plan. Here, however, other members of the campaign team walk door-to-door. Instead of mailing a candidate pre-walk card, a note is sent indicating that "a volunteer will be stopping by soon." Door-to-door workers usually have a clean-cut appearance and are somewhat familiar with the themes of the campaign. Training sessions and scripts are an excellent idea. The importance of careful records as to who was home and the interests of the contacted voters is stressed. A follow-up note might say, "Thanks for chatting with one of my volunteers." At crunch times, this sort of canvass can serve as a "rapid-response" operation, a so-called "door-to-door blitz." If the opponent levels a powerful charge during the final days of the race, a canvass blitz might help limit its impact. This was the Pallone strategy.

Voter Registration Drives

Volunteers are frequently used to find and register new voters. While the number varies greatly from one district and community to another, often only 50 percent of the voting-age residents are registered to vote. A voter registration process is a relatively uncomplicated affair. On a walk sheet, nonregistered voters will be in houses not listed. A campaign volunteer might visit these homes and try to persuade the resident to fill out a voter registration card. The volunteer brings the completed cards back to campaign headquarters, where they are compiled into a list and then delivered to the local board of elections. (Campaigns must check state laws for registration guidelines, particularly as they relate to the legality of the second step.)

Registration does not necessarily imply a vote on Election Day. Nevertheless, previously unregistered voters tend to be less partisan and, as such, less committed to opposing candidates. Moreover, because these are new voters, it is possible they will not be listed on opposition lists. If so, the only campaign material that they receive during most of the race may come from the candidate's headquarters. Voter registration drives are time-consuming and somewhat unpredictable, but they are a good way of keeping volunteers busy, and they can be a big help if the campaign faces an uphill battle. In districts with a large, mobile college student population, registration drives can make or break candidates.

Absentee Ballots and Mail-in Voting

New voting options have opened up in recent years, especially the expansion of absentee-style voting. Two states in particular, Oregon and Washington State, have made heavy use of mail-in ballots. North Carolina's "no excuses voting" plan gives voters three weeks prior to the election to vote at satellite voting stations. Advocates say that increased ease of voting is a boon for the democratic process, and that absentee-style processes are quick, convenient, and less costly than traditional go-to-the-polls-on-Election-Day voting. Moreover, the public seems willing to move in this direction. There is even a growing interest in online voting possibilities.

This shift will mean a great deal to campaign operations. Careful attention will have to be paid to the exigencies of turnout. The entrance of a new pool of voters changes the shape of the electorate. Absentee voters may be unable to get to the polls on Election Day because of an illness or disability, or they might know that they will be outside the district (as often happens with students, vacationers, and military personnel), and now, with loosening absentee rules and mail-in balloting, operatives will confront greater numbers of people whose work or low level of political interest have previously kept them from the polling booths.

The new electorates brought about by the new rules may be difficult to measure until researchers have more precedent from which to work. They also change the strategic timing of electoral contests as well as the types of work that need to be done. Campaign workers note the deadline for submitting absentee ballots, making sure that every would-be voter has a ballot form well in advance of the due date. A follow-up letter or telephone call often helps seal the ballot, so to speak. Next, in jurisdictions that provide such information, absentee lists can be secured from the board of elections or the secretary of state's office. Volunteers carefully review these registries and mail literature to absentees throughout the race. For those not then residing in the district, it may be the only concrete information they receive.

Mail-in ballots can be used to encourage participation among low-frequency voters—those who are registered but either have skipped a few elections or vote only in presidential contests. Senior citizens often fall into this category. They should be mailed a packet containing an absentee application and, if allowed by law, information on the candidate. Campaigns that engage in this kind of activity often find that "Election Day" is elongated to three or four weeks. Instead of building up to a single moment in time, a campaign must spread its most intense efforts—media buys, news events, and campaign mailings—over a month-long period, with particular attention paid to the first few days after the voting window begins.

Literature Drops

Literature drops are also targeted to swing areas. Unlike the canvass, drops do not entail meeting the voter but simply placing a piece of campaign literature on the porch or in the door jamb. It can be done by anyone, including volunteers unfamiliar with the candidate—even kids. The idea is to cover an area quickly and provide material somewhere other than in the mailbox (which is illegal). Drops are much less expensive than mailings (no postage is needed), but their overall effectiveness is debatable. They are perhaps most helpful in improving early name recognition or during a last-minute push.

Telephone Banks

Telephone banks are an excellent way to reach a large number of voters in a short period of time. They keep volunteers busy, particularly those not able to walk door-to-door, and they are relatively cheap.

There are three functions in a full-service telephone operation: persuasion, identification, and activation. A persuasion pitch simply targets voters with a brief message. A script is devised, and a volunteer conveys this information. Similar to an indirect voter contact activity, such as a television ad, the voter is not called upon to respond. The goal is to provide the voters with information. In a voter identification process a pitch is provided, followed by a few short questions regarding the voters' preferences in the coming election—who they will be voting for, what their primary concerns are, and so on. This information is carefully recorded, and the voters are marked "for," "against," or "undecided." Sometimes a numbering scheme is devised along the same lines. Voters labeled "against" are removed from the phone list, and if they demonstrate a serious dislike for the candidate, they may be removed from the mailing lists. Let sleeping dogs lie. "Undecideds" are given another call, mailed information on the candidate, and perhaps even visited by a volunteer. This group is cultivated extensively throughout the race. Activation calls are placed in order to urge persuaded voters to go to the polls on Election Day. At a minimum, this list is made up of those noted as "favorable" during the identification phase, but it can include others deemed likely to support the candidate. This can be done a few days early or on Election Day.

Telephone banks allow for tight control. Callers are given a list of voters and a carefully honed message. The number of contacts projected during a given time period can be predicted with a good deal of accuracy. This is done by multiplying the following figures:

- The length of a call (including the projected downtime between calls);
- The number of volunteers;
- The number of hours per evening called; and
- The number of days per week of telephoning.

Some nights will have more volunteers than others, and some nights will see fewer hours in service, but in general terms, a campaign can calculate about how long it will take to make a series of telephone contacts in a given period—helpful information when the campaign maps out its overall strategy and the timing of campaign activities.

There are some advantages to hiring a telemarketing firm to carry out this operation, mainly, the speed at which it can be done. At the end of the race, for instance, it may be necessary to complete 5,000 contacts over one weekend. This task would be difficult for most volunteer teams, but it could be accomplished easily by a large telemarketing firm. They generally charge a fixed rate for each completed call, perhaps $.50 or $.75, depending on the length of the script and the location of the district in relation to the telephone bank.

There are a number of benefits to keeping the operation local—and volunteer-based. It is much easier to monitor the callers, perhaps leading to higher-quality control. Often a local law firm, real estate office, or labor union donates the use of its phones during the evening. This approach offers greater security and more flexibility as to when calls are made (Yeutter et al. 1992). Most important, voters often snub professional telemarketing pitches. If the call is coming from a volunteer, perhaps even a neighbor, the voter is much more likely to listen and be receptive. In a way, it bridges the gap between efficiency and effectiveness. It is quick, somewhat personal, and relatively inexpensive.

Coffee and Handshakes

Opportunities for direct voter contact activities are vast. A growing number of candidates are using coffees or cocktail parties. A supporter invites his or her neighbors to a small gathering at home, and the candidate drops by for a visit. Hosting several gatherings on the same evening allows the candidate to touch base with a large number of voters. This can be a rather pleasurable form of campaigning. Knowing when a factory shift changes can mean a lot of voter contact over a short period—several hundred workers might pass in fifteen minutes. Factory gate and commuter station activities can be especially effective if the candidate hands out coffee and donuts, for example, as well as a small piece of literature. Moreover, shift and commuter changes usually occur when little else is going on in the campaign, perhaps as early as 7:00 A.M. Giving voters an opportunity to chat on a train platform helps candidates build strong connections.

It is possible to go overboard with handshakes, however. Some consultants deal with candidates who believe that the best way to meet voters is to visit the local mall or fair or to stand on the street corner. "Thousands of folks go to the fair," the candidate exclaims, but this type of shotgun approach is antithetical to new-style campaigning. The candidate has no sense of people's residency, partisan predisposition, or even registration status. Untargeted activities are an inefficient use of precious time. Productive campaigning is not about meeting as many people as possible but rather meeting the right folks and providing the right message.

GET-OUT-THE-VOTE DRIVES

Efficiency is critical because time is the enemy. An excellent illustration of the importance of last-minute campaigning is Rosemary Shea's first bid for the Oneonta, New York, School Board. (Shea is the mother of one of the authors of this book.) With one hour to go before the polls closed, the campaign team had exhausted its list of favorable voters. In fact, two or three calls had been made to each. Determined to work until the last minute, the candidate scoured the list of those who had not voted. With fifteen minutes to go, she drove across town to visit a household of three would-be Democratic voters. She convinced them to get into her car and be driven to the polls so that they could fulfill their "civic duty." With seconds to go, all three cast their votes. Out of the thousands of votes cast, Shea won that election by the same number, three votes.

Get-out-the-vote (GOTV) efforts can be the most important activity undertaken during a campaign. The history of campaigns is filled with elections won and lost by a handful of voters, including Campaign 2000's close presidential vote in Florida. In every election scores of congressional, state legislative, and even senatorial and gubernatorial races are decided by less than 1 percent of the votes cast. Carefully orchestrated, last-minute pushes can mean the difference between success and failure.

While democracy calls on everyone to vote on Election Day, the goal of a GOTV drive is to concentrate on those most likely to vote for the candidate. There are a number of ways to determine this, including voter ID calls, demographic and survey research, and geography. Party enrollment is often used. All things being equal, a person's party enrollment is the best single predictor of his or her vote choice. Conceivably, the canvass records will produce a list of favorable voters. A good rule of thumb is to target roughly 10 percent of the votes needed for victory: "If you are running a state legislative race and need 15,000 votes to win, you must have at least 1,500 identified supporters whom you will push to the polls" (Allen 1990c, 38). Whatever criteria are used, it is important to remember that last-minute pushes are designed to get the candidate's voters to the polls, not simply to kick up turnout.

Effective GOTV Techniques

Every consultant and party operative advocates a slightly different GOTV approach. Some rely upon canvassing, doorbell ringing, direct mail, and other tactics. Following is a technique that relies upon volunteer efforts and has proven to be quite effective.

Early Planning. The team begins planning the GOTV about thirty days before Election Day. This means establishing a written plan of action and assigning a coordinator. The plan lays out specific tasks, deadlines for accomplishing these jobs, and the people responsible for completing them. Moreover, it lists the resources needed for implementation.

GOTV Mailer. Three to five days before the election, a mailer is sent to voters in all swing and favorable election precincts throughout the district. If the swing group is not needed, it may be dropped. This mailing stresses the importance of the election and the difference that every vote can make. It is a good idea to include an anecdote of an election won by just a few votes. If the campaign is strapped for cash, a pamphlet can be dropped in target areas during the weekend prior to the election.

Telephoning. On the eve of the election, the telephone operation is put in full gear. The target group for this phase is more refined than the mailer group. If at all possible, the entire 10 percent GOTV group is contacted. The message on the phone is similar to the message in the mailer.

Poll Watching and Pickup. Many jurisdictions allow for "poll-watching." On the morning of the election, volunteers go to each polling place, find a comfortable place to sit, and then record the names of each person who votes. The resulting lists are picked up throughout the day, perhaps at about two-hour intervals, and then brought to the headquarters. The names of those who have voted are scratched off a master list. This process indicates which registered voters have gone to the polls, letting the campaign know who should get reminder calls.

Reminders and Assistance. Most people vote early in the morning or just after work. By about 4:00 P.M., a smart campaign puts a telephone operation into action, focusing on those in the target group who have not yet voted. Very often people need assistance to get to the polls: child care and rides to the polls are commonly offered. This process continues throughout the evening, relying upon updated lists from the poll watchers in order to scratch off recent voters. Prospective supporters are called until the polls close.

Other GOTV Aids

The mailer/poll-watching/telephoning/assistance operation forms the core of a GOTV drive, but several other activities might help. A rally might be held in a targeted area the weekend prior to the election. Massive literature drops can work, as can yard sign blitzes. Unless the candidate is down in the polls and a large turnout is deemed the only chance, the campaign steers clear of untargeted activities such as waving signs at intersections, handing out leaflets at shopping malls, and blanket canvassing. Again, GOTV efforts are not about getting voters to the polls but about getting the *right* voters to the polls.

As for the candidate, this can be a difficult time. Months, if not years, of work are coming to an end. It is a good idea for consultants to give the candidate a specific task, perhaps calling his or her best supporters and thanking them for their work. An alternative is to have the candidate walk door-to-door in the highest swing neighborhood in the district. More than anything else, he or she needs to be kept busy—for everyone's sake!

Some Thoughts on Recount Procedures

The gravity and complexity of recount procedures held the public's attention during the six weeks following the 2000 presidential contest. Many people were surprised with the perplexity of recount procedures and the fragility of election results. Every time the ballots were counted, the vote totals changed. Indeed, the basis of George W. Bush's legal argument was that, while accuracy is important, so is finality—and in an imperfect world perfection is not possible. In the end, many Florida votes ballots were not included in the official results of Campaign 2000. This outcome of the first presidential election of the twenty-first century says a lot about the importance of well-executed recounts. The legal process varies from state to state, and even from county to county, but there are several key elements in any recount blueprint.

In a well-prepared campaign, laws structuring the applicable recount procedures should be compiled ahead of time. An attorney with a working knowledge of state election law should be brought on board. Legal questions should be clarified well before Election Day—both in terms of initiating a recount (if the campaign loses) and opposing a recount (if the campaign wins). Among those who would sit on a recount team, both legal and political, responsibilities should be clear, contact information shared, and all the necessary addresses and telephone numbers of election offices, election commissioners, and appropriate judicial authorities should be readied. The reason: recounts are generally initiated in rapid order, usually on Election Night or the following morning. (Some jurisdictions have automatic recounts for close elections.)

Often, the first step is to secure the ballots and voting machines. In New York State, for example, a court order from a county justice is necessary to impound all voting machines in a given county. This step is critical, especially if the campaign suspects fraud. From this point the work of the lawyers begins. A recount process is time-consuming and labor-intensive; attention must be paid to the details. As both Gore and Bush learned in November and December of 2000, aggressive legal teams can be inspired to work hard for long hours. The focus is often on mistakes in voter tabulation. In the Florida case, it was a combination of poor ballot design, voter error, faulty voting procedures, improper instructions, and even allegations of voter intimidation. Less frequent, but still surprisingly common, is outright election fraud (Sabato and Simpson 1996). In any event, attention must be paid to both the legal implications of the recount and the attendant communications issues, for the court of public opinion is no less important than the court in which the lawyer's arguments will be heard.

Operatives on all sides, however, should understand that election results are very hard to overturn, even when the evidence seems clear. One attorney relates the story of a election that his client lost by thirty votes, in which a precinct that went fifty-five to one hundred twenty-five for the opposition showed clear indications of machine malfunction, even if the exact problem could not be located in the device itself. With a seeming under vote of one hundred votes,

> [W]e canvassed the precinct and got about 150 affidavits from people who said they had voted for the Democrat. I checked them against the precinct sign-in list and every one of them had been there. At the hearing, I proffered the affidavits to show that my client had been the victim of a machine malfunction. The judge said he trusted the machine. My client decided not to take an appeal. (Still 2000)

Indeed, at times, candidates believe it is more dignified to simply bow out gracefully than to fight to the end.

GRASSROOTS IN CYBERSPACE?

One of the most promising new aspects of grassroots electioneering is what now can be accomplished over the Internet. No one knows this better than Jesse "The Body" Ventura, the former professional wrestler elected governor of Minnesota in 1998 as a third-party candidate. One commentator went so far as to suggest that Ventura is the first "cybergovernor" (Noble 1998).

Ventura faced two well-known, well-financed opponents, and most observers considered his early efforts more comical than serious. During the course of the campaign he had only two paid staffers and a minuscule war chest. Yet, his supporters relied heavily on the quickest, cheapest means of communicating a message—the Internet.

The Ventura team used his Web page to build, expand, and promote his campaign. A database volunteer team was assembled, dubbed the D-Team, to input data, upload digital pictures from the campaign trail, post messages on the bulletin board, and arrange charts and figures. Most importantly, they arranged dozens of chat-room sessions between voters and Ventura and followed him on a seventy-two-hour statewide campaign tour on Election Eve. Ventura's Internet effort was primarily volunteer-driven. It became a significant tool for reaching out to voters.

How many votes did the Ventura cyber-brigade deliver? It is hard to say, but some estimates suggest as much as 3 percent of the votes in the Ventura column can be attributed to their efforts—just enough to put him over the top. Ventura's

Web master commented, "There is no way on Earth that we could have organized the tour without the Internet. And without the tour, we might not have had those votes. If you remove the Internet, we would not have won" (Noble 1998). Minnesota is well suited for an Internet campaign: the state has a history of independent-thinking voters, a large Web-savvy professional class, and Minneapolis—one of the most "wired" cities in the country.

Ventura's use of the Internet is no longer considered exceptional. Nearly every serious statewide and congressional campaign develops a sophisticated Web site. Web pages can describe the candidate's biography and policy positions, link the candidate to the party, schedule events, solicit donations, provide chat-room opportunities, and tap volunteers who might be willing to help the candidate. Volunteers, in turn, get tasks and their directions via the Internet. They know where to go and what to do. Often these Web sites are constructed by professionals, but sometimes volunteers rise to the challenge. After the sites are established, volunteers are used to input data, upload and download material, and answer and send emails. Grassroots has moved into cyberspace.

CONCLUSION

As with all other facets of electioneering, political judgment in grassroots campaigning is vital. In some places it is common to find door-to-door volunteers on Sunday; in others, this is taboo. On any day, campaigns should be wary of calling before 9:00 A.M. or after 8:30 P.M. Yard signs are acceptable in some places but considered in bad taste elsewhere. Professionals must understand the social, religious, and political norms of any area in which they campaign.

Political wisdom is usually learned on the job—often through mistakes. Take, for example, the crisp Saturday morning in October when a zealous campaign operative rounded up a team of volunteers to walk door-to-door. Their race was located in the Long Beach area of New York's Nassau County. After two hours of work, the group became increasingly discouraged. Although cars were in the driveways, no one appeared to be home. Those who did answer the door, refused to open it more than a few inches. The canvass was soon canceled. Later investigation found that the area contained a large number of Orthodox Jews. Saturday was their Sabbath, and they were insulted by insensitive campaign workers. It took considerable effort to repair the damage.

Without supervision, well-intentioned workers can cause great damage. Campaigns must channel volunteer enthusiasm properly. Strange though it may seem, many campaigns languish without volunteers because they cannot find work to fill the time. A strong volunteer workforce is a rare commodity in politics. Smart campaigns bring the candidate to many of the volunteer functions in order to express gratitude and maintain interest. Pizza, bagels, soda, and coffee are served, and on Election Night there will be an extravagant blowout.

Smart electioneering uses this model throughout the campaign operation. To win an election, the race must be fun. Sour looks and hot tempers corrode the relationships necessary for a smooth campaign. Even as targeting and media politics have overtaken many traditional campaign activities, politics remains a very human endeavor. As such, campaigning can be one of the most rewarding missions that anyone can undertake. The rush on Election Night is unmatched. Candidates, consultants, and campaign staff always want to win, but professionals never forget that it is only an election. Win or lose, the world will continue.

Chapter Thirteen

Conclusion:
The Future of Political
Campaign Organization

Political strategists speak in terms of military planning, because "[p]olitics and war follow the same principles: armies face off in battle, each with different plans, different strengths and weaknesses, limited resources, generals with different styles, and all sharing the same goal of crushing the enemy" (Sweitzer 1996, 46). For a political strategist, campaigns are civilized warfare. For a political tactician, however—the one who must implement wide-ranging battle plans—a different conceptual model is required. Tactical operations take the form of commercial marketing. The language of voter contact speaks of "gross rating points," "spot production," "list management," and "demographic research." Each electoral cycle brings new marketing tools—novel methods of segmenting the electorate and selling the candidate. As the new millennium began, consultants talked about the marketing power of the Internet and the ways in which it might help campaigns target voters never imagined in the 1950s. Adlai Stevenson, who railed against those who "merchandise candidates for high office like breakfast cereal," would surely be astounded at the present state of affairs.

For the past half century, political campaigns have absorbed innovative technologies with amazing speed. Databases, video editing, digital phones, and laptop computers have become standard equipment. Advanced technologies such as Geographic Information Systems (GIS) are used widely in high-profile campaigns and sometimes even down-ballot races. As with all other areas of life, the tools that an organization uses tend to transform the organization itself. To see the future of American political campaigns, one need only look at the leading edge of the technological revolution. This chapter provides a conceptual framework for the microeconomics of consultant-centered campaigns, highlights some of the technologies that reinforce new-style electioneering, and discusses the implications of these forces on the relationship between candidates and the electorate.

PROFESSIONALISM AND MASS CUSTOMIZATION

As party identification became a less important determinant of voting behavior, individual politicians had to build identities of their own. Television was the preferred means of promoting individual candidates. The congressional class of 1974 had a whole new look—young, energetic political outsiders with blow-dried hair. Tammany-style politics were gone. To win, candidates had to go on television, a costly medium requiring specialized expertise. Few pols knew how to backlight a candidate without creating a "halo effect." The language of ad production—with its "Nagras," "Chroma Keys," and "crystal syncs"—was foreign to campaign managers. Furthermore, the moving arts require forms of creativity not found in other visual media. Television demands professionals. Political campaigns were forced to outsource the production of campaign ads to those who already knew the business.

The microeconomics of the situation enabled consultants to penetrate the campaign market rapidly. Direct mail illustrates the point: learning postal regulations for a mass mailing requires scarce time and turning to a professional can significantly shorten the production schedule. But figuring out how to size, sort, and seal a mailing is only the beginning. Direct mail depends on clean data, efficient stuffing machines, and, most importantly, expertise in building productive lists that yield high-dollar contributions. Database professionals must know how to "merge & purge," "de-dupe," and practice "good data hygiene." Once a campaign operative has mastered the legal, technical, creative, and organizational demands of the mail business, there is no point in restricting the acquired expertise to a single candidate. Working on a number of campaigns at once helps to distribute the costs among a larger group of clients, thereby reducing per-unit overhead and increasing profits. The organizational structure of campaigns is thus forced to change.

In the 1970s a competitive U.S. Senate campaign wishing to send out a mass mailing would rely on a volunteer coordinator, who would assemble a team of supporters and spend an evening folding letters and stuffing envelopes. In the new millennium, the job is outsourced to a professional mail house. Consulting firms like the Strategy Group in Chicago can manage the process from start to finish. Professionals develop the artwork, write the copy, arrange for printing, target addressees, and then ship the mailing. Not only does professional administration reduce the number of volunteer hours needed by the campaign, but mail houses quite possibly save raw dollars and cents. A direct-mail consultant counsels, "A lettershop is cheaper than pizza and beer for your volunteers" (Malchow 1990). The new economics of electioneering devalues the role of volunteer coordinator—a position once filled by itinerant college students and battle-hardened party members—while at the same time increases the need for independent fundraisers. (The money to hire professionals is itself raised by professionals.) While a pool of talented volunteers might be persuaded to go without pizza during the final hours of a campaign, a direct marketing firm will not forgo its consultancy fees.

In the golden age of parties, campaigns were constituent parts of a centralized chain of command. In the early days of new-style campaigns, the breakdown of party structure meant a trend toward multiple hierarchies, with each candidate running its own operation. As this transformation toward candidate-centered campaigns was taking place, the candidates came to rely on dispersed outside consultancies. Even the resurgence of the national parties reflects this trend. The parties are no longer just a pecking order of elected officials and staff. They are clearinghouses for money, expertise, information, and political intelligence. The result is a party structure in which campaigns are far more adaptable to changes in the political environment.

One way to reconceptualize new-style operations is to look at a recent development in the private sector: mass customization. This seeming oxymoron was popularized by B. Joseph Pine II, who advocated a convergence of mass production efficiency with the individualized attention of hand-tailored craftwork. "Through the application of technology and new management methods," Pine wrote, new-style manufacturers are "creating variety and customization through flexibility and quick responsiveness" (1993, 44; emphasis omitted). The rise of mass customization has distinct parallels with the rise of new-style campaign techniques and in many ways, the future of political campaigns can be divined from the history of industrial manufacturing.

American industrialism arose from a major transformation in economic organization—a movement from the craft of individual artisans to the repetition of mass production. "Economies of scale" could reduce a product's cost-per-unit by increasing a factory's quantity of output. In this way, development costs were distributed among a large number of identically produced items. The downside of mass production was its lack of flexibility. Focusing on a single product hobbled a firm's ability to generate "economies of scope"—its capacity to enter new product lines. Furthermore, to maintain market share, large manufacturers dictated consumer demand rather than responded to it. But as consumers began to insist on a wider variety of goods, the old "stability and control" model began to fall away as the new marketplace demanded a "better understanding of customer requirements" (Pine 1993, 44).

Manufacturers responded by "[d]eveloping, producing, marketing, and delivering affordable goods and services with enough variety and customization that nearly everyone finds exactly what they want" (47). The retail computer industry has been completely reconfigured by mass customization. In 1964 the only mass-market computer was the IBM System/360 (36). In the new millennium, customers design their own systems online. Shoppers looking to buy a Dell or Gateway machine go to a company Web site, choose a computer that meets their needs, and then configure the system according to their own particular requirements. Network cards, hard drives, external storage, and screen sizes are selected one at a time—all according to the customer's personal specifications. Thousands of combinations are possible.

The parallel with politics is clear. Political consultants routinely mix and match preexisting campaign slogans, color schemes, policy stands, and media strategies to suit a range of clients. Campaigns are neither handcrafted nor mass-produced. Most are created by adapting pretested components to the needs of various localities, candidacies, and constituencies.

"Modularity" is the key. New-style industries use parts that are interchangeable not just within a product line, but across product lines as well. Standardized components are fitted to a variety of manufactured goods, meaning that costs can be contained by producing a multiplicity of modules that can be combined into a wide-ranging diversity of items for consumption. Writes Pine, "Economies of scale are gained through components rather than the products; economies of scope are gained by using the modular components over and over in different products; and customization is gained by the myriad of products that can be configured" (1993, 196). In the political world, CNN creates short news segments that can be played on any of its many outlets, including CNN Europe, CNNenEspañol, CNN Radio, CNN Headline News, CNNfn, CNN Airport Network, CNNsi, and CNN.com. The modular construction of video news reporting has increased the scope and flexibility of the journalistic environment.

Campaign scholars Judith Trent and Robert Friedenberg write that "candidates adapt" to varied political audiences "by making use of 'speech modules' " (2000, 182). Each module is "a single unit of speech," they write, and "candidates will have a speech unit, or module, on each of the 10 or 20 issues on which they most frequently speak" (182). These "talking points," as they are called in the industry, are recycled from one event to the next, with only small variations in phrasing. They can be used in letters, brochures, op-eds, debates, or any other textual form of communication.

But "speech modules" are only the beginning. Modularization can be seen throughout the campaign process. Campaign data come in standardized formats, and campaign commercials have a consistent regularity. A presidential advance staff can quickly assemble an immense campaign rally—with sound trucks, lights, and a handsome backdrop—because each piece of the puzzle has been used several times previously. When a campaign staffer learns how to coordinate sound and video at small events, this expertise can soon be fitted to larger and larger settings. A smart advance person figures out which pieces of the technology—electronic equipment, wiring, and so forth—are unique to local vendors and which are standard nationwide. Once the transferable elements of sound and video production are understood, the technique has been, in effect, modularized, and the swift production of large events becomes possible.

Modularization requires political wisdom. A mass-production approach would demand only that the procedures that created a successful campaign event be repeated step by step for each venue. An artisan's approach would tailor each campaign event to the specific needs of every campaign stop. A mass customization approach, however, merges the efficiency of repetition with the power of individualization. Political professionals must be able to distinguish the elements of a successful event that could work only in a particular time and place from those that can be transferred to other contexts. This task demands a broad knowledge of campaigns or, at the very least, close attention to industry trends. Communications consultants can learn how to build a Web site from hard experience, but the smart professional looks to the modularized advice collected from the experience of others: "Tell voters what others are saying about you," "Translate into Spanish," "Make the site personal, but relevant," "Use entertaining features to get people's attention," and so on (Jalonick 2000b, 56, 58). Over time, campaign professionals learn what works and what does not work—and more importantly, what can be reused time and again.

The professionalization of political campaigns stems partly from the efficiency of well-executed modularization. A whole industry of consultants has arisen—an industry that profits most when it recycles techniques from one campaign to the next. Political professionals develop "formulas" to guide electoral targeting and GOTV operations. They specialize in particular types of campaign messages or field tactics. As James Carville has said, "In campaign politics an idea is like a fruitcake at Christmas—there's not but one, and everybody keeps passing it around" (Matalin and Carville 1995, 35). There is a danger to being overly predictable—the general who fights the next war like the last risks defeat—but if the modularized components of campaign management are continually remixed and rematched, with new techniques replacing those that have become outmoded, a consultant's general methods of operation can remain strategically viable. To win—and profitability is maximized by repeated victory—campaign operatives must keep their techniques current. They must continually broaden their knowledge by working on a variety of campaigns, meeting with other consultants, and keeping up with the most recent changes in their chosen field. In other words, consultants must become "professionals" in the sense that their careers revolve not around individual candidates or the nuances of democratic governance but around campaigns and elections per se.

Indeed, political consultancy has evolved into a mature profession. It has a professional organization, standards of conduct, an industry magazine, and a collection of norms and practices that set consultants apart from the old party bosses and even their own candidates. Professional consultants have more in common with their colleagues on the other side of the partisan aisle than with outspoken ideologues within their own party. But most importantly, the profession has been locked in place by the increasing complexity of new-style campaigns. This was true as far back as 1980, when journalist Sidney Blumenthal wrote, "The arrival of new techniques based on computers—direct mail, voter identification methods, sophisticated polling—reinforces the role of consultants" (1980, 3). The reason, according to Blumenthal, is simple: "In order to have access to the new technology, a candidate needs a consultant. He can't run a viable, much less a respectable, campaign without one" (3).

CUTTING-EDGE TECHNOLOGY

Mass customization of political campaigns depends on the increasing power of database management and the astounding proliferation of communications technologies. These two developments go hand in hand. Database management produces lists of voters, and these voters can be targeted by new modes of communications. At the beginning of the new millennium, consultants for down-ballot races were still urging managers to rely on hard-copy records. Campaign managers "[m]ake a 3 by 5 card for everyone contacted by the campaign" and color-code the records of people who offer assistance to "show which campaign activities, such as lawn sign placement, phone canvass, or clerical work, the volunteer will work on" (Shaw 2000, 35–36). These sorts of tactics make sense for small races, insofar as the start-up costs for computer databasing remain fairly high. As the costs of data management decline, however, even down-ballot campaigns will enter the Digital Age.

Database Management

The 1996 presidential primary effort of political commentator Pat Buchanan was, in many ways, a new millennium campaign. At its heart was a technological advance that the campaign called "Electronic Field Operations." The idea was to integrate data from a wide variety of sources—donors, 1-800-GO-PAT-GO callers, and phone bank operations—and then use the database as the foundation of all voter contact, updating it in real time as the race moved forward. The campaign set up a military-style "Tactical Operations Center," which "contain[ed] representatives of all the major staff sections to ensure that all parts of the force [were] supporting and communicating with one another" (Hathaway 1996, 43). The database team was able to monitor all campaign plans, intervene when necessary, and quickly retrieve data. As a result, the Buchanan campaign was able to react to late-breaking events as they occurred. In Alaska, for example, partway into caucus voting, it was learned that the Wasslia polling site would be open later than expected, so the database "was queried for all the eligible voters in the district and within 10 minutes the in-house phone bank had a list of over 1,500 voters which they called in the final 90 minutes of the election." As a result, "Wasslia reported a 2:1 Buchanan win, a vote margin that accounted for almost half of his statewide margin of victory" (43).

The key to information management is data integrity. Each data record must correspond to a prospective voter, and all the data appended to the voter's record must (1) be accurate and (2) be in a form that corresponds to all the other records in the database. In Buchanan's campaign, for example, all the imported data had to fit into a standardized file structure and then be deduplicated "by building a matchcode based on zip code, name, gender, and [commercially obtained] addressing information" (Hathaway 1996, 43). The process becomes slightly more complicated with the addition of each new record. The first record in a database has no match, obviously, but the second will be matched against the first, the third against the first and second, and so on. The cost of data integrity increases incrementally. By the time a database has reached 100,000 or so voters, deduplication can become a troublesome and time-consuming job.

The high capital costs of databasing are eventually recouped by the benefits of reduced operating expenses and increased reaction speed. With individualized records, campaigns can combine polling, voter identification calls, electoral targeting, and voter contact results into a unified operation. An example is "Chi-Square Automatic Interaction Detection (CHAID), a statistical tool designed to maximize the value of political targeting by making the most of voter identification phone calls. It matches ID call data to known demographics for prospective voters in the campaign database, and then draws out all the demographic factors that correlate with the undecided and soft-support voters (Malchow 1997, 37). Once the target groups are identified, the campaign can use traditional voter contact techniques to persuade and motivate the voters.

In Oregon's 1996 special election for the U.S. Senate, CHAID "identified a subset of Democrats who were even more undecided than the Independents: those who lived in the Eugene and non-Portland media markets and who did not live in the most highly-educated neighborhoods" (Malchow 38). CHAID is an idealized example of campaign modularization. "The program is not a substitute for political judgment," it seems, "[b]ut it provides a way to refine and measure that judgment" (38; see also Malchow 2000).

While some may look forward to the use of increasingly sophisticated statistical technologies—neural net pattern recognition and genetic algorithms that model the evolution of "selection formulae" through "thousands of 'generations' " (Malchow 1997, 39)—new-style campaigns are already putting data to good use in the form of innovative list management. A database marketing consultant says, "[P]olitical fundraising can learn a great deal from commercial database marketing where analysis and overlaid information provide insight that would be literally impossible without the process" (Halatyn 1998, 48). New donors can be identified by looking at the statistical characteristics of existing donors, just as persuadable voters can be identified by looking at persuaded voters. In a North Carolina Senate campaign, one candidate "utilized database overlays" in an effort to locate "soccer moms": "Public voting records, U.S. Postal Service sequencing lists and local directory information provided a target list of more than 10,000 priority voting targets," and an "intensive mail and phone campaign" was combined with voter ID calls to "find likely supporters and undecided voters to continue last-minute mail communications" and even a traditional door-to-door canvass operation (Crone 1998, 51).

Data overlays form the basis of "tactical cartography." One of the reasons that Geographic Information Systems (GIS) are becoming an important part of campaign operations is their ability to represent numerical data in a comprehensible format. For example, "By overlapping the boundaries of TV coverage with the location of a targeted voter group, campaigns can better understand the need to reach segmented audiences" (Lindauer 1999, 49). It is the power of visualization.

Data overlays can give a political operative a statistical listing of targeted precincts, relating the numbers to demographic characteristics and past campaign operations. Numerical readouts, however, are sometimes difficult to understand at first glance. But when strategists can literally see clusters of support, opposition, and, more importantly, uncommitted voters waiting to be persuaded, the full force of database technology comes into view.

In the recent past, the use of GIS was constrained by lofty hardware requirements, but at the turn of the twenty-first century, high-end desktop computers could easily handle most off-the-shelf GIS software. As such, the visual display of campaign data began trickling down to lower-level campaigns and elections.

While GIS provides long-term efficiency benefits, the capital costs of building an integrated political GIS database are still quite high. Traditional campaign structures cannot develop the necessary technological resources over the course of a single election cycle. As a result, campaigns become increasingly dependent upon outside consultants and vendors. The contemporary political marketplace offers clean voter lists, demographics, electoral histories, and consumer data, along with the data management tools that can help build donor, supporter, and voter contact files. As the cost of technology falls, and as more campaigns take advantage of digital campaign management, the days of the three-by-five file card are giving way to outsourced data management.

Campaign Communication

With powerful database management tools, the nature of traditional voter contact changes dramatically. No longer are voters targeted just by ward or precinct. They can be targeted individually, according to their own particular voting and demographic patterns. Mailings can be tailored with an eye to market segmentation, and telephone campaigns can be personalized to individual voters.

A relatively new entry to the field of voter contact is "call center" technology, which is seen in the private sector as a leading form of mass-customized marketing. Moving far beyond the phone bank or the answering machine, call centers track consumer data and configure appropriate messages for each contact that they make. In one scenario from the financial services industry, communications software "generates a real time script that lets the customer service representative offer products or services tailored to the caller. For example, a customer seeking to stop a check may also be offered a new car loan, because the representative will know the customer is almost finished paying off his previous loan" (Wreden 1998). The political uses of such technology are obvious. If each communication with a persuadable voter can be coded into a campaign database, then the candidate's message can be refined on a virtually one-to-one basis. Mass communication gives way to mass customization.

Call center consultant Rosanne Desmone suggests that recent technological advances like "predictive dialers," which get the voter on the line before transferring the call to a call center agent, "dramatically increase the time that agents spent talking to donors—achieving 45 minutes of talk time per agent per hour compared to 22 minutes or less when dialing manually" (1999, 40). More importantly, "By capturing, processing, and reporting real-time critical performance data, such as agent talk time, average call length, call abandon rate, live answer rates and close rates, dialers enable fundraisers to change strategies and/or implementation to maximize telecampaign results" (48). Political telemarketing can be used for both fund-raising and voter contact. In Jeb Bush's 1998 campaign for governor of Florida, Bush "timed his Dade County Spanish-speaking media with a bilingual mail drop and made a personal phone call in Spanish to over 60,000 Cubans and Hispanics through [a] TEAMVoice™ CTI broadcaster" (Porter 1999, 54).

New-style campaigns also depend on sophisticated Web sites. Campaign 2000 demonstrated a quantum leap in Web site design. One of the most sophisticated sites in 1996 was that of the Clinton–Gore campaign, which, in addition to informational material, also gave visitors the chance to map their own Electoral College victory. Four years later, the old Clinton-Gore site seemed positively archaic. Web sites for both Al Gore and George W. Bush offered policy information on virtually all subject areas, used streaming audio and video so that visitors could watch new ad campaigns, and sought contributions via secure Web transaction systems. So confident was the Gore campaign of the Web site's completeness that its chairman could tell a conference call of top advisers that all necessary talking points could be found on www.algore2000.com.

Campaigns are moving strongly into the Internet marketplace. *Campaigns & Elections* magazine devotes a section of each issue to campaign Web sites. Companies like Aristotle, which got its start selling voter and donor lists—now available by credit card over the Web—have moved into Web site production, banner ads, Web-based contributions, and GIS. The Aristotle approach mirrors preexisting trends in the private sector. "Direct marketers always have yearned for more customization, personalization, and automation," and "by combining our traditional direct mail knowledge with the power of Internet technology, the holy grail is within reach" (Jeffrey B. Morris 1999, 50). One marketing consultant envisions a process whereby representatives in a widely scattered sales force "customize their own direct mail programs" using a "database . . . built in real-time, with each rep selecting the components of [his or her own] mailer" (48). Jeb Bush integrated mass media, direct mail, and political telemarketing to hit the Spanish-speaking population in Dade County with a one-two-three punch. According to Bush's telecommunications adviser, audio and visual resources must become part of a campaign's plan. "The key is to marry advanced telecommunications with digital technology and direct the voting public to an Internet site" (Porter 1999, 54).

Capital Costs

Mergers of communications and technology require substantial funding. A single telemarketing seat can cost thousands of dollars, even before the telemarketing agent is hired (Desmone 1999, 40). Sophisticated Web design can run tens or even hundreds of thousands of dollars for initial setup. Voting lists are expensive. New-style campaigns cost a lot of money because they rely on specialized expertise. For telephone services, a consultant who argues, "There is no substitute for experience," says "[c]andidates left to fend for themselves without the aid of a well constructed, organized and timed telemarketing campaign usually never really get a chance to get into the game" (53). A consultant's article in *Campaigns & Elections* entitled "Can Political Candidates Afford to Allow Their Data to Be Managed by Anyone but a Professional?" suggests that professionals "can take the burden of mission critical database management and related targeted communications off of the plate of the campaign manager" (Grefe 1998, 18). Consultants have a vested interest in outsourcing, but the logic is nonetheless compelling. Competition necessitates technical competence; technical competence is capital-intensive; and because campaign operations cannot afford to absorb the start-up costs, competitive campaigns must rely on outside consultants.

Consider Web site design. User-friendly software can help almost any technosavvy supporter to build a candidate's Web site. The difficulty is that Web sites built by amateurs end up looking amateurish. Web surfers are accustomed to visually attractive sites that never crash. They will inevitably be disappointed with a poorly designed site. Even worse, unless the designer is thoroughly familiar with server platforms and the fine distinctions among Web browsers and versions, the candidate's Web site may crash the *user's* computer—quite possibly losing a vote in the process. Top-notch sites require first-rate talent, if for no other reason than that Internet security is a growing necessity. To be hacker-proof—a particular concern for political sites, which are prime targets for computer mischief—the designer must know more about server technology than do nearly all other Internet users. When the campaign starts to deploy E-commerce applications to collect campaign contributions, the need for paid professionals becomes even greater. The campaign can hire either an outside consultant or it can contract with an existing E-commerce firm that has experience in political contributions. The relative value of volunteer Web designers is diminished, and it is becoming more and more doubtful that an in-house campaign staffer will be capable of designing a stable, secure, and up-to-date campaign Web site.

The capital costs of research, development, and experience cannot be shouldered by any single candidate operation. A candidate's loyalists will not be able to build professional Web sites, manage complex databases, layer demographic and electoral variables on GIS, and develop an integrated television, radio, Internet, call center, and mail outreach program. Polling and electoral targeting are becoming more sophisticated. The abundance of information available at the turn of the twenty-first century made opposition research an advanced skill. The new resources do not make campaigning much easier. Rather, campaigning becomes more complicated. The competitive nature of electoral politics ensures that each new technology escalates the need for campaigns to be faster, stronger, and more capable of doing battle with other technosavvy campaign operations. In the new millennium, only the uninformed would try to run a major campaign without drawing on experienced consultants using cutting-edge technology.

Knowledge comes at a price. In the late 1800s the capital costs of campaign management were borne by the major parties, as knowledge was stored in Tammany-style organizations. If, in the new millennium, traditional parties were still intact, there might be no need for the consultant industry. But in the 1960s and 1970s, with the rise of individualized campaign operations, party structures loosened, and consultants picked up the slack. Consultants, for their part, are loyal to party organizations insofar as they represent certain political ideals and a ready stock of clients. They have little interest in joining party hierarchies, and they treat their selection of candidates as a business decision. James Carville's minimalist criteria are representative: "I will work for a Democrat who I can get along with who is neither a bigot nor a crook" (Matalin and Carville 1995, 55).

The decline of parties led to a fragmented marketplace and the rise of independent consultancies; the resurgence of political parties can be attributed partly to the parties' recognition that they can serve as consultancy brokers, harnessing the power of professional expertise by distributing money and referrals to candidates in targeted races. But even as parties respond to the new environment, the fact that they are using, not remaking, consultant-based campaign techniques demonstrates a concession to the new reality: independent campaign operatives have taken over the management of American political campaigns.

The value that campaign consultants provide is specialized expertise. Imported from the private sector, television advertising and research-driven market segmentation were used heavily in the 1952 Dwight Eisenhower campaign, which used the services of television advertising pioneer Rosser Reeves, whose best-known slogan was, "M&M's—Melts in your mouth, not in your hands." In 1968 Richard Nixon relied on a handpicked media team, including Roger Ailes, executive producer of the popular *Mike Douglas Show*. In 1996 Bill Clinton used Bob Squier of Squier Knapp Ochs, a Washington-based media firm that handled a wide variety of clients. As if to demonstrate that the component parts of media consultancy truly are interchangeable, Ailes, who also worked for Ronald Reagan and George Bush, would later return to television as president of Fox News Channel, and Bob Squier, whose knowledge of damage control was virtually unrivaled, helped America Online respond to bad publicity when customers complained about busy signals interrupting their online service. Political professionalism, borne of private sector marketing, had returned to its point of origin, carrying new tools useful in the business world.

George Stephanopoulos, when he first met James Carville, reflected on the changes that had taken place since Kennedy's time:

Theodore H. White's *The Making of the President, 1960* described the major political advisors of the day as a few dozen Washington lawyers, "who in their dark-paneled chambers nurse an amateur's love for politics and dabble in it whenever their practice permits." By 1991, that description had the dated feel of a sepia-toned photograph, harking back to an era when political consultants, like tennis players in long pants, were not paid for their work. There were still amateurs who loved the game in 1991, but campaigns were now run by professionals. (1999, 45)

From 1991 to the turn of the twenty-first century, the campaign marketplace began to require increasing specialization.

According to one observer, general consultants like James Carville, who supervised a political campaign from top to bottom, "are dinosaurs of the consulting world" (Glasser 2000a). The tremendous profits that can be made by skillful entrepreneurs and the increasing complexity of political campaigns make for a campaign context in which specialization is sometimes prized over broad-spectrum talent. A large campaign might find itself hiring a strategist who bills by the hour; a pollster who charges a flat fee per survey; an opposition researcher who runs up billable hours; a media consultant who bases costs on a mix of production fees and commissions; an ad placement consultant who takes an additional cut of all media buys; a telemarketer who will invoice the campaign for a retainer plus a cost per call; and a direct-mail consultant whose fees will vary according to the type of mail requested, the lists used, and the size of the mailing sent. The strategist, in turn, might purchase demographic data from an outside contractor and voter lists from yet another, and the media consultant might work with a Web master who subcontracts visual production, site hosting, and E-commerce services to yet another set of professionals. Campaign management becomes the business of integrating subcontracted professional services.

Mitigating Forces

Despite the powerful centrifugal forces that break up campaigns and distribute their parts to a wide range of outside contractors, campaign decentralization is limited by a variety of constraints inherent in political operations. In most small, municipal-level campaigns, the economic benefits of consultancy are not always realized. Examples of consultant-free campaigns abound. Councilman Ed Baum, a Republican in a small Ohio city, gained his seat with a self-run campaign that cost only a few thousand dollars. Baum's team was made up of friends and acquaintances, and his strategy was developed by reading a few good books. He built name recognition with yard signs and he ran ads in the local paper. After his victory, Baum sat down and figured out what went right and what did not so he could do even better next time. The need for a political consultant in this sort of race seems remote. Little, if any, efficiency would be gained by turning to a professional. But aside from pure economic calculations, a number of other factors mitigate against the power of consultants in campaigns and elections.

First, the public is not infinitely malleable—some candidates just do not persuade voters. In media-driven California, Michael Huffington's losing 1994 campaign for Senate and Al Checchi's disastrous bid for the gubernatorial nomination in 1998 both suffered from backlash against candidates who seemed to be buying the election through paid media. Huffington was seen as an "empty suit" whose $30 million campaign was orchestrated by his then-wife, Arianna. Checchi's advertisements and campaign materials, coordinated by top consultants Mark Penn and Bob Shrum, reflected the sort of corporate professionalism that one might expect from a $40 million campaign run by an airline executive, but they were never able to connect the candidate with the voters. Said media consultant Alex Castellanos, "You know, sometimes the problem is not the label on the can, it's the dog food. And sometimes there's just dog food dogs don't like" (1998). In campaign politics, media makes a difference, but rarely can it make *all* the difference.

Second, loyalty counts. Even as candidates look to outside consultants, they continue to rely on inside advisers. Wise candidates form kitchen cabinets of trusted friends and colleagues. During the electoral season, the group might become a formal campaign committee. In office, a few of these loyalists might go on the official payroll. Even in the off-season, public officials depend on the counsel of their close advisers. Both major party presidential candidates in 2000 commanded this sort of loyalty. Al Gore had long depended on his former chiefs of staff—Peter Knight, Roy Neel, Jack Quinn, and Ron Klain—all of whom worked high up in the vice president's campaign. George W. Bush's inner campaign circle was filled with staffers who had demonstrated their loyalty for years in the governor's office. Candidates turn to these clusters of intimates for confidential advice, alternative interpretations of a consultant's polling data, and a listening ear to hear the musings and frustrations of candidates in the middle of a tough campaign. Consultants, who must treat politics as a business, who may be employed by a party committee, who are probably working for several clients at once, and who may well fade from view days after the election, are not always privy to the internal decision-making processes of candidates.

Third, the same technological forces that complicate campaigns can also simplify, to a degree, the campaign process. This is achieved by the production of off-the-shelf solutions to standard campaign problems. With over 500,000 electoral offices in the United States, there is a rich market for campaign advice and technology. Again, no one size fits all, but the similarities that allow professional consultants to modularize components of their campaigns also create a mass market for the tools of the trade. Campaign books provide generalized advice. The cable industry reminds professionals that digital "interconnects" make ad placement easier by consolidating transmission and billing. With respect to campaign data, a new-style candidate at ease with computer technology can, over the course of a long weekend, download a county's demographics, retrieve voter lists, layer this information on top of prior electoral data, and then display the results on a computer-generated map. In this way, candidates and their loyalists have the ability to maintain campaign operations close to the vest as they contain the costs of electioneering.

Fourth, good management demands that the number of consultants be limited. As more consultants get involved in a campaign, management issues come to the fore. With each layer of consultants comes a new possibility of media leaks, cost-control problems, and an overall inability to manage a large and growing operation. With respect to out-of-state consultants, campaigns are well advised to weigh the benefits of "a broad, national perspective on what works and what doesn't" against the reality that "overextended national consultants delegate important work to second and third tier assistants" (Faucheux 1996). Simple communication can become problematic. Even if the consultants are drawn from within the state, the task of bringing a large number of profit-driven consultants to work together can sometimes overwhelm even the ablest of political candidates. That was one of the problems on the Checchi campaign, it seems, where battles reportedly broke out among consultants who became overly aggressive in seeking fees (Glasser 2000b).

Finally, there is an inherent skepticism of outside consultants that potentially affects strategic goals. Joe McGinniss decried the use of public relations tactics in political campaigns (1969). For an electorate that demands authenticity in its candidates, there will always be something untoward in the hiring of people whom James A. Thurber and Candice J. Nelson call "campaign warriors" (2000). Mercenaries are little more respected in politics than in battle, and the very fact that a campaign has hired a high-priced, out-of-state consultant can be used against the candidate. Is it a sign of desperation? Does it mean that the candidate is trying to buy the election? And there are larger questions. If consultants use the same tricks of the trade over and over again, will American politics become homogenized at the expense of originality? Given the propensity of the electorate to seek out "authentic" candidates—Jesse Ventura's campaign succeeded partly because the candidate so often departed from the routine campaign messages—any hint that a campaign is mass-customized tends to chip away at a candidate's image. For many, the rise of political consultants signifies a move away from the politics of personal connection and toward an era of hypermediated political connections.

POLITICAL CONNECTIONS

It is a worthy question: Did the people of earlier times have a closer connection to power than those of the new millennium? In some ways, they did; in other ways, they did not. At no time did a golden age of politics exist. Never did money fail to provide some degree of access, nor was there a time when campaigns did not attempt to change the public mind for purely political reasons. The Civil War was a violent extension of partisan and sectional politics. Later, Mark Hanna took in $250,000 from John D. Rockefeller's Standard Oil, the fortunes of which were endangered by William Jennings Bryan. What passes for mean-spirited politics at the beginning of the new millennium pales in comparison to the partisan witch-hunts of Joseph McCarthy. But there is a sense in which all these comparisons are quite irrelevant. First, each tends toward the extreme. The Civil War, Rockefeller, and McCarthy are outliers in the American experience. Second, the forms of voter contact provided by campaign organizations have changed so radically that any comparison of old- and new-style campaigns is problematic.

One of the most common bases of comparison is the infamous politics of George Washington Plunkitt. Plunkitt boasted personal knowledge of everyone whom he represented. While there may be self-aggrandizement in his claim, certainly the urban political machines, which merged social and political affairs, fostered a more personalized connection between voters and elected officials. The old party hierarchies had a one-to-one relationship with many of their members. But a close read of *Plunkitt of Tammany Hall* (Riordon 1995) shows a far more attenuated relationship between candidates and constituents.

Plunkitt got his start when he built a political following of voters who would cast their ballots the way he wanted. The voters in his base of support became Plunkitt's "marketable goods" (Riordon 1995, 8). Plunkitt used his newfound assets to link up with party leaders at district headquarters, which, in turn, was beholden to the city and state organizations, respectively, on up to the national party level. In the world of the old party machines, hierarchies of power were stratified through multilayered echelons. The idea that one of Plunkitt's loyal supporters could speak with a Democratic governor or president is all but unthinkable. On one hand, the old party structure was highly personalized. Plunkitt had an immediate relationship with his initial supporters, as indeed his first loyalists were a cousin and his friends. On the other hand, there was virtually no contact between low-level supporters and leaders up the chain of command. Party hierarchies mediated relationships between leaders and voters by inserting many layers between them.

New-style campaigns have fundamentally changed the old-style party relationships, bringing with them novel forms of voter alienation. As campaign scholar Christopher Arterton has noted,

> Modern politics have eviscerated [the old party] networks, replacing them with polling and mass communications. In the process, the individual voter has become a cipher, a statistical construct rather than a living, breathing person. Targeting involves creating an electoral majority by sending out messages to voters on the basis of the probability of support, depending on certain demographic characteristics or known "facts" about the individuals in a given group. Given the large number of citizens involved, campaigners cannot treat (or even conceptualize) these voters as individuals. In fact, to some degree, the individuals themselves are unimportant. As long as the total number of supporters can be pushed over the 50 percent mark, one voter is more or less substitutable by another. (2000, 22)

Depersonalization becomes a hallmark of American politics in the period that followed the decline of traditional parties.

In some ways, however, the fall of old party hierarchies resulted from the forging of new relationships between voters and candidates. When Ronald Reagan campaigned in the 1980 primaries, he "went over the heads" of the party leadership by speaking directly to Republican voters. The appeal was made on the airwaves—it was in no sense a personal, one-to-one relationship—but Reagan's politics were a great deal more personalized than the classic "smoke-filled rooms" of Plunkitt's day. Nixon, for his part, could run apart from the Republican establishment because television allowed him to bypass the party leadership. George McGovern received the Democratic nomination in 1972, in large part, because he had mastered the art of direct mail. Jimmy Carter made effective use of television to present himself as an outsider at precisely the moment when the political marketplace demanded such a president. Ronald Reagan was the "Great Communicator," aided by public relations consultant Michael Deaver. In 1992 Bill Clinton used the "town hall" format to great effect, dispensing with the probing questions of skeptical reporters.

Clinton's town hall meetings are instructive. On one hand, the real audience was the television viewership—in this sense, it was a mediated event. On the other hand, the questions were posed to candidates by "real people" outside the usual channels of party politics. Does this make politics more or less distant? In a curious way, the randomly selected recipients of a survey call or the carefully chosen subjects of a mall intercept have become powerful new voices in the electoral process. The nature of democratic representation has truly changed.

Blumenthal noted that "consultants . . . embody many of the virtues espoused by the turn-of-the-century Progressives. They are usually dispassionate critics of politics, wary of control by party bosses" (1980, 7). The corrosive power of new technologies, in the hands of independent consultants, has, for better or worse, sealed the fate of traditional party hierarchies. Precision targeting and sophisticated marketing techniques hold out one-to-one customer relationships as their main goal. New-style campaigns do not foster the warm relationships that one finds in sentimental depictions of American politics, in which public officials know each voter personally, but neither do they promote the remote interactions of mass media advertising. Arterton sees a possibility, at least, that Internet technology may help "establish a new, more personalized connection between candidate and voter," perhaps even helping to "restore some balance and mutual respect to the relationship" (2000, 22).

Of course, it is possible to romanticize new-style politics. Consultant-turned-pundit Dick Morris sees the Internet as a new "*vox populi* in cyberspace" that will change government by reforming elections and reducing the power of money in campaigns (1999b, 27). A serious review of elections and campaigns, however, suggests that technology has neither brought candidates and voters closer together, nor has it pushed them further apart. Rather, the nature of the relationship has been so profoundly altered that comparisons between old- and new-style politics are difficult to render. When a candidate's voter contact strategy targets swing voters, does it make politics more or less personalized? When party leaders enlist independent consultants to win state senate races, have the parties consolidated their power or ceded it to outsiders? The critical transformation that has taken place in American elections has filtered down from presidential campaigns to mayoral races, and as students of politics seek to appreciate changes in American government, they must unravel the nature of new-style electioneering.

Central to the new understanding of political campaigns is the recognition that professional electioneering is a new craft. It is no longer a high art, if it ever was such, in which the intuitive faculties of candidates would impress the electorate with spontaneous oratory and principled debate. Nor is it a science in which the voter is held up for detached observation by pollsters and then manipulated by media consultants. Instead, in the competitive environment created by the two-party system, campaign operatives must constantly refine their expertise, mixing technology and creativity in the search for electoral success. Consultant-centered campaigns are less beholden to the old party structures than their predecessors were, as candidates have released themselves to set up their own campaign operations and have come to rely on professionals who know the strategies and tactics of campaign management. In this sense, new-style electioneering is both art and science—the product of ingenuity as well as research, experience, and analysis. As such, consultant-based campaigns are best understood as a new campaign craft.

References

Abramson, Paul R., John H. Aldrich, and David W. Rohde. 1999. *Change and Continuity in the 1996 and 1998 Elections*. Washington, DC: Congressional Quarterly.

Adamany, David. 1969. *Financing Politics: Recent Wisconsin Elections*. Madison: University of Wisconsin Press.

Adamany, David W., and George E. Agree. 1975. *Political Money: A Strategy for Campaign Financing in America*. Baltimore: Johns Hopkins University Press.

Agranoff, Robert. 1972. *The New Style in Election Campaigns*. Boston: Holbrook.

Ahuja, Sunil, Staci L. Beavers, Cynthia Berreau, Anthony Dodson, Patrick Hourigan, Steven Showalter, Jeff Walz, and John R. Hibbing. 1993. "Modern Congressional Theory Meets the 1992 House Elections." *Political Research Quarterly* 47:891–908.

Alexander, Kathy. 1994. "Television Is the Name of the Game." *Atlanta Constitution*. October 16, B1.

Alford, John, Holly Teeters, Daniel S. Ward, and Rick K. Wilson. 1994. "Overdraft: The Political Cost of Congressional Malfeasance." *Journal of Politics* 56:788–801.

Allen, Cathy. 1995. "Women on the Run." *Campaigns & Elections,* October.

———. 1990a. "Peer-Pressure Politics." *Campaigns & Elections,* June.

———. 1990b. "Impressing the Press." *Campaigns & Elections,* April.

———. 1990c. "GOTV." *Campaigns & Elections,* October.

Anderson, Margo J., ed. 2000. *Encyclopedia of the U.S. Census*. Washington, DC: Congressional Quarterly.

Ansolabehere, Steven, and Shanto Iyengar. 1997. *Going Negative: How Political Advertisements Shrink and Polarize the Electorate*. New York: Free Press.

———. 1995. "Winning through Advertising: It's All in the Context." In *Campaigns and Elections American Style,* edited by James A. Thurber and Candice J. Nelson. Boulder, CO: Westview.

Arnold, Marguerite. 1999. "TV Spot Production: A Political Campaign Primer." *Campaigns & Elections*, September.

Arterton, Chris. 2000. "New Relationships." In "20/20 Vision." *Campaigns & Elections*, April.

Atlas, Mark. 1989. "Gambling with Elections." In *Campaigns & Elections: A Reader in Modern American Politics,* edited by Larry J. Sabato. Glenview, IL: Scott, Foresman.

Backstrom, Charles H., and Gerald Hursh-Cesar. 1981. *Survey Research.* New York: Macmillan.

Baer, Denise. 1995. "Contemporary Strategy and Agenda Setting." In *Campaigns and Elections American Style,* edited by James A. Thurber and Candice J. Nelson. Boulder, CO: Westview.

Bailey, Michael A., Ronald A. Faucheux, Paul S. Herrnson, and Clyde Wilcox, eds. 2000. *Campaigns & Elections: Contemporary Case Studies.* Washington, DC: Congressional Quarterly.

Baker, Peter. 1996. "Contrasting GOP Strategies Mark Senate Primary in Va." *Washington Post.* May 26, sec. A.

Balz, Dan. 1996. "Clinton Broke Republican Grip on Some Suburban County Strongholds." *Washington Post.* November 10, sec. A.

Bayer, Michael J., and Joseph Rodota. 1989. "Computerized Opposition Research." In *Campaigns & Elections: A Reader in Modern American Politics,* edited by Larry J. Sabato. Boulder, CO: Westview.

Beaudry, Ann, and Bob Schaeffer. 1986. *Winning Local and State Elections.* New York: Free Press.

Beck, Paul A., and Frank J. Sorauf. 1992. *Party Politics in America.* New York: Harper-Collins.

Beiler, David. 2000. "The Body Politic Registers a Protest." In *Campaigns & Elections: Contemporary Case Studies,* edited by Michael A. Bailey, et al. Washington, DC: Congressional Quarterly.

———. 1994a. "Abraham vs. Romney." *Campaigns & Elections,* October.

———. 1994b. "Day of the Iguana." *Campaigns & Elections,* June.

———. 1994c. "The Harder They Fall." *Campaigns & Elections,* May.

———. 1994d. "Return of the Plainsman." *Campaigns & Elections,* July.

———. 1990. "Precision Politics." *Campaigns & Elections,* February/March.

Benenson, Bob. 1995. "Jesse Jackson Jr. Wins House Seat." *Congressional Quarterly Weekly Report* 53:3836.

Bennett, Matthew. 2000. Telephone interview with Michael John Burton. July 17.

Berelson, Bernard R., Paul F. Lazarsfeld, and William N. McPhee. 1954. *Voting.* Chicago: University of Chicago Press.

Bike, William S. 1998. *Winning Local Elections: A Comprehensive Guide to Electoral Success.* Juneau, AK: Denali.

Bilbank, Dana. 2000. "The Year of the Latino Voter? Only in Campaign Rhetoric." *Washington Post.* May 21, sec. B.

Blumenthal, Sidney. 1980. *The Permanent Campaign: Inside the World of Elite Political Operatives.* Boston: Beacon.

Bogart, Leo. 2000. "Politics, Polls, and Poltergeists: A Critical View of the 1996 Election." In *Election Polls, the News Media, and Democracy,* edited by Paul J. Lavrakas and Michael W. Traugott. Chatham, NJ: Chatham House.

Boorstin, Daniel J. 1964. *The Image: A Guide to Pseudo-events in America.* New York: Harper and Row.

Bovee, John. 1998. "How to Do Opposition Research on the Internet." *Campaigns & Elections,* September.

Bradshaw, Joel. 1995. "Who Will Vote for You and Why: Designing Strategy and Theme." In *Campaigns and Elections American Style,* edited by James A. Thurber and Candice J. Nelson. Boulder, CO: Westview.

Braun, Gerry. 1999. "Bilbray Catches Heat from Assembly Woman over Trip Down Under." *San Diego Union Tribune.* August 12, sec. B.

Broder, David S. 1971. *The Party's Over: The Failure of Politics in America.* New York: Harper and Row.

Brown, James, and Philip M. Seib. 1976. *The Art of Politics: Electoral Strategies and Campaign Management.* Port Washington, NY: Alfred.

Brown, Ron, and Nello Giorgetti. 1992. "Downballot Doldrums." *Campaigns & Elections,* June.

Bryan, William Jennings. 1913. *Speeches of William Jennings Bryan.* New York: Funk and Wagnalls.

Buckley v. Valeo. 1976. 424 U.S. 1.

Bumiller, Elisabeth. 2000. "Giuliani Accuses Mrs. Clinton of Negative Calls, Disguised as Polling." *New York Times.* February 23, sec. B.

Butler, David, and Austin Ranney. 1992. *Electioneering: A Comparative Study of Continuity and Change.* New York: Oxford University Press.

Castellanos, Alex. 1998. Interviewed for PBS, *The :30 Second Candidate.* Transcript at http://www.pbs.org/30secondcandidate.

Cisneros, Henry. 1999. "Winning the Crucial Hispanic Vote in 2000." *Campaigns & Elections,* August.

Cohen, Mary W., ed. 1992. *Congressional Campaign Finances: History, Facts, and Controversy.* Washington, DC: Congressional Quarterly.

Connell, Mike. 2000. "A Guide to Finding a Smart Internet Strategy for 2000." *Campaigns & Elections,* December/January.

Conway, Margaret M. 1985. *Political Participation in the United States.* Washington, DC: Congressional Quarterly.

Conway, Margaret M., and Joanne Connor Green. 1995. "Political Action Committees and the Political Process in the 1990s." In *Interest Group Politics,* edited by Allan J. Cigler and Burdett A. Loomis. Washington, DC: Congressional Quarterly.

Cotter, Cornelius P., James Gibson, John F. Bibby, and Robert J. Huckshorn. 1984. *Party Organizations in American Politics.* New York: Praeger.

Cover, Albert D. 1977. "One Good Term Deserves Another: The Advantage of Incumbency in Congressional Elections." *American Journal of Political Science* 21:523–41.

Craney, Glen. 1990. "Kentucky." *Congressional Quarterly* 48:3311.

Crespi, Irving. 1988. *Pre-Election Polling.* New York: Russell Sage Foundation.

Crone, Brad. 1998. "Finding Priority Precincts with Database Overlays." *Campaigns & Elections,* December/January.

Cross, Al. 1994. "Kentucky Derby." *Campaigns & Elections,* July.

Dahl, Robert A. 1961. *Who Governs?* New Haven, CT: Yale University Press.

Daves, Robert P. 2000. "Who Will Vote? Ascertaining Likelihood to Vote and Modeling a Probable Electorate in Preelection Polls." In *Election Polls, the News Media, and Democracy,* edited by Paul J. Lavrakas and Michael W. Traugott. Chatham, NJ: Chatham House.

Davis, Lanny J. 1999. *Truth to Tell: Tell It Early, Tell It All, Tell It Yourself.* New York: Simon and Schuster.

Dawidziak, Mike. 1991. "Use Ethnic Targeting to Focus Mailings." *Campaigns & Elections,* November.

Deaver, Michael K., with Mickey Herskowitz. 1987. *Behind the Scenes.* New York: William Morrow.

Desmone, Rosanne. 1999. "Exponential Boost: The New Contact Center." *Campaigns & Elections,* October/November.

Diamond, Edwin, and Stephen Bates. 1992. *The Spot: The Rise of Political Advertising on Television.* Cambridge: MIT Press.

Dimock, Michael A., and Gary C. Jacobson. 1995. "Checks and Choices: The House Bank Scandal's Impact on Voters in 1992." *Journal of Politics* 57:1143–59.

Dinkin, Robert J. 1989. *Campaigning in America: The History of Election Practices.* New York: Greenwood.

Dowd, Matthew. 1992. "Bottom of the Ninth: If You Target Them, They Will Vote." *Campaigns & Elections,* November.

Duncan, Phil, ed. 1993. *Politics in America 1994.* Washington, DC: Congressional Quarterly.

Duncan, Philip D. 1999. "Incumbent in the Cross Hairs." *Campaigns & Elections,* December.

Dunn, Anita. 1995. "The Best Campaign Wins: Local Press Coverage of Nonpresidential Races." In *Campaigns and Elections American Style,* edited by James A. Thurber and Candice J. Nelson. Boulder, CO: Westview.

Dwyer, Diana, and Victoria A. Farrar-Myers. 2000. *Legislative Labyrinth: Congress and Campaign Finance Reform.* Washington, DC: Congressional Quarterly.

Edmondson, Brad. 1994. "Crime Crazy." *American Demographics* 16:2.

Egan, Timothy. 1996. "Of Marriage, Money and a Lawmaker's Woes." *New York Times.* May 2, sec. A.

Ehrenhalt, Alan. 1991. *The United States of Ambition.* New York: Random House.

Fairbank, John. 1993. "Proving Conventional." *Campaigns & Elections,* April/May.

Fairbank, John, and Paul Goodwin. 1993. "When Two's a Race and Three's a Crowd." *Campaigns & Elections,* January.

Farinella, Marc. 1992. "Research Resources." *Campaigns & Elections,* January.

Faucheux, Ron. 1998. *The Road to Victory, 2000: The Best of the Best from Campaigns & Elections.* 2nd ed. Dubuque, IA: Kendall/Hunt.

———. 1996. "Should You Hire Out-of-State Consultants?" *Campaigns & Elections,* February.

———. 1993. "Don Beyer, Mike Farriss, and the Wizard of Oz." *Campaigns & Elections,* December/January.

Fenno, Richard F. 1996. *Senators on the Campaign Trail: The Politics of Representation.* Norman: University of Oklahoma Press.

———.1989. *The Making of a Senator: Dan Quayle.* Washington, DC: Congressional Quarterly.

———.1978. *Home Style: House Members in Their Districts.* Boston: Little, Brown.

———. 1973. *Congressmen in Committees.* Boston: Little, Brown.

Ferejohn, John A. 1977. "On the Decline in Competition in Congressional Elections." *American Political Science Review* 71:166–76.

Ferguson, Andrew. 1996. "Live Free or Cry: The Truth about New Hampshire." *The Weekly Standard,* January.

Fiorina, Morris P. 1981. *Retrospective Voting in American National Elections.* New Haven, CT: Yale University Press.

Fowler, Linda L. 1995. "Campaign Ethics and Political Trust." In *Campaigns and Elections American Style,* edited by James A. Thurber and Candice J. Nelson. Boulder, CO: Westview.

———. 1993. *Candidates, Congress, and the American Democracy.* Ann Arbor: University of Michigan Press.

Fowler, Linda L., and Robert D. McClure. 1989. *Political Ambition: Who Decides to Run for Congress.* New Haven, CT: Yale University Press.

Frantz, Douglas. 1999. "Plenty of Dirty Jobs in Politics and a New Breed of Diggers." *New York Times.* July 6, sec. A.

Frendries, John, and Alan R. Gitelson. 1999. "Local Parties in the 1990s: Spokes in a Candidate-Centered Wheel." In *The State of the Parties,* edited by John C. Green and Daniel M. Shea. Lanham, MD: Rowman and Littlefield.

Friedenberg, Robert V. 1997. *Communication Consultants in Political Campaigns: Ballot Box Warriors.* Westport, CT: Praeger.

Friedman, Lawrence M. 1993. *Crime and Punishment in American History.* New York: Basic Books.

Glad, Paul W. 1964. *McKinley, Bryan, and the People.* Philadelphia: J.B. Lippincott.

Glass, Andrew J. 2000. "Campaign 2000: Internet: Internet Vital to Campaigns; TV Still Best Way to Reach Voters, but Web Best Way to Raise Funds, Panel Says." *Atlanta Constitution.* May 11, sec. A.

Glasser, Susan B. 2000a. "Hired Guns Fuel Fundraising Race." *Washington Post.* April 30, sec. A.

———. 2000b. "Winning a Stake in a Losing Race." *Washington Post.* May 1, sec. A.

———. 2000c. "Consultants Pursue Promising Web of New Business." *Washington Post.* May 3, sec. A.

Goodliffe, Jay. 2000. "The 1998 Utah Second Congressional District Race." In *Outside Money: Soft Money and Issue Advocacy in the 1998 Congressional Elections,* edited by David B. Magleby. Lanham, MD: Rowman and Littlefield.

Green, John C., and Daniel M. Shea, eds. 1999. *The State of the Parties: The Changing Role of Contemporary American Parties,* 3rd ed. Lanham, MD: Rowman & Littlefield.

Greenblatt, Alan. 1995. "Republican Wins Minnesota Seat." *Congressional Quarterly Weekly Report* 53:3835.

Grefe, Edward A. 1998. "Can Political Candidates Afford to Allow Their Data to Be Managed by Anyone but a Professional?" *Campaigns & Elections,* December/January.

Grey, Lawrence. 1999. *How to Win a Local Election.* Rev. ed. New York: M. Evans.

Gross, Donald A., and Penny Miller. 2000. "The 1998 Kentucky Senate and Sixth District Races." In *Outside Money: Soft Money and Issue Advocacy in the 1998 Congressional Elections,* edited by David B. Magleby. Lanham, MD: Rowman and Littlefield.

Gruenwald, Juliana. 1995. "Wyden, Smith Vie for Center in Race for Packwood Seat." *Congressional Quarterly Weekly Report* 53:3755.

The Guide to Background Investigations. 1998. Tulsa, OK.: Source Publications.

Guzzetta, S.J. 2000. *The Campaign Manual: A Definitive Study of the Modern Political Campaign Process.* 5th ed. Anaheim, CA: Political Publishing.

Halatyn, Tom. 1998. "Using Data Files to Raise More Bucks." *Campaigns & Elections,* December/January.

Hallow, Ralph Z. 1997a. "Brad O'Leary." *Campaigns & Elections,* September.

———. 1997b. "Brad O'Leary's Fundraising Secrets." *Campaigns & Elections,* September.

Harris, John F. 1998. "Clinton's Campaign Consultants Reaped Millions from TV Ads." *Washington Post*. January 4, sec. A.

Hart, Neesa. 1992. "Buddy, Can You Spare a Grand?" *Campaigns & Elections*, September.

Hart, Roderick P. 1994. *Seducing America: How Television Charms the Modern Voter*. New York: Oxford University Press.

Hathaway, T. R. 1996. "Bright Ideas from Pat Buchanan's Integrated Campaign Database." *Campaigns & Elections,* August.

Helton, Charmagne, and Kathey Pruitt. 1998. "Millner Pulls TV Ad Erroneously Reporting Barnes Parole Vote." *Atlanta Constitution*. August 6, sec. E.

Henry, Gary T. 1990. "Practical Sampling." *Applied Social Research Methods Series*. Newbury Park, CA: Sage.

Herrnson, Paul S. 2000. *Congressional Elections: Campaigning at Home and in Washington*. Washington, DC: Congressional Quarterly.

———. 1998. *Congressional Elections: Campaigning at Home and in Washington*. Washington, DC: Congressional Quarterly.

———. 1994. "Party Strategy and Campaign Activities in the 1992 Congressional Elections." In *The State of the Parties,* edited by Daniel M. Shea and John C. Green. Lanham, MD: Rowman and Littlefield.

———. 1988. *Party Campaigning in the 1980s*. Cambridge: Harvard University Press.

Hershey, Marjorie R. 1984. *Running for Office: The Political Education of Campaigners*. Chatham, NJ: Chatham House.

Hesla, Maren. 1992. "Credibility Crusade." *Campaigns & Elections*, January.

Hewitt, John. 1999. "Sending Effective Press Releases." *Campaigns & Elections*, April.

Himes, David. 1995. "Strategy and Tactics for Candidate Fund-Raising." In *Campaigns and Elections American Style,* edited by James A. Thurber and Candice J. Nelson. Boulder, CO: Westview.

Hines, Cragg. 1992. "The Reagan–Bush Era; Reagan's Simple Message Hit the Spot." *Houston Chronicle*. August 16.

Hockaday, Tom, and Becki Donatelli. 2000. "Fundraising Capabilities." In "20/20 Vision." *Campaigns & Elections,* April.

Hockaday, Tom, and Martin Edlund. 1999. "Banner Advertising as a Voter Outreach Tool." *Campaigns & Elections,* May.

Hood, John. 1993. "The Third Way." *Reason* 24:40–43.

Hutchens, Jon. 1996. "Buying Cable Time: How to Get Your Money's Worth." *Campaigns & Elections,* June.

Hyman, H. H., and P. B. Sheatsley. 1950. "The Current Status of American Public Opinion." In *The Teaching of Contemporary Affairs,* edited by J.C. Payne. Washington, DC: National Council of Social Studies, 11–34.

Idelson, Holly. 1990. "Michigan." *Congressional Quarterly* 48:3318.

Ifill, Gwen. 1992. "Democrats Exercising Their Legs and Lips." *New York Times.* July 20, sec. A.

Institute of Politics. 1997. *Campaign for President: The Managers Look at '96*. Hollis, NH: Hollis.

Ireland, Doug. 1995. "The Rich Rise of Lamar Alexander." *The Nation* 260:517–22.

Jacobson, Gary C. 1997. *The Politics of Congressional Elections*. 4th ed. New York: Addison Wesley Longman.

Jalonick, Mary Clare. 2000a. "Bringing in the Bucks on the Web." *Campaigns & Elections,* April.

———. 2000b. "Greatest Hits II: Democratic House Candidate Sites." *Campaigns & Elections,* July.

Jamieson, Kathleen Hall. 1998. "Facing Up to It; What Those Polls Are Telling Us." *Washington Post.* March 22, sec. C.

———. 1992. *Dirty Politics.* New York: Oxford University Press.

———. 1984. *Packaging the Presidency.* New York: Oxford University Press.

Johnson, Dick. 1995. "Victory His, Jesse Jackson Jr. Heads to Congress." *New York Times,* December 14, sec. B.

Johnson, Wayne C. 1992. "First Do No Harm." *Campaigns & Elections,* July.

Johnson-Cartee, Karen S., and Gary A. Copeland. 1997. *Inside Political Campaigns: Theory and Practice.* Westport, CT: Praeger.

Johnson-Cartee, Karen S., and Gary A. Copeland. 1991. *Negative Political Advertising: Coming of Age.* Hillsdale, NJ: Lawrence Erlbaum Associates.

Jones, Ruth S. 1991. "Campaign and Party Finance in the American States." In *Campaign and Party Finance in North America and Western Europe,* edited by Arthur B. Gunlicks. Boulder, CO: Westview.

———. 1984. "Financing State Elections." In *Money and Politics in the United States: Financing Elections in the 1980s,* edited by Michael Malbin. Chatham, NJ: Chatham House.

Jones, Stanley. 1964. *The Presidential Election of 1896.* Madison: University of Wisconsin Press.

Joyella, Mark. 1994. "Beating the Son King." *Campaigns & Elections,* March.

Kanfer, Ron. 1991. "Direct to the Bank." *Campaigns & Elections,* July.

Kaplan, Robert L. 2000. "Getting the Most Out of Your Professional Fundraiser." *Campaigns & Elections,* February.

———. 1993. "Setting Up a Peer-to-Peer Fundraising Program." *Campaigns & Elections,* January.

———. 1991. "Psychology of Silence: Raising More Money by Psyching Out Donors." *Campaigns & Elections,* November.

Kayden, Xandra, and Eddie Mahe Jr., eds. 1985. *The Party Goes On.* New York: Basic Books.

Koelemay, Douglas. 1994. "Clay vs. Corbett: How a State Senate Incumbent in Alabama Was Out-Campaigned in an Upset Primary." *Campaigns & Elections,* September.

Krasno, Jonathan S. 1994. *Challengers, Competition, and Reelection.* New Haven, CT: Yale University Press.

Krehbiel, Keith, and John R. Wright. 1983. "The Incumbency Effect in Congressional Elections: A Test of Two Explanations." *American Journal of Political Science* 27: 140–57.

Krueger, Richard A. 1994. *Focus Groups: A Practical Guide for Applied Research.* Thousand Oaks, CA: Sage.

Kurtz, Howard. 1992. "Hotline to Campaign Central; Daily Clip Sheet Keeps the Pack Ahead." *Washington Post.* February 29, sec. D.

Lau, Richard. 1994. "An Analysis of the Accuracy of 'Trial Heat' Polls during the 1992 Presidential Election." *Public Opinion Quarterly* 58(1):2–20.

Lavin, Michael R. 1996. *Understanding the Census: A Guide for Marketers, Planners, Grant Writers, and Other Data Users.* Kenmore, NY: Epoch.

Lavrakas, Paul J. 1993. "Telephone Survey Methods: Sampling, Selection, and Supervision." *Applied Social Research Methods Series.* Newbury Park, CA: Sage.

Lindauer, Charles. 1999. "Tactical Cartography." *Campaigns & Elections,* April.

Longley, Lawrence D. 1992. "The Institutionalization of the National Democratic Party: A Process Stymied, Then Revitalized." *Wisconsin Political Scientist* 7:9–15.

Luntz, Frank I. 1988. *Candidates, Consultants, and Campaigns: The Style and Substance of American Electioneering.* Oxford, England: Basil Blackwood.

Magleby, David B., ed. 2000. *Outside Money: Soft Money and Issue Advocacy in the 1998 Congressional Elections.* Lanham, MD: Rowman and Littlefield.

Maisel, L. Sandy. 1990. "The Incumbency Advantage." In *Money, Elections, and Democracy: Reforming Congressional Campaign Finance,* edited by Margaret Latus Nugent and John R. Johannes. Boulder, CO: Westview.

Malbin, Michael J. 1995. "1994 Vote: The Money Story." In *America at the Polls: 1994,* edited by Everett Carl Ladd. New Brunswick, NJ: Roper Center for Public Opinion Research.

Malchow, Hall. 2000. "Predicting Voter Turnout: Applying New Tools." *Campaigns & Elections,* April.

———. 1997. "The Targeting Revolution in Political Direct Contact." *Campaigns & Elections,* June.

———. 1990. "10 Ways to Design In House Mail That Works." *Campaigns & Elections,* June/July.

Manes, Susan. 1990. "Up for Bid: A Common Cause View." In *Money, Elections, and Democracy: Reforming Congressional Campaign Finance,* edited by Latus Nugent and John R. Johannes. Boulder, CO: Westview.

Marquette, Jesse F. 1991. *Response Form Effects in Election Polling Process.* Phoenix: American Association for Public Opinion Research.

Martindale, Rob. 1994. "Ex-Teacher Tops Veteran Lawmaker." *Tulsa World,* September 21, sec. A.

Matalin, Mary, and James Carville. 1995. *All's Fair: Love, War, and Running for President.* New York: Touchstone.

Mayhew, David R. 1974a. "Congressional Elections: The Case of the Vanishing Marginals." *Polity* 6:295–317.

———. 1974b. *Congress: The Electoral Connection.* New Haven, CT: Yale University Press.

McDevitt, Bob. 1996. "Fundraising: Quick Tips for Candidates." *Campaigns & Elections,* September.

McGinniss, Joe. 1969. *The Selling of the President 1968.* New York: Trident.

McLuhan, Marshall. 1964. *Understanding Media: The Extensions of Man.* New York: McGraw-Hill.

Melder, Keith E. 1992. *Hail to the Candidate: Presidential Campaigns from Banners to Broadcasts.* Washington, DC: Smithsonian Institution Press.

Menefee-Libey, David. 2000. *The Triumph of Campaign-Centered Politics.* Chatham, NJ: Chatham House.

Mentzer, Bruce. 2000. "Banner Ads: The New Entry in Paid Political Media Plans." *Campaigns & Elections,* July.

Meredith, Todd. 2000. "Fundraising Events: The Dollars Are in the Details." *Campaigns & Elections,* February.

Milbank, Dana. 2000. "The Year of the Latino Voter? Only in Campaign Rhetoric." *Washington Post,* May 21, Section B.

Mitchell, Alison, and Frank Bruni. 2000. "Bush and McCain Swap Strategies for Next Battle." *New York Times,* Feb. 21, sec. A.

Morris, Dick. 1999a. *Behind the Oval Office: Getting Reelected against All the Odds*. Los
    Angeles: Renaissance.

————. 1999b. *Vote.com*. Los Angeles: Renaissance Books.

Morris, Dwight, and Murielle E. Gamache. 1994. *Gold-Plated Politics: The 1992 Congres-
    sional Races*. Washington, DC: Congressional Quarterly.

Morris, Jeffrey B. 1999. "You Can Use the Internet to Drive Your Direct Mail." *Target Mar-
    keting,* September.

Napolitan, Joseph. 1986. "Some Thoughts on the Importance of Strategy in a Political Cam-
    paign." In *The National Republican Congressional Committee Campaign Starter
    Manual*. Washington, DC: Republican Congressional Campaign Committee.

————. 1972. *The Election Game and How to Win It*. Garden City, NY: Doubleday.

Nelson, Michael. 1995. "Evaluating the Presidency." In *The Presidency and the Political
    System,* edited by Michael Nelson. Washington, DC: Congressional Quarterly.

New York Times. 1996a. "Dole's Speech Accepting the G.O.P. Nomination for President," 16
    August.

New York Times. 1996b. "Clinton's Speech Accepting the Democratic Nomination for Pres-
    ident," 30 August.

Nie, Norman H., Sidney Verba, and John R. Petrocik. 1976. *The Changing American Voter.*
    Cambridge: Harvard University Press.

Nieves, Evelyn. 1992. "Spelling by Quayle (That's with an E)." *New York Times*. June 17,
    sec. A.

Nimmo, Daniel. 1970. *The Political Persuaders*. Englewood Cliffs, NJ: Prentice-Hall.

Noble, Phil. 1998. "Ventura Win Marks Dawn of New Era: Age of Digital Politics." *Roll
    Call*. December 7.

O'Neill, Tip, with Gary Hymel. 1994. *All Politics Is Local and Other Rules of the Game*.
    Holbrook, MA: Bob Adams.

O'Neill, Tip, with William Novak. 1987. *Man of the House: The Life and Political Memoirs
    of Speaker Tip O'Neill*. New York: Random House.

Ouzounian, Richard. 1997. "Satellites, Feeds and Computers." *Campaigns & Elections,*
    August.

Pelletier, Paul. 1999. "Closing the Deal: Ten Fundraising Tips." *Campaigns & Elections,* May.

Persinos, John F. 1994. "Gotcha!" *Campaigns & Elections,* August.

Pew Research Center. 2000. "Internet Sapping Broadcast News Audience." Text at
    www.people-press.org/mediaoorpt.htm. June 11.

Phillips, Gerald M. 1984. *How to Support Your Cause and Win*. Columbia: University of
    South Carolina Press.

Pine, Joseph B. 1993. *Mass Customization: The New Frontier in Business Competition*.
    Boston: Harvard Business School Press.

Pomper, Gerald M. 1974. *Elections in America*. New York: Dodd, Mead.

Porter, Rick. 1999. "The Magic Campaign Combination in the Age of Access." *Campaigns
    & Elections,* October/November.

Pressley, Sue Anne. 1994. "The Comeuppance of Texas Icon Mirrors Nation's Political Re-
    volt." *Washington Post*. December 7, sec. A.

Randolph, Sallie G. 1989. "The Effective Press Release: Key to Free Media." In *Campaigns
    & Elections: A Reader in Modern American Politics,* edited by Larry Sabato. Glen-
    view, IL: Scott, Foresman.

Reeves, Richard. 1994. "Synar's Defeat Gives Politicians the Jitters." *Tulsa World.* Septem-
    ber 28, 27.

Rieter, Howard L. 1993. *Parties and Elections in Corporate America*. New York: Longman.

Riordon, William L., ed. 1995. *Plunkitt of Tammany Hall: A Series of Very Plain Talks by Ex-Senator George Washington Plunkitt*. New York: Signet.

Robberson, Tod. 1996. "Those Who Dig Dirt Are in Demand." *Washington Post*. November 1, sec. B.

Robbin, Jonathan. 1989. "Geodemographics: The New Magic." In *Campaigns and Elections: A Reader in Modern American Politics,* edited by Larry Sabato. Glenview, IL: Scott, Foresman.

Roberts, Steven V. 1987. "Preserving Reagan's Legacy." *New York Times*. May 7, sec. A.

Sabato, Larry J. 1991. *Feeding Frenzy: How Attack Journalism Has Transformed American Journalism*. New York: Free Press.

———. 1989a. *Campaigns and Elections: A Reader in Modern American Politics*. Glenview, IL: Scott, Foresman.

———. 1989b. "How Direct Mail Works." In *Campaigns & Elections: A Reader in Modern American Politics,* edited by Larry J. Sabato. Glenview, IL: Scott, Foresman.

———. 1981. *The Rise of Political Consultants: New Way of Winning Elections*. New York: Basic Books.

Sabato, Larry, and Glenn R. Simpson. 1996. "Vote Fraud!" *Campaigns & Elections,* June.

Sabato, Larry, Mark Stencel, and S. Robert Lichter. 2000. *Peepshow: Media and Politics in an Age of Scandal*. Lanham, MD: Rowman & Littlefield.

Salmore, Barbara G., and Stephen A. Salmore. 1989. *Candidates, Parties, and Campaigns*. Washington, DC: Congressional Quarterly.

Schapiro, Beth S. 1992. "It's a Man's World: Unless You Know the Right Questions to Ask." *Campaigns & Elections,* June.

Schlesinger, Joseph A. 1991. *Political Parties and the Winning of Office*. Ann Arbor: University of Michigan Press.

Schuman, Howard, and Stanley Presser. 1981. *Questions and Answers in Attitude Surveys*. San Diego: Academic Press.

Scudder, Virgil. 1997. Interviewed in "Spin." *Campaigns & Elections,* April.

Selnow, Gary W. 1994. *High Tech Campaigns*. Westport, CT: Praeger.

Semiatin, Richard J., and Tari Renner. 1994. "Much Ado about Nothing? The Impact of Check Bouncing on Members Returning to Congress." Paper presented at the 1994 Annual Meeting of the Midwest Political Science Association, Chicago, April 14–16.

Shaw, Catherine. 2000. *The Campaign Manager*. 2nd ed. Boulder, CO: Westview.

Shea, Daniel M. 1999. "The Passing of Realignment and the Advent of the 'Base-Less' Party System." *American Politics Quarterly* 27(1):33–57.

———. 1996a. *Campaign Craft: The Strategies, Tactics, and Art of Political Campaign Management*. Westport, CT: Praeger.

———. 1996b. "Issue Voting, Candidate Quality, and the Ousting of a Ten-Year Incumbent. *American Review of Politics,* 17:395–420

———. 1995a. *Transforming Democracy: State Legislative Campaigns and Political Parties*. Albany: State University of New York Press.

———. 1995b. "Lessons from a Challenger Upset: The Voters Have the Floor." Unpublished Manuscript.

Shea, Daniel M., and Stephen C. Brooks. 1995. "How to Topple an Incumbent." *Campaigns & Elections,* June.

Shea, Daniel M., and John C. Green, eds. 1994. *The State of the Parties*. Lanham, MD: Rowman and Littlefield.

Sheingold, Larry. 1993. "One More Hurrah: How Milton Marks Beat the Odds." *Campaigns & Elections* 14:40–41.

Shirley, Craig. 1997. Interviewed in "Spin." *Campaigns & Elections,* April.

Shrum, Robert. 1997. Interviewed in "Spin." *Campaigns & Elections,* April.

Sifton, Elisabeth. 1998. "The Serenity Prayer." *The Yale Review* 86 (1):16–65.

Silverberg, Carl. 2000. "The Secret Ingredient for Successful PAC Fundraising: Discipline." *Campaigns & Elections,* June.

Simon, Paul. 1999. *P.S.: The Autobiography of Paul Simon.* Chicago: Bonus Books.

———. 1995. Interviewed for CBS, *60 Minutes.* "Capitol Hill Nine: Retiring Senators Discuss Why They Chose to Leave Public Office," December 17.

Simpson, Dick. 1996. *Winning Elections: A Handbook of Modern Participatory Politics.* New York: HarperCollins.

Snider, Steve. 1990. "What Makes a Press Release Sing." *Campaigns & Elections*, January.

Sorauf, Frank J. 1995. "Competition, Contributions, and Money in 1992." In *Campaigns and Elections American Style,* edited by James A. Thurber and Candice J. Nelson. Boulder, CO: Westview.

———. 1988. *Money in American Elections.* Boston: Scott, Foresman.

Squier, Robert. 1998. Interviewed for PBS, *The :30 Second Candidate.* Transcript at http://www.pbs.org/30secondcandidate.

Stephanopoulos, George. 1999. *All Too Human: A Political Education.* Boston: Little, Brown.

Still, Edward. 2000. Listserv posting to Law-Courts List-serv, December 9.

Sweeney, William R. 1995. "The Principles of Planning." In *Campaigns and Elections American Style,* edited by James A. Thurber and Candice J. Nelson. Boulder, CO: Westview.

Sweitzer, Don. 1996. "Kill or Be Killed; Military Strategies Can Help Win Campaigns." *Campaigns & Elections,* September.

Sweitzer, Don, and David Heller. 1996. "Radio Tips: 10 Ways to Give Your Campaign Ads More Punch." *Campaigns & Elections,* May.

Swint, Kerwin C. 1998. *Political Consultants and Negative Campaigning: The Secrets of the Pros.* Lanham, MD: University Press of America.

Thibodeaux, Bessie. 1999. "The Road Home: Direct Mail Fundraising." *Campaigns & Elections,* May.

Thomas, Robert J., and Doug Gowen. 1999. *How to Run for Local Office: A Complete Guide for Winning a Local Election.* Detroit, MI: R and T Enterprise.

Thurber, James A., Robin Kolodny, and David A. Dulio. 2000. "Consultants on Candidates: Survey Taps Surprising Attitudes." *Campaigns & Elections,* May.

Thurber, James A., and Candice J. Nelson. 2000. *Campaign Warriors: Political Consultants in Elections.* Washington, DC: Brookings.

———. 1995. *Campaigns and Elections American Style.* Boulder, CO: Westview.

Thurber, James A., Candice J. Nelson, and David Dulio. 2000. *Crowded Airwaves: Campaign Advertising in Elections.* Washington, DC: Brookings.

Tourangeau, Roger, and Kenneth A. Rasinski. 1988. "Cognitive Processes Underlying Context Effects in Attitude Measurement." *Psychological Bulletin* 103(3):299–314.

Traugott, Michael W., and MeeEun Kang. 2000. "Public Attention to Polls in an Election Year." In *Election Polls, the News Media, and Democracy,* edited by Paul J. Lavrakas and Michael W. Traugott. New York: Chatham House.

Trent, Judith S., and Robert V. Friedenberg. 2000. *Political Campaign Communication: Principles and Practices.* 4th ed. New York: Praeger.

Tron, Barrie. 1996. "Staging Media Events: What We Learned from the 'Contract with America.' " *Campaigns & Elections,* December/January.

Troy, Gil. 1991. *See How They Ran: The Changing Role of the Presidential Candidate.* New York: Free Press.

Tufte, Edward R. 1975. "Determinants of the Outcomes of Midterm Congressional Elections." *American Political Science Review* 69:812–26.

Tuttle, Stephen. 1996. "Arizona Primary of Secondary Concern." *Arizona Republic.* February 4, sec. H.

Uslaner, Eric M. 1981. "The Case of the Vanishing Liberal Senators: The House Did It." *British Journal of Political Science* 11, pt. 1:105–13.

Varoga, Craig. 1995. "The Lone Star Upset." *Campaigns & Elections,* March.

Visser, Penny S., Jon A. Krosnick, Jesse F. Marquette, and Michael F. Curtin. 2000. "Improving Election Forecasting: Allocation of Undecided Respondents, Identification of Likely Voters, and Response Order Effects." In *Election Polls, the News Media, and Democracy,* edited by Paul J. Lavrakas and Michael W. Traugott. New York: Chatham House.

Wachob, Bill. 1991. "Tapping the Local Till." *Campaigns & Elections,* July.

Wachob, Bill, and Andrew Kennedy. 2000. "Beating B-1 Bob: Underdog Ends Conservative's Congressional Career in California's 46th District in 1996." In *Campaigns & Elections: Contemporary Case Studies,* edited by Michael A. Bailey et al. Washington, DC: Congressional Quarterly.

Wallace, Amy. 1994. "Stunning Blow for a Hired Gun." *Los Angeles Times.* November 14, sec. A.

Wattenberg, Martin P. 1998. *The Decline of American Political Parties 1952–1996.* Cambridge: Harvard University Press.

Wayne, Stephen. 1982. "Great Expectations: What People Want from the Presidency." In *Rethinking the Presidency,* edited by Thomas E. Cronin. Boston: Little, Brown.

Weaver, Mark. 1996. "Paid Media." In *Campaign Craft: The Strategies, Tactics, and Art of Political Campaign Management,* by Daniel M. Shea. Westport, CT: Praeger.

Weitzner, Larry, and Adam Geller. 1999. "Winning Tough Re-Elections: Start with Early Media." *Campaigns & Elections,* August.

Westneat, Danny, and Tom Brown. 1998. "Self-Funded Races Rarely Succeed." *Seattle Times.* September 3, sec. B.

Whillock, Rita Kirk. 1991. *Political Empiricism: Communication Strategies in State and Regional Elections.* New York: Praeger.

White, John Kenneth, and Daniel M. Shea. 2000. *New Party Politics: From Jefferson to the Information Age.* Boston: Bedford/St. Martin's.

White, Theodore H. 1961. *The Making of the President, 1960.* New York: Atheneum Publishers.

Wilson, Chris, and Mike Burita. 2000. "Winning in Unfriendly Territory." In *Campaigns & Elections: Contemporary Case Studies,* edited by Michael A. Bailey et al. Washington, DC: Congressional Quarterly.

Wreden, Nick. 1998. "On-Target Marketing." *Information Week,* August 31.

Yang, John. 2000. "Battle Tested: Poll Helps Bush Craft Anti-Gore Message." ABCNews.Com, March 23.

Yeutter, Clayton, Jeanie Austin, James S. Nathanson, and Jane Hershey Abraham. 1992. *The RNC Campaign Encyclopedia.* Washington, DC: Republican National Committee.

Index

About the Authors

DANIEL M. SHEA is Associate Professor of Political Science at Allegheny College. Prior to teaching and conducting research, Professor Shea was Regional Coordinator of the New York State Democratic Assembly Campaign Committee. He is the author of *Transforming Democracy* (1995) and co-editor of *The State of the Parties, 1st, 2nd, and 3rd Editions* (1994, 1996, 1999).

MICHAEL JOHN BURTON is Assistant Professor of Political Science at Ohio University. Professor Burton served as assistant political director to Vice President Al Gore in the mid-1990s before returning to academia.